Brian McConnell is a veteran Scotland Yard and Old Bailey journalist who is now a freelance writer and the author of several books, including one on the rise and fall of the Kray brothers.

# Holy Killers

## True Stories of Murderous Clerics, Priests and Religious Leaders

### Brian McConnell

**HEADLINE**

First published in 1994
by HEADLINE BOOK PUBLISHING

First published in paperback in 1995
by HEADLINE BOOK PUBLISHING

10 9 8 7 6 5 4 3 2 1

ISBN 0 7472 4440 5

Typeset by
Letterpart Limited, Reigate, Surrey

Printed and bound in Great Britain by
Cox & Wyman Ltd, Reading, Berks

HEADLINE BOOK PUBLISHING
A division of Hodder Headline PLC
338 Euston Road
London NW1 3BH

# CONTENTS

# INTRODUCTION

'Whoso sheddeth man's blood,
by man shall his blood be shed.'

*Genesis ix, 6*

'Thou shalt not kill.'

*Exodus xx, 13*

The road to hell is paved with the skulls of clergymen, according to the cynics, but then too many clerics throughout the ages have chosen the path of crime as well as creed. They have exhorted their flocks from the pulpit to 'walk in the paths of righteousness' and then broken God's law, lied, coveted, thieved, committed adultery and even murdered with knife, gun, rope, torch or bomb.

In fiction the villain is seldom if ever the clergyman. The culprit is usually the butler, the maid or that most frequent rascal, the family doctor. What is strange is that no one appears to have ever counted, listed, analysed or published the collected crimes of real-life holy killers.

Edmund Pearson, the distinguished American chronicler of true crime, thought that

> Persons who find much interest in assassination by a gangster or gunman ought to know that these events are feeble in their charm compared to a murder, if one could be unearthed, by an archbishop. And a thoroughly good poisoning perpetrated by the Professor of Christian Ethics in a respectable school of divinity; a well planned shooting or bludgeoning by a fashionable curate; or almost any sort of homicide by the Dean of a cathedral would be more precious to the discriminating amateur than all the vulgar atrocities which may be committed in the underworld of Memphis, Tennessee.

Mr Pearson wanted his churchmen slayers to be too highly ranked. But the world had already begun to hang, guillotine or burn (by the electric chair) their lesser but more interesting brethren, who could not find a convocation or synod to hide their crimes from public view. A fellow American, incidentally, produced the fascinating information that at any one time in the United States of America there is a higher percentage of clergymen in jail than actors; although he did not specify their respective crimes.

There is historical evidence that in Britain for many years news of clerical crimes was suppressed because the clergy enjoyed the privilege of trial in an ecclesiastical court. Punishments handed down by such tribunals were less severe than in secular courts and presiding bishops were forbidden to impose the death penalty, which was the tariff for so many offences. Anyone who could read was classed as a clerk (a legal term for clergyman) and could claim immunity by reading, or even reciting from memory, the beginning of the 51st Psalm:

> Have mercy upon me, O God, according to thy
>   loving kindness;
> According unto the multitude of thy tender mercies
>   blot out my transgressions.

The court official would then say, *Legit ut clericus* ('He reads like a clerk') and each prisoner who did so would save his neck. The passage became known as the 'Neck Verse'.

Henry VII, worried about so many regular offenders, ordered that convicted clerks could claim the privilege only once in a lifetime and had to be branded in the hand before they were released so they could be identified if they were accused again. Yet for some considerable time gentlemen of the cloth still escaped the pain, odium and contempt associated with capital punishment.

In this century, because hanging ceased to be the penalty for so many crimes, the public conception of wayward parsons became limited to naughty vicars, like the philandering Reverend Harold Davidson, Rector of Stiffkey, Norfolk, who came to London regularly to 'protect fallen angels from the flames of hell'. He became so intimate with the angels that a church court found him guilty of immoral conduct, had him 'removed, deposed and degraded' from all clerical offices and, to use church language, unfrocked him.

Then there was the Very Reverend John Wakeford, sixty-two-year-old Archdeacon of Peterborough – next in rank to the bishop – who went openly into a local hotel in clerical garb with a young woman and signed the register, 'J. Wakeford and wife'. He denied it, maintaining that the words 'and wife' were forgeries, examples of malicious spite by two other church divines, one of them his own brother-in-law. Wakeford fought the church all the way to the Privy Council, the highest legal court in the Commonwealth, but lost. He, too was unfrocked. 'He is either mad or bad,' said his own counsel.

The Reverend Henry James Proctor, at his Abode of Love at Charlinch in Somerset, invited his flock into the billiard room to watch an act of public worship – him having sex on the sofa with a disciple to produce a second Messiah.

Sex and religion have always been a powerful mix. Frank and Laura Jackson were aware of that when they set up the Church of the Theocratic Unity. Laura, an ugly creature of large proportions, called herself The Swami (Hindu religious teacher) and with her husband ensnared starry-eyed young women, promising them health, wealth and fame. It turned out to be a lucrative vice ring. Each of the girls had to go into the dock to tell her story before the couple were sentenced to long terms of imprisonment.

Holy killing as a result of sexual passion, frustrated or achieved, has always been a major embarrassment for the churches. The Reverend Peter Vine from Exeter, Devon, raped and murdered an eleven-year-old girl to whom he was supposed to be giving Bible lessons, then killed a man sent to arrest him, and was hanged. The Reverend James Hackman of Gosport, Hampshire, developed a passion for a Miss Reay, a young woman living under the protection of Lord Sandwich. Unable to further his sexual ambitions, he waited until she left a Covent Garden theatre, shot her, tried to kill himself, failed, and ended his life on the hangman's rope in 1779. A hundred years earlier, in Stanton Lacy, Shropshire, the Reverend Robert Foulkes was bequeathed a young lady to look after in a parishioner's will, a more common testamentary occurrence than is generally supposed. He took her to his bed; she bore him a child, whom he murdered to avoid the embarrassing publicity that would follow. He too was hanged.

The Gordon family, wealthy merchants of Edinburgh, had in their residence a personal priest, the Reverend Thomas Hunter. He fell for the maid and was seen in bed with her by the two Hunter sons, so he murdered them both in case they talked. He, too, was executed.

With the abolition of hanging, the law, if not the Church of Scotland, took a different view of murder. When James Nelson applied to become a minister it was revealed that he had beaten his mother to death fourteen years previously and had served a long jail sentence. The argument that we should all have an unremitting capacity for forgiveness and that he should be admitted to the ministry was put to the elders of the church. They refused him a dog-collar but only by forty-three votes to forty-two.

Contrast that with the nineteenth-century case of Father Francis Salesius Riembauer. His name is still quoted in the High Court in London, not so much on religious grounds, but as the principal in one of the classic cases of circumstantial evidence.

Riembauer seduced any girl he fancied. When a brother clergyman found him making overtures to his cousin he threatened the offending cleric. Riembauer cheekily wrote to his bishop, bemoaning the worldliness of his parish and asking to be sent to a more saintly and spiritual place. At his new living, he persuaded a girl named Anna to go to bed with him and marry him despite his vows of celibacy. When the randy reverend took on another girl and married her – each time officiating at his own marriage – Anna challenged him. He murdered Anna, buried her, and the crime was not discovered for many years. He was found guilty but out of deference to the cloth, because of his age, and because of the unsatisfactory state of the evidence he was sentenced to life imprisonment.

Clergy in Britain remained very much respected, even idolised, thanks to the adeptness of their superiors – particularly in the established Church of England – at protecting the 'good name' of their brethren, covering up dishonesty and other more grave offences 'for the good of the church'. That is why we did not hear much about sacerdotal sex, ecclesiastical adultery or priestly sexual child abuse until the 1990s. News that the Bishop of Galway had fathered a son was only revealed when the boy was in his teens and the mother finally went public and told her story.

By posting clerics to far-off livings, demoting them from office, removing their titles and their licences to perform certain ceremonies, banishing and separating them from their victims and (where appropriate) refusing to make any complaints to the police the church ensured little or no publicity and, therefore, no scandal. Only very occasionally would a flagrant offence like killing be exposed.

Few nations and few faiths, though, have a greater record of scandals than the Roman Catholic Church in France. In the magnificent reign of Louis XIV, the 'Sun King', when no one, prince or peasant, could go about his or her business without the knowledge, consent or connivance of the church, there flourished Catherine Monvoisin, née Deshayes, otherwise 'La Voisin'. According to her biographer, she was 'a strange and horrible creature – the last of the great sorceresses'. She graduated from reading palms and crystal ball-gazing to interpreting the grounds in coffee cups. Clients were so satisfied with the way the fortune teller got rid of unwanted husbands and wives that her fame reached the ears of the aristocracy.

The Princesse de Tingry, who begged for love philtres and charms that would make her more erotic, was given a severed hand and a toad. The Duchesse de Vivone wanted a Black Mass to devote herself and the unborn child in her womb to the Devil. The Comtesse de Soissons and the Duchesse de Vitry wanted black magic to make them the King's mistresses. The ravishingly beautiful Marquise de Montespan, who ruled the King's heart and bore him seven children, wanted the Black Mass to engineer the poisoning of her principal rival, Madame de La Vallière.

These sacrilegious ceremonies, in which the Devil is invoked in place of God and various obscene rites performed in ridicule of the proper ritual, could only be celebrated with a real priest. According to Montague Summers' *The Geography Of Witchcraft*, the hunchback Abbé Guibourg

celebrated innumerable Satanic masses at the insistence of Madame de Montespan in order to secure her supreme power and eternal fidelity on the part of the King. A long black velvet pall was spread over the altar and upon this the royal mistress laid herself in a state of perfect nudity. Six black candles [made from the limbs of the executed] were lit, the celebrant robed himself in a chasuble embroidered with esoteric characters wrought in silver, the gold paten and chalice were placed on the belly of the living altar, to whose warm flesh the priest pressed his lips each time the missal directed him to kiss the place of sacrifice [De Montespan's vagina].

All was silent save the low, monotonous murmur of the blasphemous liturgy. The Host was consecrated, then the Precious Blood. An assistant crept forward bearing an infant in her arms. The child was held over the altar, a sharp gash across the neck, a stifled cry, and warm drops [of blood] fell into the chalice and streamed upon the white figure beneath. The corpse was handed to La Voisin, who flung it callously into an oven fashioned for that purpose which glowed white-hot in its fierceness.

The Marquise de Montespan was banished. La Voisin was tortured for three days, her confession committed to *L'Archives de la Bastille*, her tongue cut out and she was burned alive at the stake. But the Reverend Abbé Guibourg? No one seems to recall the fate of the organiser of the holy killers.

Pearson, the American crime-writer with the professional taste for charming and precious holy killings, would not have been disappointed at his own country's record. George Morton Field, a man of God with a stern religious code, was the richest man in Mustoch, Kansas. He built the local church and poured money into the community to ensure the parishioners' Christian discipline and welfare was maintained. When no visiting rota preacher was available, Field himself would mount the pulpit and deliver one of his sermons, promising all sinners eternal damnation.

He was such a powerful preacher that buxom, rosy-cheeked gospel singer Gertie Day could hardly refuse his request to remain behind after choir practice. When Gertie discovered she was pregnant she was hysterical and eventually demanded that Field should pay for the baby's upkeep. The church benefactor thought that mother and baby would be better off in another world, so when she called at the temple to collect a down payment of $2,000 she was blown to smithereens or atoms or wherever bomb victims go.

Sheriff James R. Carter poked around the church ruins, found the remains of a fuse, a piece of the timing device, a charred piece of paper and some handwriting, 'The wrath of God will slay all sinners.' It was George Morton Field's text for his next sermon. God's wrath did not slay him immediately. His death came eleven years later in bed in the state penitentiary.

The Reverend Jacob S. Harden, of Mount Lebanon, New Jersey, was attracted to a young girl parishioner who inveigled him into promising to wed her, despite the fact that he was already married. Instead of asking for God's guidance, advice he had urged upon others, he asked a fortune teller. She told him that his wife would soon die. Harden hastened that prediction by poisoning his wife with arsenic. The young girl left him. The clairvoyant gave evidence against him. The parson was convicted and hanged.

The Pilgrim Fathers, when they founded New England, took with them all human failings, including the seed of future sinful clerics. In Cambridge, Massachusetts, the Reverend V. T. Richeson of the Immanuel Church was staying with the head of the Baptist Missionary Society of America while he prepared for his wedding to the daughter of the house, Miss Violet Edmonds. Richeson appeared to have forgotten his intimate friendship with Miss Avis Linnell, a young student of singing, whom he had met during his previous ministry at Hyannis Port, Cape Cod.

As the marriage date approached, a group of girls at the Boston YWCA, where Miss Linnell was living, heard cries and groans from her room, broke the lock, forced the door and found her naked in the bath in agony. She lasted fifteen minutes.

Potassium cyanide killed her, said the doctors. The minister, whose name was linked to the lady by popular gossip, was miles away in Cambridge at the time. Alas, a chemist remembered the clergyman calling at his shop to ask for some poison to kill a dog, mercifully and quickly, and the pharmacist had recommended and supplied potassium cyanide. The reverend had asked the druggist to say nothing about the prescription, for had not St Francis of Assissi called all God's animals his 'brothers' and 'sisters', to be treated with quiet compassion?

Then a woman remembered the minister using her telephone and asking, 'Is that the Boston YWCA?' That must have been the call in which he told the singing student to take the medicine and a hot bath to get rid of her unwanted pregnancy.

On the day Richeson was due to be married, a grand jury indicted him on a charge of murder. The reverend tried to commit suicide with the jagged edge of a marmalade tin but failed. His bride-to-be and her powerful missionary father stood by him as did many supporters who claimed he was a victim of dual person-ality. Despite all the pleas made on his behalf, he had to be carried to court to be sentenced and thence to the electric chair.

One can only wonder, if a psychiatrist had examined the Reverend Herbert H. Hayden, what conclusion he would have reached. Is it normal for a well-to-do incumbent of a church, a person of standing in the community, to seduce the staff, and when they com-plain, kill them? Or does it betray a certain arrogance:

you can't touch me, I'm a man of the cloth?

Mary Stannard, a twenty-two-year-old maidservant, was found near Rockland, Connecticut, in a field belonging to the Reverend Hayden, with her throat cut, her skull fractured, and what looked suspiciously like arsenic in her stomach. Mary had once been in service at Hayden's home, and had subsequently told friends, and anyone else who would listen, about his sexually passionate nature. She herself was no innocent, for she confessed at the same time that she was pregnant by him for the second time. She added that the clergyman had said he would give her some medicine to induce an abortion, and that she was going to meet him in a nearby field to pick berries and discuss her future.

Hayden was questioned and although he could not remember where he was at the time of Mary's death, his wife volunteered the information that he was at home chopping wood. Released pending inquiries, he was re-arrested when it was discovered that the dead girl had arsenic in her body and that he had purchased an ounce of arsenic from a local chemist.

Hayden was not without friends. He was a minister of the cloth. The murdered girl was, by her own admission, 'a fallen woman'. A parishioner testified that he had found an ounce of arsenic, intact, in the clergyman's barn, evidence which upset the police who had already made a thorough search of the same barn.

The trial of the minister was delayed for a year while a professor went to England to have samples of the arsenic found in the barn analysed in case any light could be thrown on the parishioner's discovery. A further sensation was caused by the calling of a clairvoyant to give evidence of the preacher's innocence. The jury found Hayden not guilty of murder, a verdict which, in that social and religious climate, came as no real surprise. And society passed any further investigation of such attitudes on to sociologists rather than doctors. Yet there were some who found it extraordinary that in those days of 1878 a minister, of all people, a figure of substance in the district, should be so incredibly unthinking that he could seduce a maidservant, a girl who already had an illegitimate child, in his own household, under the very nose of his wife.

Sheriff Ben Totten of Ottowa County, Oklahoma, was not a particularly religious officer. A farmer had told him about finding the body of a young girl in the hills, a girl who had been pretty once and had no place being found alone, dead in the cold, wet autumnal weather. While recovering the body the sheriff wondered what went on in a nearby house about which people spoke with awe, and why it was called the House of Deuteronomy. A local person told him that the word meant 'the second law'. It was the second book of Mosaic law, the fifth book of the Pentateuch, the last of the first five books of the Bible. Totten muttered about there being only one law in his territory and continued to wonder.

Doctors told the sheriff that the girl had been dead about two weeks. There was a .38 calibre bullet in her skull. No one had reported anyone of her description missing, no homestead for miles around could help. So Sheriff Totten went to the House of Deuteronomy, which he quickly learned was named by the head of the mission, Dr Alan Heeber, after his favourite Biblical quotation:

And this shall be the priest's due from the people,

from them that offer a sacrifice . . . the first fruit . . . of thy corn, of thy wine, and of thine oil, and the first fleece of thy sheep, shalt thou give him.

Deuteronomy xviii, 3 & 4.

The sheriff examined the well-stocked back barn, where he saw that the first fruits had indeed been given by generous supporters in the form of groceries, vegetables and other household needs. Dr Heeber, assistant pastor James Garrett and all the staff swore they had never seen the dead girl. One defector from the mission, however, identified her as a former resident, Josie Byers, from Fayetteville, and the more the sheriff asked questions the more people began remembering girls who had come to the mission and suddenly disappeared.

A series of raids on the red light districts of local towns produced girls who had been taken to the mission, farmed out to the white slave traffic and had never returned. Dr Heeber and his assistant had been collecting $250 for each girl delivered to the whorehouses. Meanwhile Heeber and his assistant had vanished to Santa Monica, California, where a beach cameraman snapped a picture of the runaway pair. When the reverend threatened to punch the photographer on the nose unless he handed over the film, the cameraman took the snaps to the police.

The photographs were circulated, Dr Heeber was arrested and taken back to Oklahoma, where he confessed that he had killed Josie because she threatened to defect and tell all. Within an hour of his admission he returned to his prison cell, took poison and died. Sheriff Totten turned to his deputies and said 'the first fruits of the vineyard were virgins he recruited into prostitution' and turning to chapter eighteen of Deuteronomy in the Good Book he concluded, 'For all that do these things are an abomination to the Lord.'

Some religious sects believe they have the God-given right to determine when masses of people will die. They have decided they, and they alone, can put a date on the second coming, their own Apocalypse, with some horrifying results: murdering some, ordering others to commit suicide. Such cults are not new, but the massacres of more than 900 people at Jonestown, Guyana, in 1978, and the slaughter of eighty-five at Waco, Texas, in 1993 – including Britons in both places – shocked many people, religious and non-religious, all round the world. (Since then, in the Ukraine, in November 1993, a threat that 150,000 worshippers would commit suicide outside St Sophia's Cathedral, Kiev, was averted by police making mass arrests.)

These are the stories of murders carried out perversely for the usual reasons – for sex or lack of it, for gain, for revenge, to eliminate someone, out of jealousy, or simply from the insatiable desire to kill. Some also kill under the pressures of a particular sectarian faith, in the mistaken belief that they are acting according to God's wishes.

We are all human, with or without cassocks and dog-collars, and all of us are subject to the same temptations. But there is something more than just scarlet sin when the butchery is carried out in the passion of intense religious belief. This has driven far too many preachers and lay believers to murder and is an affront to reason as well as a blasphemy. It makes holiness, which is as sacred as life, into killing, which is as profane as death. It has reared again the understandable but unfortunate argument that capital punishment is a Christian duty. Yet in some of the following accounts there will be found that supreme gift, the unremitting capacity for forgiveness. Pray that one religion, one denomination or sect at least will find a way to rid us of this supreme wickedness.

Brian McConnell
Dulwich Village, London
January, 1994

## Chapter One

# THE POSSESSED ANGLICAN

'I had to destroy her. No, not my wife, but the Devil in her.'

Michael Taylor, father of five.

On Sunday, October 6, 1974, the feast of St Faith, the third-century virgin and martyr who was burned to death on a brazen bed, Michael Taylor killed his wife. With his bare hands, he tore her eyes out. He tore her tongue out. He tore her face almost from the bones and she died choking on her own blood.

Calling his mother-in-law's pet poodle which was sniffing outside his terraced council home he killed it with a violent blow of the hand or foot and by wringing its neck as if it were a chicken. Then he walked out of the house, naked except for his socks and covered in blood, wearing his wife's gold rings on his hand.

A psychiatrist was to say later that the case was unique in his experience of more than a thousand murders.

The slaughter happened in Yorkshire, but it raised questions that would test beliefs far beyond the boundaries of the Ridings. Could Yorkshireman Michael Taylor have been possessed by the Devil? Could such possession lead to his murdering someone near and dear to him, or anyone else for that matter? And should exorcism, the religious rite to drive out evil spirits, to which he had been subjected, have been the response to his suffering?

These questions erupted into vociferous public debate because Taylor had undergone exorcism the night before the murder, and because the horrific film *The Exorcist* was still a fresh topic of conversation in church pew and public house bar, over the garden fence and in the supermarket queues.

The film was based on an actual well documented case. A house in Daly City, a southern suburb of San Francisco, which was occupied by a young couple with a baby, seemed to be possessed by 'a whole army of demons'. A crucifix flew from the bedroom wall, landing on a bed twelve feet away; a steak knife flew round the house, terrifying the occupants. The principal tenant said, 'We believe the Devil himself is present and has made his presence known by attacking us personally. Often he knocks one of us unconscious. He will choke us, twist our arms behind our backs.'

After two years of such manifestations, the couple called in Father Karl Patzelt of Our Lady of Fatima Church, San Francisco, who treated the matter with scepticism. He declared that the events were 'disturbances caused by the Evil One', declining to call it possession, but suggesting that the occupants may have been suffering from obsession. Yet he eventually carried out the exorcism rites between August 19 and September 8, 1973, with the ritual words, 'I cast thee out, Most Unclean Spirit.' At the end of the period, the occurrences ceased.

In the film, Max Von Sydow plays a Jesuit priest and exorcist and the film-makers, as evidence of its factual basis, brought in Father John J. Nicola, a practising Roman Catholic exorcist, to advise them. The screenplay was nevertheless sensational. Canon John Pearce-Higgins, a leading Anglican exorcist, of Southwark Cathedral, London, declared that the film was 'filthy, indecent, blasphemous' and predicted that 'it will produce a new crop of schizophrenics and a small number of cases of genuine possession.'

Father Peter Vincent, vicar of St Thomas's Church, Gawber, two miles west of the old Yorkshire coal mining district of Barnsley, also condemned the movie:

'The one thing the film does not show is the truth about the Church's work of exorcism. If the Cross means anything it means that Jesus was conqueror over the power of the Devil and his evil spirits. Exorcism is the casting out of evil spirits and Satan himself by the power and victory of Jesus, and when exorcism is carried out in the name and by the authority and cover of the blood of Jesus the evil spirits must go.

'The film is an exploitation of the gullible minds of the public who like a bit of sensation and may well get more than they bargained for, I'm afraid.

'No film can be good if it corrupts the mind and reverses the principle of good being more important than evil. I cannot warn you enough to avoid this kind of film. If you know of anyone who is disturbed by *The Exorcist* tell them to get in touch with me or Father Cheetham at Grimethorpe or the Reverend Ray Smith and we can call on a team who will help.'

Within three short months of Father Vincent's warning he carried out a ceremony of exorcism on Michael Taylor, a thirty-one-year-old out-of-work resident of Ossett, eight miles away. Next morning Michael literally tore his wife to death with his bare hands.

Ossett is one of those clustered Yorkshire towns with a population a little over 20,000, a golf course, market days Tuesday and Friday and not much else visible. But there is Christianity there and apart from the churches of different denominations a Christian Fellowship group gathered people from different churches for

23

Bible readings, hymn singing and prayers in private homes.

Although religion did not dominate the lives of the Taylors, Michael, his wife Christine, and their five sons aged from six to twelve years were more than nominal Christians. They mistrusted or were at least unsure of the Church of England, the established church of the nation, which was why they acted as hosts to the very first meeting of the Fellowship in their terraced council house in Havercroft, Ossett on Tuesday, September 24, 1974.

Marie Robinson, a twenty-two-year-old single former music teacher, was there with her guitar. Although not ordained in any ministry, she celebrated a form of Holy Communion and a form of exorcism. Mrs Barbara Wardman, a neighbour of the Taylors, said Marie 'thought it would be nice' to introduce the worshippers to some simple form of faith and an act like breaking bread. She had some ready-sliced bread in the cupboard and some Ribena, a blackcurrant cordial, and 'it would be just like Holy Communion.'

She added, 'Everyone seemed to enjoy it. Afterwards, everyone went home and got fish and chips and seemed quite happy.' Miss Robinson stayed overnight with the Taylors and next day, the Wednesday, they had a singing and prayer meeting. During the prayers, Michael Taylor spoke in tongues.

'Speaking in (or with the gift of) tongues' is known as 'glossolalia,' a soliloquy of ecstatic spiritual emotion. When a high state of emotional fervour is reached in group worship the result can be a torrent of words expressed in a language unfamiliar to speakers or listeners. The Bible acknowledges it in the miracle of Pentecost in the Acts of the Apostles (ii: 4): 'And they were all filled with the Holy Ghost, and began to speak with other tongues, as the Spirit gave them utterance.' Worshippers in the early church practised it, as did the Irvingites (1829) named after Edward Irving of Annan, the Scottish divine, who was later found guilty of heresy and deprived of his ministerial status.

In the Taylor household, Mrs Wardman, the neighbour, recalled, 'While Michael was saying prayers he suddenly spoke in tongues. It is the gift of the Holy Spirit. It's rather beautiful. Michael had just received the gift and was rather afraid of it and inclined to speak in a normal voice at first.'

At the same meeting, twenty-five-year-old Mrs Mavis Smith who lived in Healey View, Ossett, recalled later:

'I was disturbed at the time Marie Robinson joined the Fellowship and attended their gospel and hymn-singing meetings in people's houses. Marie decided at that meeting I had an evil spirit and she said she'd exorcise it. Christine [Taylor] was there, with one or two others. Marie said some prayers over me and beckoned the spirit to leave. But a strange sensation came over me. I felt it was getting out of hand. Then I broke into tears. I told her to stop the prayers. She did and I decided to leave.

'I felt that if I'd gone any further with the exorcism I might have gone home and done something dreadful – even perhaps to the children. Marie certainly has an influence over people, especially when they're like Michael and me, nervy and depressed. Something very wicked must have come over Michael because he loved his wife so much.'

The neighbour, Mrs Wardman, said Taylor was upset by Marie's attempt to exorcise evil spirits from Mrs Smith. 'I would not say he was violently upset. When I told him to calm down, he did calm down.'

On the Sunday, September 29, Taylor went to morning service at Father Vincent's church, St Thomas's, and later to a Fellowship meeting in his own home. Marie was there. She began to shake as if possessed and gibbered and chanted 'in tongues'.

The diary of death began two days later. On Tuesday, October 1 Taylor was very depressed. He had applied for a job and been rejected. On Wednesday, October 2, he told his mother and his neighbours, Mr and Mrs Wardman, that he had seen the Devil, who had told him to go and kill himself in his car. Guitar-playing, would-be priest Marie Robinson called at the Taylor household later. Taylor, she recalled, 'kissed me on the lips. It was not a Christian kiss and we bounced off each other, repelling each other.'

On Thursday, October 3, Taylor approached neighbours in the street, knelt before them, and told them that the world was coming to an end. The same day he went to another meeting of the Fellowship, this time in Barnsley, at the home of Ron Smith, choirmaster at St Thomas's, and his wife, Margaret. Father Vincent was there.

Taylor told the company that he had been seduced by the Devil. The group voted that they should hear him in detail and that he should confess all that had taken place. A prayer of absolution, known as 'the infilling of the Holy Spirit', said to be a form of exorcism, was recited, although the word 'exorcism' was not at that stage mentioned. After the meeting ended, Taylor went home. His mother-in-law said, 'He looked strained and tired and was afraid to go out in the dark.'

Friday, October 4: Michael told his wife, 'Get rid of all the crosses in the house and all the religious books.' This she did. When it was time to go to bed, he left the radio switched on because, he said, 'I am frightened of the silence of the night.'

Saturday, October 5: John Eggins, a member of the Fellowship, who lived at Wakefield, the old woollen centre on the River Calder, a few miles east, thought that Taylor and his family needed a rest and would benefit from a car ride in the fresh air of the Yorkshire dales. With John at the wheel, Christine and the five children were all apparently grateful for the break but the peaceful journey was suddenly broken by sullen Michael uttering a piercing scream. The children were scared. Christine said of Michael, 'He desperately needs help.'

John turned the car round and headed for Father Vincent's vicarage at Gowber. By 7.30 p.m., Taylor was behaving irrationally, violently and noisily. He picked up the vicarage cat and flung it through a window. When a meal was placed before him to placate him he threw it to the floor. His children were put to bed upstairs for their peace and safety.

Sally, the vicar's wife, took the view that there was an enormous force of evil emanating from Taylor and that this was undoubtedly a case of demonic possession. Taylor needed exorcising and that was a task which could take all night. Her husband, the vicar, agreed and Mrs Vincent felt that others experienced in exorcism ought to be there. She summoned by telephone the Reverend Raymond Smith, a Barnsley Methodist minister, and his wife, Margaret, who described themselves as practitioners in exorcism, Donald James, a Methodist lay preacher and John Eggins, the afternoon driver, making a team of six.

They counselled Taylor to undergo the night-long exorcism. It was clear from Mrs Taylor's words that she was convinced that Marie Robinson, the guitarist communion celebrant, was connected with some Satanist group and had pledged Michael, her husband, to the Devil. Michael's violence of speech and action, his threat to murder someone and the fact that he invoked the power of the moon persuaded the listeners that the exorcism should continue. There was only one dissenting voice. Reverend Smith, the Methodist minister, added that although he was a practitioner in exorcism, he believed that Taylor was not in need of church ministration but needed psychiatric care. Father Vincent indicated the wish of the majority that the exorcism should continue.

The six had taken Taylor to the vestry at the side of the church where he was laid on his back on a pile of red and gold hassocks. One by one they stood over him, asking questions, finding answers, putting suggestions, saying prayers and announcing that they were casting out devils one by one.

Taylor later told doctors that he had a striking recollection of what took place that night. Words, he said, had been put into his mouth by the exorcists and he had been led to admit sins he had never committed. They named each devil by its own evil. They included bestiality, lewdness, blasphemy, heresy and masochism. A wooden crucifix, given him by Marie Robinson and worn round his neck, was repeatedly put in his mouth as the exorcists prayed for him. As he writhed and thrashed on the floor he was held down forcibly. Every time he puffed out his cheeks and gasped and panted for breath the exorcists claimed another demon had been expelled from his body.

(Doctors call this hyperventilating, which is often associated with hysteria.)

Eventually, the wooden crucifix which hung from his neck by a leather thong was wrenched from him and burned on charcoal in a dish in the vestry. The silver crucifix given him by his wife was buried in the church grounds.

At 6 a.m. Taylor and the exorcists were exhausted. They claimed that the possessed had been rid of forty demons, although there were, alas, one or two still within him, among them violence and murder. Reverend Smith, the Methodist minister, said that only the spirit of murder remained, and that could not be expelled. Margaret, his wife, said, 'I feel that there is a doll somewhere for Michael – like the witchcraft dolls into which people stick pins – and unless this is found and burned we will never cast out the spirit of murder. I have had word from God that if he goes home this morning he will murder his wife and children.'

There came a time when Father Vincent was asked: 'When he left you at eight o'clock on the morning of Sunday, October 6, 1974, you firmly believed he was going to kill his wife?'

Father Vincent: 'Yes.'

Those at the vicarage could not compel him to stay. False or unlawful imprisonment includes preventing a person from leaving a building and that includes a church. The exorcists tried to contact a medical welfare officer. On the sabbath it would be difficult anyway, but bureaucracy makes it impossible for such a person to visit a house without the owner's or tenant's permission. They called the police who recommended that a doctor be invited to call, but here Mrs Taylor objected. 'Michael will be cross

29

if a doctor is called into the matter.'

At 8.30 a.m. Mr Eggins drove the Taylors home, wisely leaving the children with their grandparents. At 9 a.m. Mr Eggins left the Taylors at their home. At 9.30 Mrs Taylor told her neighbour, Mrs Wardman, 'My husband needs a doctor. We're going to have a good rest.' She added, 'Don't come near me. There is something in me.' That something was believed by some to be more devilish than she could have imagined.

It was 10 a.m. when Michael Taylor attacked his wife with his bare hands, tearing out her eyes and her tongue, tearing the flesh from her face until she choked to death from her own blood.

A policeman called by neighbours found him on his hands and knees with his forehead touching the ground. His arms, hands and body were bloody. The officer asked, 'Where did all that blood come from?'

Taylor replied, 'It is the blood of Satan.'

Later at the police station, Detective Inspector Brian Smith asked him: 'Did you kill your wife?'

Taylor replied: 'No, not her. I love her. I destroyed the evil within her. It had to be done. I am relaxed. What had to be done has been done. The evil in her has been destroyed. Chrissie was good. The evil had been put into her by them. I had to kill it. It came through religion. They primed me for this last night.

'We went to the church in Barnsley and stayed all night. The people at the church, they will tell you. It was a long night. They danced around me and burned my cross. But they were too late. My cross was tainted with evil.

'They tried. Oh, how they tried, but I had to do it. I had to destroy. I am relaxed now. I am at peace. It was terrible. They had me in the church all night. Look at my hands. I was banging them on the floor. The power was in me. I could not get rid of it and neither could they. I was compelled by a force within me which they couldn't get rid of. I felt compelled to destroy everything living within the house. Everything, including the dog. Everything living – but that was a lesser evil.

'I am relaxed [now]. It is done, it is done. The evil in her has been destroyed. It was in Christine. It used my wife, my love. Oh Hell, I loved that woman. I destroyed the evil within her. It had to be done. No, no, not Chrissie, Chrissie, Chrissie, she was good. I loved her. I loved her so.'

A society doubtful about the existence of God and suspicious about the presence and power of Satan could not be satisfied with that explanation. A human rather than a supernatural agency had to be found. If Taylor was possessed and therefore hardly in possession of his own faculties, there had to be someone else responsible. The public wanted something more tangible than the Biblical goat on whose head the high priest laid the sins of the people before sending it into the wilderness. That human agency, that scapegoat, was Marie Robinson. Everyone seemed to place some blame upon her.

Michael Taylor himself said that she had 'seducing eyes'. That the Devil seduced him was another allegation he had made. When the communion of Ribena and ready-sliced bread was celebrated at his home he said of Robinson:

'The evil came upon me. We had a battle of wits. She seduced me with her eyes. I can still see those eyes. I saw her standing before me and I was naked. She was looking at the sun. She turned and her eyes became slits and I felt

31

the evil within me but I fought it – Oh how I fought it – but it overcame me. I sought for knowledge for myself. She tried to give it to me. But this is not the way. They were wrong. They were all wrong. They tried to bring me peace of mind but instead they filled me with the Devil.'

His wife, Christine, told friends and neighbours before she died that 'Marie had begun to act strangely looking out of the window at the full moon. There had been a battle of wits between Michael and Marie and talk about the Bible and then Marie would again look out of the window at the moon. It had gone on like that until dawn. I was frightened to leave Michael and Marie alone because one would have hurt the other and there was already a handful of my hair in the ashtray. Michael told me that he looked at Marie and although she was fully dressed, he saw her naked and he knew that when she looked at him she saw him naked too.

'I saw their eyes had become narrowed. They were hissing and I was terribly frightened but dare not show it. Michael and I wanted to resume our quiet life and decided we would not attend any more Fellowship meetings, but we were then up all night. As soon as it began to get dark, Michael went to the window and started to stare at the moon and go on about it. We sat downstairs in the sitting room all night making the sign of the Cross over each other to keep each other safe.

'Marie had gone then, but that ceremony conducted by Marie was all a sad mistake.'

Michael's mother, a prematurely white-haired woman of fifty-two, explained:

'I believe Mike thought that Marie Robinson had put the Devil in him and he was attacking her for it. That terrible Sunday morning, Mike thought he was destroying

her, not his own wife. Before Mike started going to these
Christian Fellowship meetings he was a normal, loving,
family man, he loved Christine. If ordinary folk are told
by evangelists and Jesus freaks that they're wicked, they
could well start believing it.'

Marie Robinson was twenty-two at the time, eight
years younger than Taylor. She was educated, having left
school with nine 'O' (Ordinary) levels in schools' certifi-
cates of education and three 'A' (Advanced) levels. She
worked as an engineering technician in the West Yorkshire County Council highways department at Wakefield,
lived with her parents in Wentworth Road, Doncaster,
and preached regularly in the village Congregational
Church at Horbury, a few miles from Ossett. A devout
Christian, she had worked with a missionary team in
France, regularly attended religious conferences and met
Michael Taylor through Christian Fellowship meetings.
She was emphatic in her denial of accusations that she
was in some way to blame.

'People are calling me a witch. They are saying that I
bewitched a man and led him to kill. I have been labelled
a Satanist and a devil worshipper. Nothing could be
further from the truth. I love Jesus Christ. He is everything to me. I have seen my friends look at me with fear
in their eyes but I don't hate them for it. It hurts me
because I loved the Taylor family.

'I believe the accusations against me are based on the
demented ramblings of a man possessed by the Devil.
That man was my friend, Michael Taylor.

'When I was introduced to Mike and his wife, Chris,
he was searching for a kind of peace. They had heard
some tape recordings of my singing and they wanted to
meet me. Mike was very depressed and he had a back

complaint and could not work to support the family. Like all men he wanted to be the breadwinner.

'Over the weeks I grew to love them all. I used to sing to the children and they all had their favourite songs. I spent so many happy evenings there I felt I belonged with them. But what I didn't realise until it was too late was that Michael had fallen in love with me. I was completely blind to it. I didn't see it until the night he attacked me, a few days before Chris died.

'We were together in the sitting room and he suddenly reached forward and kissed me. I was shocked because it was not a Christian embrace, the sort we use in our Fellowship, and I pushed him away. The rebuff made him angry. Within minutes his face seemed to change and I sensed almost at once Mike had been taken over by evil spirits. He tore at my hair and hit me in the face. Chris tried to drag him away but he pushed her out of the way and threw me on to the floor. For a moment I felt the taste of death in my throat.

'I kept saying the name of Jesus. Chris joined in too, and it seemed to calm him almost immediately. I believed that saved my life.

'I never believed that Mike could possibly care for me in that way. You see Mike and Chris were so beautiful, completely entwined like the roots of the tree. But Chris knew of his feelings towards me. They were that close. She even offered to divorce Mike there and then so that he could marry me if it would make him happier. I told him I didn't want him in that way. I loved him as I loved all my friends. Mike must have misunderstood. I had never encouraged him in any way, believe me. Yes, I had kissed him first.

'It seemed that Mike was looking for more than that.

34

The trouble was that he put me on a pedestal – he expected so much of me. I tried to help him but I failed miserably. The next day I seemed to keep saying to myself, "You're useless, Marie, do away with yourself." I was in a state of shock.

'Three days later a member of the Fellowship told me of the killing. I was numbed by the horror of it and I was tormented by self-accusations. I thought I was to blame. But I am convinced now that it was not Mike who brutally killed his wife. It was the Devil.

'It has been said that Mike was driven to kill by the exorcism ceremony in church the night before. I cannot say if that is true. In my humble opinion, Mike should not have been exorcised when at least one person present [the Methodist minister] did not agree it should go ahead. I believe a united front is essential to defeat the enemy, but perhaps they felt it was so urgent they had to act quickly. Most important, I believe Mike should not have been left alone if they felt demons were still present within him. He may well have been better off under sedation in hospital. I just don't know.

'Some people have said it was my evil influence that drove Mike to kill. But I never tried to influence Mike except to help him. I want people to understand that. Looking back, I believe Mike must have been possessed with an evil spirit before I met him. It could have been through dabbling with spiritualism of some kind. I talked over Chris's death with a psychiatrist friend. He reassured me that I could not have influenced Mike in an evil way. I don't blame myself for this tragedy. Why? Because God has reassured me and I have complete peace of mind.

'Soon after Chris's death I was asked to leave the

Christian Fellowship. They didn't give me any reasons, except that a bishop and some ministers felt it unwise for me to stay on. But until the court hearings I didn't even realise they were calling me a Satanist. Why couldn't they have been more honest?'

Michael Taylor was charged with the murder of his wife. A newspaper reporter called to tell Marie that evidence had been given of her demonic influence on Taylor.

She said, 'I felt physically sick. People think it strange that I have laid hands on people, spoken in tongues, and carried out a service of exorcism at these meetings. But why should this make me a Satanist? I believe these are gifts Jesus can make available to any devout Christian when he feels it is necessary. I am not a disciple of Satan. However, just as I know there is a God I know there is a Devil and I find worship of him abhorrent.

'Too many people are dabbling with ouija boards and the occult. They don't understand the dangers. There have been other aspects of the case which have made me sad. Like the burning of the wooden cross I actually gave to Mike's wife. The clergyman took it from Mike and burnt it during his exorcism. They felt it radiated evil. Chris asked me to buy it for her at a Christian choir gathering. It was a simple 85p varnished wooden cross inscribed with the words, "Jesus Lives," and many Christians have bought them. How could such a simple gesture be misinterpreted?

'There has been gossip that I take occult books to work with me. I have three books on the Christian fight against evil in my bedroom. They were loaned to me and I can't even remember the titles. This tragedy has not made me wary of people, perhaps just wary of myself. I have made mistakes and I have learned from them. As for Mike, I don't think I could ever meet him again. But I will always pray for him and his children.'

At his trial, a jury found Michael Taylor not guilty of murdering his wife by reason of insanity. The judge, Mr Justice Caulfield, ordered that he should be detained at Broadmoor, the hospital in Berkshire for mentally ill criminals. That confirmed in the view of many that the law does not recognise demonic possession. After all, when a person is praying he is talking to God but when he claims that God or the Devil is talking to him, then the law says he is a schizophrenic.

Coroners usually adjourn their inquiries into the deaths of murder victims until after criminal trials have ended and then merely rubber-stamp the trial jury's verdicts. In this case, Mr Philip Gill, the West Yorkshire coroner, reconvened the inquest on Mrs Christine Taylor in the public interest.

His verdict was that she came to her death by misadventure, an accident resulting from some lawful venture. Was anyone then to blame and if so whom?

Mr Harry Ognall, QC, later Mr Justice Ognall, who defended Michael Taylor at his trial said:

'Michael Taylor was a decent, hard-working, public-spirited and well-liked young man. He was described by a friend as cheerful, friendly and in no way a violent man. He was a devoted father and a loving husband for whom marriage was one long courtship. He then encountered the Christian Fellowship and this particular branch of the Fellowship was a group of tormented souls who simply fed neuroses to a neurotic and in a few short days he was a homicidal maniac.

'In that condition he was the subject of what we submit

were grotesque and wicked malpractices posing in the guise of religion. And, in the light of all the evidence, supervised by members of two branches of the Christian Church, he was made to confess sins of which he was wholly innocent and indeed did not understand and was subjected to indignities which defy comprehension.

'At the end he was allowed to go home with the spirit in his heart and no reason in his head, and within minutes he had killed the darling of his life with unspeakable brutality.

'He [Taylor] was a mere cypher. The real guilt and certainly moral responsibility for this appalling crime lies elsewhere. We submit that those laymen who have been referred to, and those clerics in particular, who purported to minister to Michael Taylor on that night should be with him now in spirit in this court building and each day he is incarcerated in Broadmoor.'

Mr Maurice Shaffner, counsel, who represented the West Yorkshire police, thought that the exorcism was the ultimate trigger mechanism which produced the final insanity which led Taylor to slay his wife.

The coroner, Mr Gill, who had the last legal word, said, 'Nothing like this must ever be allowed to happen again. But it could unless the warnings are heeded and action taken. I am greatly disturbed that these warnings have not been heeded by those concerned before. Exorcism itself – it is a recognised part of the Church's ministry, but it can have dangers. Those who dabble in it are playing with fire.

'Those who believe in exorcism must always consider also seeking medical advice. Exorcism must be performed only by those trained and properly skilled in the work. There is a danger that novices may be overwhelmed by emotion at such religious gatherings.'

The church also had its say. Father Vincent said that he was satisfied that his authority for conducting exorcism was vested in him by the New Testament and the Lord Jesus Christ and he gave evidence on oath on the matter at his trial. But he was probably ignorant of or ignored the Church of England study on exorcism carried out two years previously. Dr Robert Cecil Mortimer, Bishop of Exeter at the time, who signed the report, said that no case should be considered suitable for a service of exorcism until physical or psychiatric disorders had been ruled out. Most bishops had accepted those guidelines as general authority.

The local bishop, Dr Eric Treacy, declared, 'I am bound to say that the attempts made at exorcism during the night before the murder were unwise. But I believe that the clergymen involved with it were actuated by good intent and had a sincere desire to help Michael Taylor. Exorcism is a type of ministry which is increasingly practised in the Christian churches. There is no order of service for this, which is administered as the situation demands. Clearly it is a form of ministry which must be exercised with the greatest possible care and responsibility.

'No clergyman in the diocese of Wakefield has my specific authority to practice exorcism, but I am aware that some clergymen will feel that it is a normal part of their pastoral ministry.'

Dr Donald Coggan, Archbishop of Canterbury, spoke from on high. 'We must get this business out of the mumbo-jumbo of magic. I do not see exorcism as something set off against and in opposition to medicine. Far from it. I think there are many cases where the more rash exorcists have by-passed the work of psychiatrists and some of the cases where exorcisms have been carried out should not have occurred at all. They should have been referred to psychiatrists. But there is no doubt that there are many cases of men and women so within the grip of the power of evil that they need the aid of the Christian church working in collaboration with the forces of medicine to deliver the person so oppressed.'

The Archbishop said 'obviously there was a grave mishandling of that poor creature [Michael Taylor]' but 'we should not condemn the ministry of liberation because there has been a bad case of it in the Diocese of Wakefield.'

In the face of so much religious talk, the medical view was illuminating. Dr Hugo Milne, the forensic psychiatrist called at the trial in defence of Taylor, said he considered Taylor had been in a trance, a hypnotic or dissociated state which was connected to the exorcism. Taylor's violent exhalation of breath during exorcism (hyperventilation) would reduce his awareness of reality and reduce his control of his behaviour.

Dr Patrick McGrath, superintendent of Broadmoor Hospital, where Taylor was detained pending trial, said he was convinced that Taylor had been brainwashed. Brainwashing is a systematic indoctrination used to change or undermine someone's beliefs, usually by the use of prolonged stress. Dr McGrath said that the case was unique in his experience of more than a thousand murderers.

None of these experts could possibly have imagined what was to come – the killing of pretty university student Anneliese Michel.

## *Chapter Two*

# THE ROMAN CATHOLIC EXORCISM KILLING

'She hadn't eaten for seventy-six days, weighed only four stone, six pounds. I refused to sign the death certificate.'

Police doctor.

Anneliese Michel, a devout twenty-three-year-old Roman Catholic university student and a virgin, had to be tied down on the exorcism bed as she cursed, blasphemed, spat and screamed. When the priests had finished ten months of rites to drive out her devils there were injuries to her genital organs, her beauty was reduced to a parchment-covered skull, and her eyes were so sunken in their sockets no one could tell whether they were open or closed.

A doctor told the police that Anneliese weighed only four stone six pounds. She had starved to death. Her parents and two priests were charged and convicted of killing her.

While the Yorkshire Protestant exorcists were ill-advised, inexperienced, somewhat amateurish and divided, Roman Catholics have a more orderly formula of discussion before deciding whether or not to perform an exorcism. The ritual ceremonies are based on the 1614 *Rituale Romanum*, but it is still no guarantee against death or homicide. Exorcism, whoever administers it, can still be very much the experiment perilous.

The case of Anneliese left even more questions unanswered than the case of Michael Taylor. Taylor, by the legal definition of insanity, did not know right from wrong when he murdered his wife, so he could not be responsible for his actions. Before the case had been forgotten Taylor was adjudged to be sane again.

Within eighteen months of being sentenced to confinement in Broadmoor, he was moved to Waddilove's Hospital, about ten miles from the scene of the murder. He was said by doctors to be no longer in need of intense security and suitable for residence in a hospital without bars. Within two years of the trial he was allowed to make unsupervised visits to his parents' home in Ossett, with a view to returning him a free man to society to rejoin his children.

The debate which followed the Yorkshire case also revealed that demonic possession and exorcism was much more common in Britain than even the Church wanted publicly to admit. Michael Taylor, the exorcised murderer, like so many of the possessed, came from a working-class background. The Reverend Trevor Dearing, vicar of St Paul's, a light industrial working-class parish at Hainault, Essex, off the main London–Southend road, estimated that in four years he drove literally thousands of demons from the bodies of his followers. 'I don't go to people offering them exorcism,' he said. 'They come to me asking for it. They come and say, "I hear strange voices," or "I see frightening things," or "I feel I am being taken over by an evil spirit."

'Let me give you an example. Margaret, a fifteen-year-old girl, brought up as an orphan, was emotionally disturbed. She had been in the care of psychiatrists. They could do nothing for her. Margaret came to our church one Tuesday evening with a friend. Suddenly, among the crowded congregation, she began screaming. She was possessed by hate, fear and anger. Helped by two colleagues and their wives, I carried the girl to the vestry. She went berserk, smashing furniture and glasses, attacking us, trying to climb walls, shouting and screaming at

44

me, "You have no power over me. I am stronger than you. Jesus died for you, but he didn't die for spirits like me."

'We had to hold her down while I commanded the spirit, "In the name of Jesus, go. Leave this girl."

'We had a trying and violent few hours. Eventually, at midnight, Margaret calmed down and we were able to take her home. In the following two weeks we had two more desperate fights with her in the vestry before the battle was won. But it was finally over. Margaret for the first time was free of the voices and strange happenings in her mind. She is now quite happy, quite normal. A happy, pleasant girl and a regular church attender.'

Mr Dearing recalled another case of 'a young attractive married woman, a good wife and mother for several years – until she was possessed by the spirit of seduction. She just couldn't help herself. The evil spirit drove her to seduce almost any man she saw, anywhere – even in the street. I don't mean that she had sex in the street, but she just used to pick up men and go with them or take them back to her house when the family were out. All the time she was tormented by feelings of guilt and remorse, but she couldn't overcome the demon that drove her on. A friend brought her to our church.

'As soon as she saw me she cried, "There's something in you that frightens me. I am seduction . . . I am seduction . . . I am seduction."

'You see, I knew then what I was dealing with. I commanded the spirit of seduction to go, repeating the order firmly over and over again, until the woman seemed calm and peaceful. She came back two or three times before I finally drove the spirit of seduction from her body. Now she is once more a faithful wife and mother, no longer tempted by seduction.'

If Dearing could help these women, could not other priests in another church have saved Anneliese from death?

Another case, according to the Essex vicar, concerned 'a woman who became involved in witchcraft and was possessed by twelve demons. From memory, they were desecration, doubt, fear, death, despair, an enchanting spirit, an animal spirit and some others. She came to one of our regular services of praise and healing and cried out for help. One by one, over the next twelve weeks or so, all the evil spirits identified themselves – "I am despair," "I am death," and so on – I cast them out.

'Incidentally, she also suffered from back trouble. It was cured instantly during one of our services of exorcism.'

Mr Dearing added that afterwards when the woman's name appeared quite innocuously in a church publication she was hounded by a member of the evil devil-worshipping cult to which she had once belonged. The woman herself recalled:

'I became violent and destructive. Usually I would make for our family Bible and tear it up, not page by page, but by tearing it straight across the covers. I had tremendous strength. Over the years we bought fifteen new Bibles to replace the ones I had torn up. A hymn book my mother had given me also went this way.

'I heard stories about the vicar's healing powers. I heard that people were getting rid of backaches and other pains and that he was getting rid of people's depressions.

'I went to his church and as the evil spirits came out I began screaming. Since then, I've found peace. My health is now good. I am more tolerant of people. I am generally a happy person. And I feel strong enough to deal with the Devil should he ever try to take me over again.'

The Reverend J. Christopher Neil-Smith of St Saviour's in more fashionable Hampstead, in north-west London, conducts exorcisms almost daily, although he points out that not all exorcisms are major cases of possession.

In minor cases, he places his hands over the head of the person concerned and tries to break the link with the Devil. One or two people present pray for the subject. But, the clergyman added, 'In a major case you must command in the name of the Father, the Son and the Holy Ghost that the spirit depart. Sometimes then there are eruptions and you have to hold the person down, but it would normally be over in quarter of an hour.'

The Reverend Dr Henry Cooper, chaplain to the Archbishop of Canterbury, normally carries out exorcisms face to face, wearing his robes, in a calm, dignified church-like atmosphere. But night calls are an emergency and for the nocturnally distressed he runs an exorcism hot-line from University College London. The telephone rings at all hours and is answered: 'Dr Cooper here. Can I help you?'

The caller then blurts out his or her story. Callers are often frightened, and cannot go home because evil spirits are stopping them, diverting them to debauchery or some other form of evil.

Dr Cooper placates them in this manner:

'Calm yourself. Don't be afraid. God will help you. Please answer these questions.

'Do you believe in God . . . ?

'Do you believe that He is stronger than any spirit . . . ?

'Do you believe He can control the spirit you think is in you or your home . . . ?

'Do you believe He cares enough to do so . . . ?

'Do you commit yourself in His love and power . . . ?'

When the caller answers 'Yes' to every question, Dr Cooper says firmly:

'It is God's will that you should be free to love and serve Him without fear, for you are His child and He loves you and gave His son to die and rise for you and now sends His Holy Spirit to be with you.

'I bid all that is evil depart from you. And go to its own place. To harm nobody. To remain there. And never to return to trouble you, the child of God. In the name of the Father, and of the Son and of the Holy Spirit. Amen.

'Will you now say with me, together, the Lord's Prayer . . .

'Now go home to bed. There's nothing to be afraid of.'

Having heard this catalogue of success from the Anglicans, one wonders how the Papists would fare. No one church has a monopoly of success in dealing with the more extreme cases as will be seen in the exorcism of Anneliese, the university student who was starved to death.

The Roman Catholic Church, which handled the exorcism of Anneliese, could not be faulted as they insisted on thorough examinations by qualified doctors, psychiatrists and clergy. Only after these reports did the bishop authorise an exorcism by a qualified experienced exorcist. While there is no specialist training to become an exorcist, the priests who perform the function often hold qualifications in medicine, psychiatry or psychology. Two influential Roman Catholic priests who served on the Anglican Bishop of Exeter's inquiry into exorcism explained their approach. Father Joseph Crehan of the Jesuit Church, Farm Street, Mayfair, London, said:

'We know that ninety per cent of these cases are bogus. There's no evil spirit there at all. People who claim that some demon stops them from entering church or prevents them from kneeling down to pray don't usually need exorcism. They more often need to be told their trouble stems from wounded pride or resentment at being rejected. It's a sort of shock treatment but it generally works.

'On the rare occasions when demon possession may be the only explanation for some odd behaviour, the priest would do nothing until he had reported all the facts to his bishop. Only after careful consideration and preparation, involving fasting and prayer, would the exorcism be carried out.'

Dom Robert Petitpierre, a Benedictine monk and acknowledged expert on the subject, explains it thus:

'We are not the only intelligences in the Universe. Some of the others are definitely unpleasant – which is what we mean by demons. Exorcism against them was a miracle worked by Our Lord as a result of the prayers of the Church, not a technique enacted by the church authorities. And it should be kept as brief as possible. There can be a connection between mental illness and the supernatural. We can have mental pressure from other human beings and we can have pressure from departed human spirits – ghosts in the house. I can give instance after instance of this, sometimes very unpleasant. There is a third possibility, of mental pressure from the non-human world.'

What then was the reason for the exorcism and death of Anneliese? Anneliese was a Roman Catholic, exorcised by trained and disciplined priests and, according to the courts, they killed her.

She seemed to build her life around an old-fashioned kind of Roman Catholic devotion. In her dormitory room at the University of Warzburg, West Germany, the pretty, pious young student of education covered her walls with pictures of saints, kept a holy water font near the door, and regularly prayed the Rosary. Timid and intense, she seemed somehow afraid of life, of the worldly atmosphere beyond her own four walls. Even in her scholastic thesis, which she finished in the spring of 1976, she seemed to focus all her thoughts on the phenomenon of fear.

By then, her parents, Josef Michel, a wealthy saw-mill owner, and his wife, Anna, had already taken her to see the parish priest in her home town of Klingenberg. She had developed some signs of abnormal behaviour at the university, refusing to eat, flying into violent rages, screaming and trying to attack those around her. Her parents and friends were deeply concerned.

In the priest's opinion, Anneliese was possessed by demons and he recommended ritual exorcism. As Roman Catholic procedure requires, the case was first investigated by a leading authority on demonic powers, possession and exorcism. That authority was Father Adolf Rodewyk, an eighty-year-old internationally-known Jesuit Satanologist from Frankfurt, and Germany's foremost practitioner in exorcism. He agreed with the priest's diagnosis and on his recommendation, the regional bishop, the Right Reverend Josef Stangl, gave permission for the exorcism to take place. From the list of trained and experienced exorcists, Fathers Arnold Renz and Erns Alt were chosen.

Anneliese's case was well documented. She was even said to be destined for possession. She was born in 1953 in Klingenberg, 150 miles from the Brocken, the highest point in the Saxony Hartz mountain range, where, according to legend, Lucifer and the witches stage their unholy annual Sabbath. The legend, although widely believed, is an illusion in which shadows of the spectators, greatly magnified, are projected on the mists about the summit of the mountain opposite. Long before Anneliese was born, Thomas de Quincey, in his *Confessions Of An Opium-Eater*, gives a powerful description of the illusion from one of his dreams.

Long before Anneliese went to the university she was treated by a neurologist for convulsive attacks. She was then not sixteen. In 1973, after she began collecting pictures of saints and after she had installed holy water in her room, she was medically diagnosed an epileptic. Her parents and her parish priest and eventually Rodewyk refused to believe that this was the sole cause of her malady.

No one suggested that she was mentally unbalanced. She knew her own mind. And she declared, 'The only conclusion for my suffering is that for reasons beyond my control and comprehension, the Devil is trying to possess my soul.'

For ten months, beginning on September 14, 1975, and continuing until not long before her death, the two priests conducted an intermittent series of exorcisms to rid the young woman of six demons they believed possessed her. The efforts were to no avail. About Easter time, her convulsions returned with renewed ferocity, and she

51

began to refuse food and drink.

The rites, performed in her college dormitory and later in her parents' home, were scenes of ecclesiastical bedlam, with flickering candles, a large statue of St Michael the Archangel, a modern gory picture of the crucifixion, and chanting priests resplendent in purple vestments. Anneliese foamed at the mouth and writhed on the bed, uttering obscenities as her parents watched in silent horror. The rites were repeated seventy-two times in the ten months. And the priests dutifully recorded the process on 434 cassette tapes.

According to Father Renz, the six evil spirits attacking her included Lucifer, Nero, Judas, Cain and Adolf Hitler, who used to shout 'Heil!' through the voice of Anneliese. The other demons used her voice, in speech ranging from high tenor to a low bass, and in languages of different ages not known to Anneliese. At least one spoke an archaic form of Latin, another language in which the possessed was not at all versed.

Lucifer spat at the crucifix, howled when sprinkled with holy water, and occasionally invited the exorcists to engage in sexual intercourse with their charge. Nero, the Roman Emperor, who spoke the archaic form of Latin, was also very interested in sex and went into lengthy discussions of the most extreme pleasures in between shrieks of 'Take that holy water away!' Cain, the first murderer in creation, seemed more interested in violence and described in exaggerated detail the torments awaiting the girl, her parents, the two priests, and all their friends and relatives when they were consigned to Hell. He imitated the voices of persons long since dead, identifying the owners, certifying that they were already in the nether regions, roasting in torment, and that those present would soon join them.

Judas, the betrayer of Christ, did not appear very often but when he did so, he confined his remarks to complaining that the thirty pieces of silver he had been given for the betrayal of Our Lord was not enough and he would require further compensation. Despite his reticence, it was during his presence that the girl had her worst physical convulsions and her voice took on the deep, low bass of the disgraced Apostle. It seemed impossible that the voice could have come from the throat of an otherwise refined, delicate young lady.

Another demon who spoke through her mouth, this time in a high falsetto, was Father Helgar Fleischmann, a priest who killed his mistress in the year 1563, and who was subsequently unfrocked, excommunicated, hanged, drawn and quartered. This experience had presumably not diminished his interest in the fairer sex and his language and the subject of his remarks were filthy and sordid beyond belief. He spoke in a long-outdated form of German unknown to anyone except linguistic scholars and historians, and certainly beyond the comprehension of the highly religious Anneliese.

Anneliese's condition worsened. The convulsive attacks become more frequent and more violent. The language was obscene and blasphemy was piled on blasphemy. The priests were violently cursed. Her sexual expressions became more and more coarse and would have been accompanied by sexual actions if she had not been tied to her bed. During all this time, Father Alt and both parents reported seeing the stigmata, the marks of Christ's wounds, appear on the girl's hands and feet.

Sometimes she gasped into the microphone of the tape recorder, 'I can't go on any more! I can't go on any more!' Then, when not actually in the grip and frenzy of one of her seizures, she spoke rationally and prayed for God's guidance, seeking his help and deliverance from the devils she knew were tormenting her.

She probably believed that God had deserted her. No help came. The sight of a crucifix threw her into a spate of spitting and cursing in such violent language that it was difficult to believe that it was uttered through the mouth of a shy, deeply religious girl from a respectable, conservative family background.

As the months passed, the voices of the demons strengthened as Anneliese weakened. The priests thought the demons were fighting for possession of her body and soul, and with each convulsion within her body the sight became more and more frightening. On April 16, Good Friday, the anniversary of Our Lord's crucifixion, Anneliese began to refuse food and had to be helped to take liquid nourishment. The violence of the attacks continued, but her body became weaker and weaker until on the night of June 30, 1976, she died.

The parents summoned Dr Kehler who knew Anneliese. He was shocked by her appearance. Afterwards, he was heard saying in a telephone conversation.

'A human being?'

'Yes.'

'Female?'

'Yes.'

'An adolescent?'

'A child.'

'She is dead?'

'Yes.'

'How tall?'

'Five feet, three inches.'

'And weight?'

'Sixty-two pounds.' [Four stone, six pounds].

The doctor asked the parents, 'What happened to her? How did she get into that condition?'

'She has eaten nothing since Good Friday,' her father replied.

'Heavens. That was weeks ago. It is now July 1.' Anneliese had not eaten for seventy-six days.

'She was possessed by the Devil,' said Herr Michel.

'Evil was in her,' his wife sobbed. 'The Devil had her in his claws. Death has released her. Now she is in heaven.'

'Perhaps so,' said the shaken doctor. 'But you must realise that I cannot issue a death certificate for a corpse in such a condition.'

'Then you may go,' the father retorted. 'We will call in another doctor.'

'No other doctor will issue a death certificate, either, and moreover I shall have to report this to the police. There is certainly going to be an investigation into the circumstances of this girl's death.'

With that Dr Kehler returned to his practice in Ashaffenburg, eighteen miles to the north and the administrative centre for the district, where he reported his visit to the police.

A team of detectives with a police doctor found Josef and Anna Michel still weeping in the living room. They glanced at the picture of Anneliese on the mantelshelf. The experienced officers, used to the sight of shot, stabbed and mutilated bodies, gasped. In the bedroom and under the sheet they saw that only the hair spread over the pillow was any reminder of the good-looking girl whose photograph they had just admired.

'Cause of death?' asked a policeman with his notebook open.

'Extreme malnutrition and dehydration amounting to inanition,' said the police surgeon. 'Death was some time last night. There are wounds on the body, particularly on the genitals, but not serious. I suspect they may have been self-inflicted. She was a virgin. There are also marks on the wrists and ankles where she's been tied. This was probably to prevent her from injuring herself from what I can gather.'

When the public prosecutor saw the report he concluded that the two priests and parents had stood passively by while the girl starved to death. It was homicide by negligence. After all, the law does not recognise demonic possession and expects one human being to go to the aid of another, particularly when it must be obvious that the person is dying. Nor does the law accept that prayer, even if permitted and approved by a competent church authority, is the answer in such circumstances.

Parents and priests all repeated the same story over and over again. Mrs Michel also remembered that when she had been expecting Anneliese, she passed a broken-down cottage in the woods on the edge of the town and an ugly old woman, with only one eye, had stared at her swollen stomach, pointed and said, 'That one will be seized by the Devil.'

Anna had run all the way home to tell her husband. Josef had gone immediately to the old cottage but found no one there. When Anneliese was fifteen, her mother recalled, she had fallen to the floor, writhed, babbled in a strange incomprehensible tongue – obviously talking in tongues – and torn off much of her clothing. To the horror of her deeply religious parents, some of the postures she assumed on the floor were highly indecent; behaviour completely out of character with their modest, chaste daughter.

The priests, answering the prosecutor's questions, replayed the tapes. A typical exchange ran:

Priest: 'I beseech you to leave this girl and never return.'

Anneliese: 'You damned pig. Keep your mouth shut. I am not leaving.'

Priest: 'Why are you here?'

Anneliese: 'I am the Father of Lies.'

Priest: 'Why have you gone into Anneliese?'

Anneliese: 'Because she is damned.'

Charges of homicide by neglect were brought against the parents and the two priests. All four pleaded not guilty. The trial lasted a month, with more than 300 witnesses and experts called upon to testify for the prosecution and the defence.

Prominent physicians gave evidence that the girl had suffered from epilepsy and that exorcism had worsened the condition. But they had to admit, under cross-examination, that they had not seen the girl while she was alive. Equally well-qualified doctors testified that her symptoms did not resemble epilepsy but they, too, had to confess they had never examined the living Anneliese.

Prosecution medical experts testified that 'exorcism was the most inappropriate means of bringing Anneliese out of her psychosis.' (Psychosis is the name for a group of mental disorders including schizophrenia.) A specialist in nervous disorders said she suffered from an emotional conflict resulting from guilt feelings arising from a sexual interest in Christ. Asked to substantiate that opinion, he said it was his faith in modern psychology, a matching answer to the priests who testified to their faith in the existence of demons which were able to take possession of human souls.

Another neurologist said, 'No demons spoke out of Anneliese. The girl spoke to the exorcists with a psycho-hysterical transposed voice.' Another psychiatrist held that 'the girl suffered from paranoiac hallucinatory psychosis in which demons were nothing more than manifestations of a deeper inner spiritual conflict.'

Eventually, the court ruled that priests and parents were guilty of negligent homicide, and sentenced them to imprisonment, suspended for three years' probation in each case.

Since his daughter's death, Josef Michel has reported that his house is haunted by swarms of huge fat flies and big, strong white mice. At night, the house is lit up by strange flashes of light which cannot be explained by natural or man-made illumination. Two years after Anneliese was buried, Sister Ursula, a nun, suffered epileptic seizures and predicted that if the girl's body was exhumed it would be found to be undefiled. When the coffin was opened, however, the body was found to be decayed.

Herr Michel's last word was, 'The guilty are the forces of darkness. You cannot put the master of gloom in the dock.'

## Chapter Three

# TO ACCUSE THE DEVIL

'The courts have dealt with the existence of God before. Now they are going to have to deal with the existence of the Devil.'

Arne Johnson's defence lawyer.

In the English case of Michael Taylor, who was exorcised and next morning killed his wife, and in the German case of Anneliese, who starved to death during exorcism, clergy were able to go into the witness box and under oath tell why they believed in the ritual of exorcism, even though in both cases it had ended in killing. In 1983, in the Connecticut Superior Court, Danbury, Conn., USA, the law and the church clashed head-on when the clergy were refused permission to give evidence in court.

The Roman Catholic Bishop of Bridgeport, seven priests and two experts on demonology queued to give evidence at the trial of nineteen-year-old Arne 'Cheyenne' Johnson, charged with stabbing to death his forty-year-old friend and next-door neighbour, Alan Bono. Johnson's counsel, Martin Minella, claimed that demons had forced his client to murder his friend. 'The devil is going to be on trial,' he declared.

Judge Robert Callaghan refused to hear such evidence. He ruled that 'Courts have not recognised such a defence and I'm not going to allow it. It's irrelevant. The profession of demonology has not reached the position of reliability at which it can be acceptable to the court.'

On February 16, 1983, Johnson and his twenty-six-year-old girl friend Helen Louis returned to Bono's boarding kennels, where she was working, and where Johnson was repairing a stereo sound system for the owner. Johnson, a curly-haired, blond, baby-faced six-footer, with no previous record of violence, suddenly pulled out a five-inch-bladed folding knife and plunged it into Bono's chest.

What troubled many people was not the killer or the victim but Helen's twelve-year-old brother, Mike, whom the church thought was possessed by demons. The boy reportedly hissed and growled and burst into fits of profanity and displays of superhuman strength. He spoke in strange tongues and recited passages from John Milton's *Paradise Lost*.

How else could anyone explain why a fat, mop-haired boy would declaim lines like:

> When night
> Darkens the streets, then wander forth the sons
> Of Belial, flown with insolence and wine.

Or:

> A shout that tore hell's concave, and beyond
> Frightened the reign of Chaos and old Night.

And:

> Satan exalted sat, by merit raised
> To that bad eminence.

Was it:

> His red right hand

and not Johnson's that plunged the knife into Bono's chest? Was this the work of a human being or the young brother, possessed by Milton's

> Demoniac frenzy, moping melancholy,
> And moon-struck madness?

Helen and Arne, from Brookfield, Connecticut, had scraped together $500 deposit on the rent to move into a bungalow in Newtons, a comfortable suburb of Fairfield County. 'It was exactly what we have been looking for,' they said excitedly. Helen's brothers, Paul, aged sixteen, Hart who was fourteen and eleven-year-old Mike came to help them move.

In the basement they found a large collection of furniture which would be better employed upstairs, but there was no room for the huge waterbed with the mirrored canopy. The previous tenants had promised to return to remove it.

Later that afternoon, as most of the family worked in other parts of the bungalow, Mike, the grossly overweight baby of the family, just a month away from his twelfth birthday, found himself alone. Something happened to him that was to remain fixed in many minds.

When they returned to their former home from which they were moving, he said, 'Someone shoved me on the water bed when I thought I was alone in that room.'

'Who was it, Mike?' someone asked.

'It wasn't someone. It was something. And it followed me all the way back here!'

Arne laughed, 'Give us a break, Mike. What did this thing look like?'

'It was an old man, burnt and black – looking like he had feet like deer.'

Imagination? Childish day dreams? A waking nightmare? At night, Mike would see 'the thing' again. Members of the family would hear strangled moans coming from the boy's room. They would steal into his room and see him tossing feverishly in bed, his hands tearing at his throat, as if trying to wrench away unseen fingers that were strangling him. Sometimes he muttered incoherently. Other times he spoke obscenely and made animal noises. Asked what was going on, he would invariably answer that he had seen the apparition again.

Arne and Helen became distraught. Their terror heightened as their new home seemed to take on an evil personality of its own. One night, the whole family was haunted by strange human voices. Whenever there was an inexplicable sound one member of the family would grab a torch and would try to track down its origin. No one ever saw a thing.

Mrs Louis, Mike's mother, found her son's sufferings so painful to watch that she called in Ed Warren and his wife, demonologists with a nationwide reputation for helping in such matters. Warren insisted that Mike Louis was first seen by a physician to ensure there was no physical explanation for his visions. Then, accompanied by his wife, a well-known clairvoyant, he sprinkled holy water over the child and held a crucifix to his forehead, reciting 'Hail Mary' over and over again.

When the boy seemed to experience some relief from the 'thing', Mrs Warren taught him a prayer called 'My Guardian Angel,' which she had composed. She asked Mike to repeat it over and over again because it might keep the 'beast' away.

The Warrens returned on each of the ensuing nights, bringing more holy water, more crucifixes and more prayers. There appeared to be some improvement but they could not shake the grip of the 'thing' that appeared to be torturing him. They could not even identify it. They instructed Mike's parents to take photographs and make tape recordings of anything the boy said in his sufferings, in case these would give some clues to the nature or identity of the demon.

Instead, the Louis family decided to ask the Roman Catholic Church for help. What Mike really needed was to have the demon exorcised from his body. On the first visit the priest would only say Mass and 'Bless this house,' but he did 'feel a presence in the house'. Whatever it was, there was no let-up in Mike's sufferings.

The Bishop of Bridgeport was informed and at St Joseph's parish church, Brookfield, the Reverend Francis E. Virgilak performed a service of deliverance, the first of three lesser forms of exorcism. At the first Mike spat and fought and tried to sink his teeth into the priest's hands as prayers were said for him. At subsequent services four priests were in attendance.

Then, the day after the last deliverance, Arne, the skilled tree-surgeon, had an accident. He knew how to tie ropes. His knots were always secure. But he fell twenty feet from the branch of a tree. Fortunately lower branches broke his fall and he escaped with a slight knee injury, but careful examination of the ropes revealed no cause for the incident.

Arne was more worried about Mike, the possessed, than himself. When the boy was in the middle of a seizure, Arne would challenge the demon, 'Take me on. Control me. Leave the boy alone.' The demon, it was claimed, did just that. On a journey between the two homes, Arne's face became twisted. He started shaking all over. His girlfriend, Helen, said, 'I could tell it just was not Arne with me.'

Later, Arne told her that he did not remember a thing about the experience. Later still in the middle of one night, beside Helen, he began talking about Hell. Then he punched his fist through a panel in a chest of drawers beside the bed. When he awoke next morning, he asked Helen how he had injured his hand. Arne Johnson continued to display similar bizarre behaviour, but because the family were more concerned with the twelve-year-old Mike, they paid little attention to the muscular tree-surgeon.

On February 16, 1982, Helen was working as a groom for their neighbour, Alan Bono, at the Brookfield Boarding Kennels. Arne, Helen and Alan had become close friends, but the tree-surgeon got the notion into his head that the kennel-man was trying to steal Helen's affections. They all went out to lunch together, returned, and suddenly there was an emergency call from the kennels. Police found Bono lying in the driveway with a five-inch knife lying nearby. He had died from multiple wounds to the chest and abdomen. A pathologist said that the knife had been plunged in, withdrawn, and plunged in again and again.

An hour later, Arne Johnson was found wandering dazed along a road two miles from the kennels. Helen told police that Arne had drunk some red wine and had an argument about some work he was doing on the stereo system for Alan. He then pounded his fist in his hand and started to walk away. Bono then grabbed Helen and her nine-year-old cousin and both girls called for help.

After that, all she remembered was seeing her boss sprawled on the front lawn in a pool of his own blood. Her boyfriend stumbled out of the yard 'like someone in a trance', acting as he had on four previous occasions in recent months when he had not seemed himself.

The lawyer who was to represent Johnson said at the outset, 'The courts have dealt with the existence of God before. Now they are going to have to deal with the existence of the Devil. The case will be unique in the higher jurisprudence system of the United States.'

He was prepared, he said, to introduce tapes, photographs and expert testimony from priests and psychic researchers to show that his teenaged client was possessed by the Devil and not responsible for his acts. 'We have substantial credible evidence that Mr Johnson had no intention to harm anyone – and that what happened was a result of demonic possession,' he declared. 'People may not really want to deal with the Devil, but he does exist.'

Warren, the demonologist, said, 'We have always felt that if they ever bring us into a court of law, we will prove that the preternatural exists – that the Devil exists. The old cliché that "the Devil made me do it" is not going to be enough. We are going to have to prove it.'

Arne's attempts to deal with the young Mike's demon, were, according to Warren, 'amateurish because the only way to order out demons from a person's body is by using the name of Jesus Christ, not to challenge the Devil yourself.'

Mrs Warren said that Arne 'had to watch someone he cared about coming under violent attack from demons. So he challenged what was within the child to take him on – and none of us ever do that, not even the priests. It was like sitting on a powder-keg. We knew there was going to be some sort of tragedy.'

Considerable interest focussed on whether the Roman Catholic priests would break the Church's traditional silence about exorcism cases and testify in court about what they saw and did during the rites of deliverance performed over young Mike Louis. And on whether or not Arne Johnson had become possessed in trying to save Mike.

After a grand jury indicted Johnson for murder, his

lawyer told the judge that he intended to pursue a defence of demonic possession at the trial, even though he had to concede such a defence was not recognised in American legal books. He planned to ask priests and psychic experts to testify that Johnson was under the influence of demons who entered into him through Mike Louis. 'I have discussed this with my client and he wishes to inform you, through me, that he intends to pursue this matter before a jury.'

The jury of seven women and five men heard Helen insist that Arne growled and beat and kicked her before the stabbing. 'He made voices come out of his mouth, growling, screaming at the same time.'

When Judge Callaghan refused to allow the demonic defence evidence, Johnson's counsel switched to self-defence, added to the fact that there was an element of drunkenness in the case. Bono had an alcohol level of thirty-three per cent in his blood compared with Johnson's twelve per cent. The State of Connecticut law says that the judgment of a motorist with a level of more than ten per cent is impaired.

After a three-day retirement, the jury found Johnson guilty of manslaughter. Judge Callaghan told him, 'I do not assume the powers of God. But you took a human life – and you showed no acknowledgement of guilt and little remorse.' He sentenced Johnson to the maximum ten-to-twenty years' imprisonment.

Mrs Louis reported afterwards that her son, Mike, showed no sign of improvement in his battle against demonic possession. 'He still sees things every day,' she said, 'My son needs exorcism. I want the exorcism for him – and for Arne who has suffered as a result of the demon, too.'

And so the debate continues, in courts, consulting rooms and church vestries, not about whether there are such people as holy killers but about whether a religious, churchgoing person can be guided by an unseen hand, a voice that no one else can hear, a power that none can withstand, to strike the fatal blow.

## Chapter Four

# MYTH OF THE HOLY MAN

'He punched her ribs for twenty-five to thirty minutes and said the Demon had gone but the Demon had killed the girl.'

Lancashire Crown Prosecution Service.

If lawyers, doctors and churchmen dispute the existence or power of demons in European Christian communities, how can they judge them in immigrant non-Christian groups?

Cedric Whitman, the American classicist, has probably never been to Oldham, the great cotton-spinning town seven miles out of Manchester. But he might have been looking into the windows of the millstone grit houses when he wrote: 'Mythology is what grown-ups believe, folklore is what they tell their children and religion is both.' That is certainly how it appears in some Muslim communities in Britain, notably those made up of migrants who quit the Hindu- and Sikh-dominated Punjab after the partition of India to seek peace and security in Lancashire.

Many of those Muslims believe in the classical Islamic myth of the existence of the djinni or jinni, a supernatural class of spirits, lower than angels but capable of appearing in human and animal forms and influencing people for both good and evil. Elders teach these myths to children like pretty Kousar Bashir, who absorbed them like a set of fairy-tales until she was twenty-one. Then, in the eyes of some of her elders, she had become possessed by the spirits about which they had taught her.

She had the options of a free society to choose, or have chosen for her, the best cure for that 'possession': the doctors at the Royal Oldham Hospital; the mullahs, the learned teachers of sacred law in the Muslim community; or the self-appointed holy men who are widely believed by many Muslims to possess healing powers unknown to the medical profession. So great is the respect shown to these holy men and the belief demonstrated in them that Kousar's family watched as they tortured her and thrashed her to death.

She lived in a quiet terraced house in St Thomas Street, on the way north to Rochdale. When she took a driving test and failed she became very depressed and even threatened to throw herself from an upstairs window. Her parents could not understand why she was so ill, but then they only spoke Punjabi and found communication with experts extremely difficult. They had to get interpreters to accompany them to see doctor after doctor.

Eventually, Kousar was admitted to the Royal Oldham Hospital for psychiatric care in April 1990. While under treatment there she told doctors that she had repeated visions of a bearded man wearing an orange robe. Wherever she went, indoors or out, to the bathroom, to the bedroom, he would appear and threaten to kill her.

When Kousar was discharged from hospital, obviously not completely cured, her family had to weigh the chances of her being made well by traditional methods from their homeland and their community. Where medical science had failed, they believed, Islamic faith could succeed.

As faithful Muslims, they consulted the Imam, the officiating priest at the local mosque, who prayed to Allah for the girl. When she did not get better the family turned to the holy men who are employed, for a fee, to expel the evil spirits from the bodies of their possessed victims. Even though some Islamic authorities warn against such practices, the Bashir family went ahead with their plans.

The Church of England has a para-psychic adviser in each of its forty-three dioceses to advise on cases of demonic possession. Alas, Muslim dwellers in Britain are not so well served. Their advisers are often of doubtful background, education and training. Eventually the Bashirs contacted the scholarly-looking and bearded fifty-five-year-old Mohammed Bashir (no relation), from McLeod Street, in the cotton, mining and brick-making town of Nelson, Lancashire. He put them in touch with a white-bearded Father Christmas lookalike, Mohammed Nourani, otherwise known as Sayeed Nourani, a sixty-three-year-old from Blackburn, another outpost of Cottonopolis. He was widely respected in the Muslim community and generally believed to possess healing powers.

He had, they said, carried out more than 200 exorcisms to drive out the jinni from the faithful; so he was invited to St Thomas Street, Oldham, to cure Kousar Bashir. Her parents came from a rural community, and believed in him.

They had been taught how the jinn could intervene in human affairs just as in *The Arabian Nights*. The jinni disguise themselves as men, women, and many different animals, particularly snakes; even bearded men in orange robes. They live in all manner of places: stones, trees, ruins, beneath the earth, in the air and in fire.

A girl like Kousar, even at the age of twenty-one, would know that at times they can be friendly to mankind, although mostly they seek to punish humans for some slight or harm done to them intentionally or accidentally. The jinni are also supposedly responsible for many diseases and all kinds of terrible misfortunes.

Free from all physical restraints, they possess extraordinary powers, so it is not surprising, human nature being what it is, that some people claim to be able to understand them, talk to them, and negotiate with them. Some even claim to know the secrets of their magic so that they can counter the more hostile spirits. They are acknowledged as the holy men.

The spirits are mentioned frequently in the Koran and devout scholars have interpreted the work of the jinni in terms of medieval science. Avicenna, the famous Arab physician and philosopher (980–1037) said 'a jinn is an airy and rational animate being with a transparent body, capable of assuming various shapes.' However, he added, 'This is not a true definition but the idea suggested literally by the name.'

To a student, this is a helpful scepticism but since Kousar Bashir was told this spirit was invisible it became merely another distortion on which the two holy men traded. On the other hand, because the jinni dislike all modern technology and the twentieth-century innovations which make everyday life more comfortable, belief in them varies considerably, from devotion in poverty-stricken Third World areas to suspicion and disbelief in wealthier western regions.

The holy men in Britain, promising to rid the possessed of their evil spirits, charge around £25 per day. It does not seem much, but then the so-called priests move in with the patient and family, sometimes staying for weeks or even months, as the bill multiplies. Some thought that Sayeed Nourani was a very holy man and not like that at all. They were not so sure about Mohammed Bashir, whom they regarded as possibly an agent on a percentage. Then they saw Nourani bless his own walking stick and hand it to Bashir, and wondered.

In the small hours of Tuesday, June 18, 1991, other members of Kousar's large family, who also lived in St Thomas Street, were awakened by an uproar of horrendous noises; shouting interrupted by wailing. Forcing their way into her home they found Kousar, the once bright-eyed attractive Asian girl, lying on the floor bloody and battered. She was dead. A doctor said that weals suggested that she had been whipped, large bruises that she had been clubbed. When they got her to the mortuary, a pathologist added that she had also been kicked, suffering broken bones in her chest and neck regions.

Detective Superintendent Bill Kerr took into custody every occupant of the house for questioning, while outside and beyond the boundaries of Oldham, the religious argument over the valid use of holy men intensified. Kerr had confirmed that among the people detained was 'a holy man'.

He explained cautiously, 'The dead woman had apparently received unorthodox treatment from religious figures in a ritual designed to beat evil spirits from her body. I can confirm that priests had been invited to the family home to give Kousar spiritual help to rid her of her depression.' He had already come to the conclusion that that help had gone far beyond what was permitted by either British or Muslim law.

So worried was the burgeoning northern Muslim community that a spokesman for the Manchester Council of Mosques issued a statement explaining that priests might try to drive out spirits. 'One theory accepted by people who come from the villages is that a person may be

77

possessed and priests may be brought in to say prayers,' he explained. 'The use of beating to drive out spirits is extremely rare. It would be unacceptable in my experience.'

Choudhary Nadir Hussain, president of the British Pakistan Muslim Welfare Association, confessed that the practice of inviting into their homes 'fake holy men' to cure illnesses by casting out jinni or evil spirits is widespread. 'Bogus witch doctors are duping deeply religious people into paying for exorcism rituals. It is nothing more than dangerous magic. They often cause more harm than good.'

Mr Hussain painted a simple word picture of Muslims from rural communities in India and Pakistan. 'They trust their priests completely. When they come to Britain their life is with the educated. They are not in the jungle. They should trust proper doctors and the hospitals, who provide good modern scientific care.

'Priests often deliberately strike terror in the hearts of people. They send them into trances, with various drugs and chants, and shout at them to terrify them. I have heard how chillies are placed in a bowl, set alight and then pushed into the face of the patient, who is forced to breathe in fiery fumes. This is supposed to drive out evil spirits, but in fact causes great pain and suffering. People should have nothing to do with these priests. They claim they are holy men when in fact they are no such thing.'

How phoney or how genuine were the holy men – Sayeed Nourani, who told people that he was a holy man with priestly powers, or Mohammed Bashir, who actually carried out the beatings on the orders of Nourani? Bashir was in fact charged with murdering the twenty-one-year-old girl. Nourani was charged with conspiracy to cause her actual and grievous bodily harm.

When the case opened at Manchester Crown Court on March 9, 1992, the jury were told that the two men had been called in to cure Kousar of her behavioural problems, but instead she had been kicked and battered to death in a bloody session disguised as exorcism.

The first real doubt about the holy men came when, on the defendants' second visit to Kousar, while they were questioning her, an aunt saw her write down on a piece of paper the name 'John Wayne'. The name of the American movie star of so many western films was immediately seized upon by the holy men as the identity of the evil jinn that was possessing the soul of the demented girl.

Day by day, the prosecution spelled out the eight days of torment, starvation and torture inflicted on Kousar by Bashir. It began on Monday, June 10 and continued until she died in the early hours of Tuesday, June 18. During that time, Bashir had hit Kousar with a heavy glass ashtray; with the walking-stick given him by Nourani, the stick which broke in two as a result of the ferocity of his blows; and with his bare fists.

That was the pattern. Nourani handed him the weapons; Bashir displayed the brutal violence, hitting the girl for anything up to two hours at a time. When questioned during the 'treatment', he always explained that he was beating not her but the evil spirit inside her.

The Crown, however, claimed that Bashir was acting on the instructions of Sayeed Nourani. On the evening of Thursday, June 13, Nourani told Bashir, 'Continue the treatment, but do not beat her up any more.' But on Sunday, June 16, Bashir was seen punching Kousar in the neck, in the ribs, on the arms and the shoulders. Bashir punched her all over her body and grabbed her hair with great force.

By that time, Kousar had not eaten for eight days or slept for four days. In the afternoon and evening of that Sunday, Bashir continually punched Kousar in the stomach and the chest, then jumped on her stomach and her chest with both feet.

At 1.30 a.m. on the Tuesday came the final attack. He hit her in the stomach with great force, then punched her ribs on both sides of her body for some twenty-five to thirty minutes. Kousar breathed three times, three deep, gasping groans, then nothing more. Bashir, the holy man, who had come to banish the evil spirit within her, was asked what had happened. He replied, 'The demon has gone but he killed the girl.'

When he realised the police were being called, he said, 'If anyone asks, say that the demon pushed the girl down the stairs and that the fall killed her.'

The pathologist easily demonstrated that was untrue. The girl had suffered severe bruising and died after receiving sixteen fractures to the ribs and a fractured breast-bone, caused by punching, kicking and stamping.

Hussain, the Muslim welfare worker, had underestimated the use of chillies as a torture. Nourani visited the house twice. On the first occasion, he drew a circle round her. She was then ordered to inhale the smoke of burning mustard oil and hot chilli powder which was pushed down her throat.

On the second day of the trial, Kousar's mother cried as she described watching Bashir banging Kousar's wrists and ankles with the heavy glass ashtray. The back room of the house was full of smoke from burning oil and candles as Nourani recited passages from the Koran to drive out the evil spirit whom he called 'John Wayne'.

Kousar's mother, under cross-examination, agreed that she herself had heard the jinn speaking. 'The jinn said he would go and not come back. It was Kousar's voice, but it was like a man talking.'

The uncle of the dead girl said that towards the end Bashir had ordered her to lie on the floor in the back room. 'He had both his knees on her abdomen and was pressing on her chest with his fists. Then he started punching. He was using all the force of his body. He was punching her ribs and stomach and while he was doing so he was asking, "Want to go or not?"

'He was saying it to Kousar but he was talking to the jinn. The child breathed three times and Bashir asked me to check her pulse. But there was no heartbeat.

'Bashir said, "The jinn has gone, but he has killed the girl." '

Bashir, a family man with eight children, giving evidence, told the court that he had no formal education and could not read or write. When he first met Nourani he had been very impressed by him, especially since they were both followers of the same religious leader. Sayeed Nourani was 'a very good man' and he had helped him in several cases of exorcism and in treating sick people. 'Some of them were possessed with evil spirits.'

He insisted that he had slapped and hit the girl to drive out the evil spirit, but claimed that members of her own family also took part in the violence.

Nourani, with his snow-white beard, went into the witness box and said he was able to cast out evil spirits from possessed people by using powers handed down to him by his elders. But he said that force or violence was never used. Islam did not permit it.

He denied that he had ever instructed Bashir to beat the girl or tie her up and he had no knowledge at the time that that was being done to her. Had he known, he would have put a stop to it.

Bashir had to try to shift the blame on to Nourani. His counsel told the jury that he had been following orders from a holy man of great distinction and he genuinely believed he had been doing good work. When he was arrested by the police, he said, 'You do a good deed and you get all the trouble.'

Against this, the prosecuting counsel said that even as he rained down blows on the unfortunate girl he assured her parents that she was suffering no pain. It was the jinn who was suffering and the pain would cease as he was finally driven out. Bashir himself had said, 'The girl don't feel the pain. The demon is the one in pain.'

The trial lasted nine days and at the end the jury returned verdicts of guilty against both men. The judge sentenced Nourani, the holy man of distinction, to five years imprisonment, and Bashir to jail for life for murder.

To Bashir, the judge said, 'You systematically tortured and thrashed and eventually killed the deceased by breaking bones in her chest and throat in no fewer than eighteen places. The amount of fractures gives a horrible indication of what she suffered in the presence of various members of the family.'

To Nourani, 'You blessed the walking stick and gave it to your assistant for the obvious purpose of it being used to thrash that poor girl. And thrashed she was, as you well know. You have been a man of good works and today is a terrible day for you. You were trusted by her family, but what you agreed should be done to her was no less than torture. You were called in to help her but you abused the trust placed in you.'

But the biggest question hanging over the principle of exorcism and this particular exorcism in the name of Islam came in the words of the counsel for Nourani who said: 'The verdict is a catastrophe for the thousands of Muslims who followed and regarded Nourani as a holy man. The conviction of this saintly man will have a dramatic impact upon the entire community and all those who believe in jinns and their exorcism.'

Police thought differently. They had picked up from Bashir, who said he could not read or write, a document which said, 'I will free Kousar and leave proof in an hour's time. (Signed) J. Wayne.'

One could almost hear John Wayne, the 'Duke' himself, saying, 'The hell it did!'

*Chapter Five*

# A SERPENT IN PARADISE

'Ladies like you
Make men pour out their hearts
And you have also thrilled the body
Making its hair
Stiffen with desire.'

Monumental inscription at
Sigiriya, Sri Lanka.

Russel Ingram, the sportsman who had never been ill in his life, lay in hospital dying. He was only thirty-two. He had trembled, fainted, sweated. His heart had beat rapidly and irregularly. Mentally, he was confused, his behaviour irrational, his speech slurred. He appeared drunk, although he had only ever taken an occasional glass of arrack, and then not recently. Russel's head throbbed. He lost his temper for no reason; picked up a knife and threatened to attack a relative; wanted to break down a door; and he had lost his memory. When he looked at the doctor and the nurses he saw two of each of them, and finally he fell into a coma.

In little more than a fortnight the medical staff had cured him and sent him home without recommending any further medication. In another four days he was unconscious and, back in hospital, he died within hours.

It was a very odd case. On both occasions, Father Matthew Peiris, the faith-healer and exorcist, had brought Russel, who was his house guest, to the hospital, and made sure his food was delivered in person every day. Seven months later, the vicar's wife, Eunice, showed precisely the same symptoms. She too fell into a coma and, after a long time unconscious, this time in hospital, she also died.

And all this happened in Paradise.

Parishioners, friends and relatives asked why Father Matthew, who had the power to drive out devils and to invoke divine aid to cure the sick, had not been able to save his wife or Russel. After all, Russel was the husband of Father Matthew's secretary and they did all live together under the same roof.

Usually in such cases of pain and suffering, Father Matthew would have prayed and cited how, according to the Good Book, the seriously ill and dying can be healed and even the dead brought back to life by faith. They only had to close their eyes and they could hear their priest's voice recounting how Our Lord raised Jairus's daughter from the dead saying 'the maid is not dead, but sleepeth' (Matthew ix: 24). He raised the only son of a widow from his coffin in the city of Nain (Luke vii: 11–17). And he raised Lazarus, the beggar 'full of sores' from the dead (John xi: 1–44, xii: 1–18). Sceptics were reminded by Father Peiris that even as recently as the 1970s, Sai Baba, the Hindu leader, raised a man who had been dead for days and whose body had begun to decompose.

No wonder the reverend father, who preached and practised faith-healing, found such a prodigious following. The faithful found it very difficult to believe that Father Peiris and his secretary, Mrs Dalrene Ingram, could have conspired together to murder first her husband, Russel, then, months later, the priest's wife, Eunice. The motive, though, was there – elimination of her husband and his wife so that they could enjoy their illicit relationship without interference.

The method of killing was diabolically clever, even ingenious. Lawyers acting for the defence said that the victims met their deaths naturally, or by accident, or from neglect or even by suicide. And, strangely, they could have done so. Proving or disproving conspiracy and murder would be a Herculean task for both prosecution and defence.

Father Matthew George Frederic Peiris was a remarkable man. After his early schooling at Prince of Wales College, Moratuwa, Sri Lanka, he came to Britain, where he graduated to the Church of England priesthood from Lincoln Theological College in 1952. He became a deacon at St Albans, the city named after the first English martyr; next a priest at the church of St Francis of Assisi, under the patronage of the Marquis of Salisbury, in Welwyn Garden City, Hertfordshire, and then curate at Hatfield Hyde in the same county.

A family man, Peiris was married to Eunice Felicia Lois, and they had three grown-up children, a son, Munilal, and two daughters, Mihiri and Mairani, all of whom lived in South Wales. Mihiri was a graduate of Ceylon University, held a Master's Degree from Cardiff University and worked in the town planning department of Cardiff City Council.

Her father was also an impressive figure. When he preached, he claimed that he could go into a trance at will, that he could talk to angels and that he could make intercessions through the Archangel St Michael. He showed the palm of his right hand which bore the stigmata, the wounds of Christ, which bled when he was in a trance, and which, in his own words, 'make me a saint'. He said that he had divine powers, and was capable of curing people possessed of evil spirits and other maladies.

Fortunately perhaps for the people of Hertfordshire, the reverend curate decided to return to his native Sri Lanka, that place of extreme beauty, the original Biblical Paradise. King Solomon called it Eden. When he looked for the treasure trove that would win the heart of the Queen of Sheba he found it there. Mark Twain said of Sri Lanka, 'Dear me, it's beautiful.' Bernard Shaw called it 'the cradle of the human race'. 'I have been in hell, otherwise Sakhalin,' said Anton Chekhov, 'and in paradise, that is to say Ceylon' [the old colonial name for Sri Lanka].

It was also known as Serendip, whence we get the word 'serendipity', meaning the faculty for making desirable but unsought discoveries by accident. Horace Walpole gave this gift to the heroes of his work, *The Three Princes of Serendip*.

If Matthew Peiris came across an unsought discovery by accident it was in the woman, Dalrene Ingram. She came to his church, St Paul's, Pettah, in Kynsey Road, in the capital, Colombo, in need of help. He was besotted by her. He had seen on the 1,144-ft high pencil of granite at Sigiriya the inscription:

> Ladies like you
> Make men pour out their hearts
> And you have also thrilled the body
> Making its hair
> Stiffen with desire.

Father Peiris was sixty. Mrs Dalrene Ingram was a very attractive married woman of twenty-seven, a typist and secretary. Her husband, Russel, to whom she had been married for eight years, had lost his job in 1976 and he and his wife needed work to keep them and their three small children in health and comfort.

Peiris, who had first become the curate at St Paul's, then the vicar, was by 1978 a very busy and important

Marie Robinson, a 23-year-old lay preacher, was labelled a Satanist and blamed in court for 'seducing' Michael Taylor of Ossett, Yorkshire, into murdering his wife with his bare hands. She denied it (*Syndication International Ltd*)

Kousar Bashir, aged twenty-one, of Oldham, Lancashire (*right*) was taught to believe in genies. Her parents hired holy man Mohammed Nourani (*below*) to drive out her evil spirit (*Quay Photographic Ltd*)

Mohammed Nourani blessed his walking stick, handed it to his assistant, Mohammed Bashir (no relation), who thrashed her to death (*Quay Photographic Ltd*)

Adelaide Bartlett and her lover, the Reverend George Dyson (*insets*), at her trial for murder at the Old Bailey (*The Hulton-Deutsch Collection*)

Adelaide Bartlett asked Dyson to get her chloroform to help her grocer husband sleep. Edwin Bartlett died of chloroform poisoning but no one knows for certain how it was administered (*The Hulton-Deutsch Collection*)

cleric. He was organising the visiting foreign dignitaries and the ceremonies for the January consecration of the new Anglican Bishop of Colombo; he was planning a world trip with his wife; and he was writing a book, to be called *Damn the Bloody Exorcist*. He needed someone to type his manuscript and, it suddenly occurred to him, someone to look after the vicarage in his absence.

The ageing vicar and the youngish secretary had the answer. Mrs Ingram could become his secretary and work on his book. He would find a job for Russel, and the Ingrams, with their children, could all move into the vicarage in Regent Street, Borella. Mrs Peiris was away visiting the family in Britain. And Dalrene could, when no one else was about, keep him company in bed. The couple cemented the illicit relationship by taking out a joint account at the People's Bank.

Peiris recommended Russel for the job of advertising agent at Associated Newspapers, the local publishers, where he started work on January 1. His bosses found him regular in attendance, mentally and physically fit, sociable, sober and keen on sport. He had been a Stubbs Shield school boxer, played football and cricket at Wesley College, Colombo, and more recently played for the firm's cricket XI, all of which was to raise the question of how such a healthy person could become so ill in such a short space of time and die.

Soon the Ingrams were attending St Paul's and the regular Thursday night exorcism services. Dalrene took an increasingly active part in these ceremonies. By the time Mrs Peiris returned to the island Father Matthew's faith-healing and exorcism work had reached a new level of popularity. He began to try to convince both his wife and Dalrene's husband, on separate occasions, that the

91

angels had warned him that they were doomed.

In the second half of April, while on a visit to South Wales, Father Matthew told his son, Munilal, that Russel was ill. Early in June, Mrs Ingram found Russel collapsed, senseless on the floor. She did not call a doctor and did not contact the Colombo General Hospital, where her own mother had been a nurse, even though the out-patients department was only half a mile away and within sight of the vicarage. Instead she allowed her priestly lover, who had no medical qualifications, to care for her husband with advice supposedly obtained from doctors by telephone.

Mrs Ingram summoned Russel's father, Alex, a retired railway engine driver, on June 10. He remembered Father Peiris pulling about four pills from his pocket together with a capsule which he gave to the sick man. 'The doctor prescribed them,' said the priest, adding 'They are just like Dispirin.'

Russel got up, but he could not eat solid food, and went back to bed in a stupor. And that was how he remained for almost five weeks. His father had a graphic phrase, 'One moment he was in the pond, next moment he was on the bank.' He was in the pond, seriously ill, for seventeen days and unconscious for twenty hours before the vicar took him to hospital.

There, Father Matthew had placed a torch on the patient's stomach and said, 'I feel a vibration. Divine guidance tells me there is something wrong with Russel in his stomach.' He even tried to prevent doctors administering sugar to Russel, saying that sugar was bad for him. The sick man was put on a drip of saline and dextrose; he recovered sufficiently to eat solids and walk about and was sent home to the vicarage with Father Peiris on July

14. Four days later, on July 18, he was re-admitted to hospital unconscious and there within hours he died. The cause of death: hypoglycaemia causing irreversible brain damage.

Hypoglycaemia is the opposite of diabetes, where there is too much sugar in the blood. Hypoglycaemia is caused by an abnormally low level of sugar in the blood. It is dangerous because the brain is critically dependent on glucose and is rapidly and irreversibly damaged if this vital 'fuel' is absent.

One treatment commonly available for diabetes is Euglucon, a 2.5 milligramme tablet. This reduces the blood sugar level, but only one tablet or even half a tablet per day is prescribed, to be taken at breakfast or during the first main meal of the day. Father Peiris had given Russel Euglucon, four tablets at one time, seven at another and no one knows what quantity at other times. When he said a doctor had prescribed them, he lied. No doctor had been consulted at all.

When Dalrene was asked why the vicar was giving Russel tablets, she answered, 'Father is looking after Russel' and 'Father knows what he is doing.'

The vicar's son, Munilal, remembered that in April, 1978, his father, who was staying with him, had told him, 'I am worried about Mummy's health. She does not look too well.' This puzzled the son because he knew his mother was perfectly well at the time. Was Father Matthew preparing his only son for his mother's death, which he had already planned?

Munilal also remembered seeing his father buy 100 Euglucon tablets in a chemist's shop. He remembered the label on the foil cover of the medicine. Euglucon was then universally available over the counter and not, as it is now, obtainable only by prescription. Doctors and chemists in Sri Lanka searched their notes and memories and found they had frequently supplied the drug to the vicar, even while Russel Ingram was in the hospital. He bought the tablets in blisters of 10, 20, 30, and 50 as well as 100.

And Munilal remembered that his father had had two trances, in one of which, he said, an angel had confirmed that Mrs Peiris was not well and in the other, an angel had told him that Russel was ill and that he, Father Matthew, should look after him.

When Russel Ingram returned to the vicarage after his spell in hospital, the situation quickly worsened. Father Peiris was lying on his own bed. 'Father is in a trance,' said Dalrene. The priest was rubbing his abdomen, saying 'This is where Russel is feeling the pain. The pancreas, the pancreas, the pancreas.' Peiris indicated the part of his anatomy where Russel was suffering and Dalrene then took some oil in the palm of her hand and rubbed it on the priest's body.

Because Russel was so ill and about to die, Father Matthew needed an independent witness in the house. He invited Russell Jackson, a lay preacher, and his wife, Bridget, to come and stay in order to pray. Jackson found the patient's room locked and was astonished to find Father Peiris, in his wife's absence, sleeping in the same room as his secretary and her children. Bridget Jackson recalled that the vicar told her that Russel was not long for this world and, shortly after Russel's death, she saw Father Matthew put a gold ring on Dalrene's finger and heard him say, 'Don't worry, Dalrene, soon I will be in the same condition as you.' Bereft of a partner! Dalrene had drawn up a will naming the priest as her executor and guardian of her three small children.

Mrs Peiris fell unconscious on the last day of January the following year. Her condition was diagnosed as hypoglycaemia, and she was admitted to hospital, where doctors noted how anxious Father Peiris was to give details of his wife's medical history. But just as he had done with Russel Ingram, he misled them and he lied. He did not tell them that she had collapsed some days before her admission. In answer to questions, he said, 'She is not a diabetic and at no time has she taken anti-diabetic medicines.' He advised the doctors not to give dextrose to the patient. The doctor at the hospital made a note of the priest's advice because he was not sure if there was some rare disease, of which he had not heard, for which sugar would be dangerous.

The vicar's wife never regained consciousness. She remained in a coma from January 31 until March 19, when she died. Another doctor wrote on the patient's record, 'Suspected poison. Inform police. Hypoglycaemic agent. Attempted suicide/homicide.' Yet another medico added, 'Cause of death cannot be given. Hold an inquest and a judicial post-mortem.'

The Reverend Matthew Peiris and Mrs Dalrene Ingram were held on suspicion of murder in May, 1979, but because of the complexity of the case it took Tirak Malapana, the deputy Attorney-General, more than four years to bring them to trial on December 6, 1983.

By then, witnesses had been found, local doctors had assembled their notes, consultants and experts had been brought in. Throughout the 163-day trial, Peiris wore his white cassock and a large crucifix. Mrs Ingram wore a white sari, the garment normally worn by women of Sri Lanka at funerals. Often the priest smiled at his son and daughters in the courtroom but they answered him with scowls.

The three trial judges decided, under Sri Lankan law, that because the case was built almost wholly on a combination of circumstantial evidence and complex medical and scientific testimony, they would try it without a jury and rule on matters of fact as well as law.

One of the main arguments mounted by the defence in the case of both deaths was that there are several natural conditions and diseases which can account for low levels of sugar in the blood. They also claimed that there was a risk that samples of blood and other medical evidence gathered while Mr Ingram and Mrs Peiris had been in hospital could have been lost, tainted, or otherwise misreported as a result of human error. Russel was wrongfully described by the defence as a drunk and they even suggested that alcohol, in addition to his low blood sugar level, could have killed him. He could have taken his own life. So could Mrs Peiris, who had been depressed.

The true account lay in the personal recollections of those close to the principal characters.

Not surprisingly, Mrs Peiris had objected to Dalrene's presence in the vicarage, but she had been assured by her husband that it was the angels' guidance that she should look after this big family; and since Eunice believed in angels, and believed and trusted her husband, she accepted the situation.

Yet Munilal, aware of his mother's distress at the scandalous live-in relationship between his father and the secretary, threatened to report the matter to the Bishop of Colombo. Father Matthew promptly advertised for a three-bedroom house to rent so that he could enjoy

Dalrene's company away from the vicarage. And the pair drew the deposit money for the rental from their joint account.

What aroused suspicion about Mrs Peiris's death, however, was that her coma, from which she never recovered, occurred not long after she had cried out in the middle of the night. Asked what it was about, Mrs Peiris had said that her husband had predicted that that Christmas and New Year would be her last.

Their son, Munilal, said that he found it strange that the divine guidance received by his father always brought bad news, and that as a Christian he thought that angels brought good tidings. The judges eventually remarked, 'Having regard to the medical evidence we accept we now know that if indeed he had a supernatural message it was inaccurate.'

It was the medical evidence that clinched the case. Russel Ingram and Mrs Eunice Peiris died from hypoglycaemia, a dangerously low level of blood sugar, causing irreversible brain damage, introduced by medicine. That medicine was Euglucon, medicine known to Father Peiris because he took the drug for his own condition.

But how did Mrs Ingram know about diabetes, low blood sugar and its effects? Was she really a conspirator? When the police searched the vicarage, they found on a shelf, available for all to read, *Body, Mind And Sugar*, a layman's guide to what happens when sugar in the bloodstream reaches too low a level and wrong dosages of medicine are administered – irreparable brain damage and death.

Strange that Mrs Ingram should have said that both her husband and Mrs Peiris had been 'stuperose'. The word, similar to 'stuporous', the state of being in a stupor, is not in general use – but it is used quite frequently in that book from the vicarage shelf.

The same book also explained how levels of blood sugar vary and can be regulated by the secretion of hormone insulin in the pancreas, by tumours, and by other quite natural causes – information which was seized upon, to no avail, by the defence.

Remember that the faith-healing vicar had appeared to go into a trance, hands on his abdomen, repeating over and over again 'pancreas', to indicate the source of Russel's illness. The reverend father had already invented his defence and wanted everyone to believe that Russel's pancreas secreted too much insulin, keeping sugar from his brain.

He was clever enough not to continually overdose either Russel or his wife. He would give medicine, then refuse it. The priest was even bringing in food for the patients every four hours; milk, soup, Marmite, passion-fruit juice, milk with egg, all in liquid form.

The judges came to the conclusion that he had provided in the food the deadly Euglucon to reduce the sugar in Russel's blood, knowing it would be fed to him through a nasal drip by the hospital staff. And Mrs Ingram knew all the time what was going on. She did not try to stop him. Hospital staff suddenly remembered at the trial seeing the priest with his arm round the secretary and thought how supportive he was in her time of need. She would benefit from both deaths. Therefore she was a conspirator and a party to the murder.

The judges, in their conclusion, said, 'We think this is the method of murder. An anti-diabetic drug was administered to Russel Ingram over a period of time. The doctors were perplexed during his lifetime as to the cause of several attacks of hypoglycaemia and unusual attacks during a period when he was getting consistently high doses of Dextrose [the antidote].

'The method of murder had been to surreptitiously administer the drug making the victim and his relations believe that there was a natural cause making him ill and thereby allay any suspicion that might arise out of his sickness. So if one is bent on committing murder that will go unrecognised as a crime it would be quite consistent for the murderer to create evidence to support a view that there was indeed a natural cause for his sickness.'

The judges found the priest and his mistress guilty of conspiracy to murder and of murder in both cases and they were sentenced to be hanged by their necks until they were dead. The killers appealed; their appeals were rejected, but their sentences were commuted to life imprisonment.

*Chapter Six*

# TO BE CARNALLY MINDED IS DEATH

from St Paul's Epistle to the Romans, read
daily by the Reverend Ronald Geeves Griggs.

Sex, arsenic and dog-collars do not go well together, as the Reverend Ronald Geeves Griggs would tell you. Every day of his life from the age of twenty-six to the day he died, he picked up the Holy Bible and read two passages. From St Paul's Epistle to the Romans, chapter eight, he learnt by heart, 'to be carnally minded is death; and to be spiritually minded is life and peace.' From St Paul's Epistle to the Corinthians, chapter thirteen, he could recite, 'And now abideth faith, hope, charity, these three; but the greatest of these is charity.' Both were important lessons to him, even though he had learned them late.

No one else to this day knows for certain how Ethel, his childhood sweetheart, bride and mother of his baby, died from a massive dosage of arsenic poisoning. Why she did so was wrapped up in the scandal of the passionate parson.

To hear the Reverend Ronald Geeves Griggs tell it, he was born for the ministry. There he was, a Digger in the 12th Battalion, Australian Infantry Force, away from home, in World War One, quaffing wine in a French bar, when one of the soldiers shrieked, 'Jesus Christ!'

A pretty girl walking by stopped and said, 'Don't talk like that about that man. That man loves the likes of us.'

Griggs looked at her in amazement and said, 'I wonder why I've never heard anyone say that before.'

The girl whirled on him, too, and said, 'Why should

you wonder? What are you doing for Christ more than I am?'

That night, Griggs (according to his story) wandered aimlessly until he found a roadside crucifix, knelt down beside it and wept. From that moment, he knew he was destined for the church. It did not occur to him that there would be a detour from pulpit to prison while he stood in the dock on trial for his life for the murder of his wife.

Griggs was born in 1900, eldest son of prosperous fruit farmers, in Franklin, Tasmania. He went to state school until he was sixteen, then, at eighteen, was just in time to join the Army in the final year of the First World War. He was sent to England, where he was stationed at Sutton Veny on the edge of Salisbury Plain, Wiltshire; went via Weymouth Camp to France, where he saw something of the fighting just before the Armistice and returned an acting corporal with the job of assistant secretary in the Officers' Mess.

He would always tell those with time to listen how, when he returned home in 1921 after seeing something of the world, he tried to fight off the idea of joining the church, but after two years became a home missionary with the Methodist Church and studied for the Wesleyan Ministry at Queen's College, Melbourne. Considering his basic education, he did well to gain two scholarships, and shone in Greek and Latin studies, and in theological drama.

In 1926 he gained a degree as a Licenciate of Theology and was sent 190 miles from Melbourne to take charge of a Methodist congregation in Omeo, a valley town in the Victorian Alps, catering for sheep and cattle farmers and miners. It was nearly seventy miles from the nearest railway station at Bruthen. Griggs bought a motor-cycle and side-car combination to reach the outlying home-steads, and he needed a horse to visit his scattered flock in the hill farms.

A month before he left Tasmania he had also acquired a bride, Ethel White, whom he had known since child-hood. Although he had spent much of the past eight years away from his Tasmanian home, three abroad during and after the war and more on the mainland studying, there was no inkling among those who knew the couple that it was anything other than a marriage made in heaven.

Ethel was a schoolteacher, a talented pianist, above all a lady; and when the Reverend and Mrs Griggs were greeted by the elders and some of the congregation of the local Methodist Church, no one could have imagined the grossly anti-social drama that was about to open. The newly-weds were town people and the local residents country folk and Mr and Mrs Griggs were perhaps better educated than most. Even so there was something amiss in the normal genial chemistry of companionship between the Griggs and the 2,000 souls of Omeo.

Ronald Griggs was a man of the world. He had been to war. Ethel Griggs was a small-town woman who had taught kindergarten and primary school but never been out of Tasmania. He was busy getting to know the spiritual needs of the people of the area while she was busy arranging the parsonage to their mutual comfort and liking. Despite the townsfolk's welcome and the apparent delight of the Griggs couple, much was to be made of the comment of a next-door neighbour: 'Been here two years and I've never been invited over their doorstep.'

That hardly explains the rift that was to appear in the marriage. Blame for that was partly laid ten miles away at the home of wealthy John Condon and his family. Griggs had met Lottie Condon, the second-born of five children, within a week of arriving in Omeo. But it was not until seven months later when Mrs Griggs – who was pregnant at the time – actually invited Lottie to stay that the chink in marital bliss became a chasm.

It may have been an innocent if perhaps ill-advised invitation. If Ethel had been older and more experienced in womanhood she would most likely not have offered it. If Lottie had been more mature she would probably have avoided the situation by not accepting. The clash of immature wills was only the beginning.

Lottie said of Mrs Griggs later, 'She seemed rather jealous of me being there. She told me she did not think I should stay there even though she had asked me. She asked me if there was anything between us, Griggs and me. I said, "No." I was lying on the couch in the kitchen. I had a bad head. She went out of the room and while she was out he put his hand on my forehead. When she came back in, Mrs Griggs asked if I thought it was right for her husband to put his hand on my forehead. She asked Griggs if he thought it was a fit thing for him to ask me to lie down on the couch while she did the ironing.'

Ethel, the home-maker and pianist, was, to some, the better-looking of the two women; Lottie, the outdoor girl and accomplished horsewoman, the more attractive to men. The man of the world, the reverend parson, was soon to discover just what that meant.

Within a few days of the frisson at the parsonage, Griggs left on his motor-cycle to conduct a service at Ensay, a little more than thirty miles out on the road to Bruthen. He would take Lottie Condon in the side-car and it had been arranged before they left, with Mrs Griggs's approval (they insisted), that they should stay overnight at the home of Methodist friends. The Condon family were wealthy and generous contributors to the Methodist cause in Omeo. The Reverend Griggs and Lottie were going to stay overnight at the home of Harry Harman, a prosperous farmer and a chief supporter of the Ensay congregation.

What could be going through the mind of Mrs Griggs at that time? Her husband had not yet been ordained minister of the church and was dependent on the financial as well as the spiritual support of the faithful. She could not stand in the way of him socialising or accepting the hospitality of the mainstays of the Methodist faith in those parts. Besides, there would be an evening service at which he would be preaching; there would be supper afterwards, and he should not ride his machine thirty miles across the mountains at night. But what was Lottie Condon, twenty years of age, unmarried and six years his junior, doing with him?

Lottie was quite frank when asked about it later. 'I remember staying at the Harmans' one Sunday night. Mr Griggs was also there. It would be about Christmas time, 1926. It would be after Mrs Griggs had spoken about Mr Griggs stroking my forehead. We occupied different rooms. I went into his room by arrangement. I decided to go. We had discussed the matter. Misconduct took place that night.'

Misconduct was a 1926 euphemism for what a later generation called adultery and a later generation still called sexual intercourse. But everybody knew the truth. The unvarnished answers that emerge from legalistic questions are often unattractive but are plain enough. And it did not appear that the Reverend Griggs and Miss Condon were merely engaged in a one-night affair.

So far the triangular argument had been private. On January 3, 1927, Ethel was shopping in Omeo when Ronald Griggs pulled up outside the shop in his combination with Lottie in the side-car. Griggs went inside the store and said, 'We have come to take you home.'

In a voice loud enough for every assistant and shopper to hear, Mrs Griggs replied, 'Take home the one you've got. I'll get home as best as I can.'

Griggs rode home with Lottie and began mowing the lawn. Lottie wandered down to the creek out of the way. Mrs Griggs returned home soon afterwards, went to her bedroom and locked herself in. That night, according to Griggs, his wife tried to throw herself on the fire, which was later trumpeted as evidence that she had attempted suicide, a difficult enough end to achieve on a domestic hearth.

In January, Ethel Griggs gave birth to a baby girl. Ronald's mother, Mrs Griggs senior, stayed with her during and after the confinement. Lottie wisely left the district. First she went down to Melbourne for six weeks, after which she went north to Wagga Wagga in New South Wales to stay with an aunt for another six weeks. And Griggs, despite his recently required responsibilities, took his motor-cycle and rode to Wagga Wagga, more than 300 miles away.

Lottie said, 'He rang me up when he got to Wagga, he came round to my auntie's place and I was with him for about half an hour. We arranged to meet in Wagga the next morning. We met at 10 a.m. and went out in the sidecar. We came back and had dinner. I told him that it would perhaps be better if we did not go together again. There was no intercourse between us at Wagga.'

If the witnesses are to be believed, the couple did not meet again for some considerable time, perhaps months. Griggs's behaviour, however, did not appear convincing. Time came for Mrs Griggs senior to return to Tasmania and the reverend persuaded his wife to take the baby and go back home with her. Despite Ethel's reluctance she eventually agreed, and he booked their passages.

Repentance dictated that he chase after them on his motor-cycle to Melbourne to stop them. He overtook them before they reached the quay. All he could say was, 'I am sorry.' Penitence demanded he spend a holiday with his wife and infant in Melbourne, and after a decent interval they returned to Omeo. But then Lottie returned to the district, and tragedy followed.

The parson's account of what happened next seemed frank enough. The Condons invited the Griggs to stay with them. They occupied the same bedroom. On returning to the room one night, Mrs Griggs began making loud accusations about her husband's behaviour.

'Do you think it right and proper that you should spend so much time outside the house alone with Miss Condon?' she demanded.

'Nothing wrong took place at all,' he replied.

'But Mrs Condon noticed it and today she told me that she wishes you would not come here so much. And she said she wished you would not ask the girls to go with you. And that you are not fit to be a minister of the church.' (Mrs Condon had several daughters.)

When the couple returned home, Mrs Griggs challenged her husband to let her have a divorce.

'On what grounds?' he asked her.

'Misconduct,' she replied.

'I think it will be better if you were to go to Tasmania

for six months. During that time we will think things over. Don't tell them – either your people or my people – that there is anything wrong. We may come together again. We can do that.'

Ethel replied, 'I have lost all love for you and I will never live with you again. I will do as you want me to do. I will go home, I will come back, but I will not stay. If you will not let me get a divorce now, we will have to get it later, because I will go for six months and when I return I will not stay.'

Griggs seemed to have jumped at the opportunity to remain behind while his wife returned to Tasmania without him. 'At any rate,' he said to her, ' I want you to go for six months and we will both think things over.'

'All right,' she agreed. 'I will come back somewhere about Christmas and I will probably go teaching after-wards.'

Two weeks later, Ethel Griggs had gone with her baby to her mother's. Mrs Condon's view that Mr Griggs was not fit to be a minister and that he should not associate with her daughters did not prevent him returning and staying at their home. If she had wanted to interfere, she was not very successful, for the lapse in the bush love affair was temporary, and Lottie and Ronald resumed it with renewed and increased passion. Once a week, 'your place or mine' was the rule. A Condon bed or a presby-tery couch, it did not matter which. Towards the end of 1928, Ethel sent word that she would be returning home on Saturday, December 31. Griggs did not tell anyone, neither the next-door neighbour, nor the shopkeepers, nor his congregation, that she was coming back. He presumably told Lottie. But after that his behaviour became more and more odd.

He spent the night of December 30 with Lottie at the Condon home, and he did not go next day to meet his wife at the Bruthen rail-head but waited until she arrived by car.

Almost immediately, Ethel fell ill. The reverend did not seek immediate medical aid and next day, New Year's Eve, went off on his spiritual rounds to conduct services and minister to others. When he returned his wife complained of more sickness. He insisted she was getting better, but on Monday, when she was worse, he went to see Dr Matthews, a local practitioner, who handed him a prescription which he took to Mr Perry, the local chemist.

On Tuesday morning the clergyman rushed to the doctor's surgery and complained his wife was no better. At 11 a.m., the doctor called at the church house, where he found Mrs Griggs had pains in her stomach accompanied by constant retching. She had taken very little of the medicine he had prescribed, so he gave her a measured dose and returned at 9 p.m. to find her apparently slightly better. She complained that she still could not rest, so he went to the surgery to get his syringe, came back yet again and injected a mixture of morphine and strychnine to make her sleep. At 1 a.m. next morning, January 3, he received an emergency call, went to the clergy house and found Ethel Griggs dead.

Dr Matthews came to the conclusion that she had been upset by the sea voyage across the Bass Strait from Tasmania, which had produced exhaustion and nervous vomiting. A goitre from which she suffered had contributed to heart failure. There was no post-mortem, and the doctor gave Griggs a death certificate which stated that his wife had died from hyperemesis (excessive vomiting, particularly during pregnancy) and exhaustion and, secondly, from cardiac failure. Mrs Griggs was buried at Omeo cemetery.

Two days later Griggs wrote to his mother-in-law, Mrs White:

Dear mother, I think you will understand when I say I cannot write very much just now. You will realise how hard it is. It seems to me that it has all been a dream, that I will wake up and find your dear girl still with me. Perhaps you will like me to tell you everything right from the start. I could not say very much in the wire, and I did not like sending it but you had to know.

I had the parsonage all clean and sweet for Ethel's homecoming; the tea ready in the kitchen, hot water ready, etc., the day seemed as though it would never pass. It was an exceedingly hot day. The motor arrived about nine o'clock, and after our little girl had been put to bed, she had a bath and we had tea. Before tea, she was just a little bit sick, but I thought it was the heat and the excitement. She did not eat very much and about half way through was sick again.

She felt ill, so I got her to bed and she lay there while I finished my work for the Sunday, watching me. She went to sleep. About eleven o'clock she woke up, from then on was very sick all night. Between the sickness she went to sleep but by morning she seemed a lot better. Had a cup of tea. She could not keep that down, though, so I thought it best that she should have nothing but soda-water. The baby was splendid.

About church time, she dropped off to sleep and at one o'clock appeared to be recovered. I thought she had better have nothing, though. I did not like leaving her but I had a service at two (o'clock) 20 miles away and started. I was back as quick as I could, she was sitting up playing with the baby, and said she had a good sleep and felt better but was feeling sick. I gave her a cup of tea and after that she seemed to get bad again so I went for the doctor. He seemed to think it was nothing but heat and excitement, gave her medicine, said he would call again in the morning. She was bad all night, sick every half-hour, so at daylight, I went for the doctor.

He did what he could, got her easy and came back at tea; she seemed much better but round two o'clock Monday afternoon, the change came and she was bad indeed – no pain but sickness, and of course she was extremely weak. The doctor was away and would not be back till six. Neighbours came in and we did what we could but although we managed to stop the sickness, she became delirious from weakness. And when the doctor came she seemed better again but he said he would come back at ten and give her something to give her rest. He did. And between six and ten she was still very weak but was in no pain and quite conscious.

The doctor gave her an injection and, as she was falling asleep, she asked, 'How long will I sleep doctor?' He said, 'Till mid-day tomorrow and you will wake up happy and well.' His words or part of them proved true. About eleven she seemed sound asleep, so I lay down as I had been up two nights,

113

never even had my collar off, I was feeling done. I was asleep for two hours and went in to look at her and she was gone. Apparently only a few minutes before.

The doctor was up in ten minutes but it was true. She had never spoken or moved and knew nothing of pain or weariness or anything. Doctor said the heart had just stopped beating and she would know nothing or feel nothing. It was really a beautiful way to go. She just went to sleep and woke in Heaven. Apart from the two days of sickness and weakness there was no pain and there was nothing at all to indicate anything serious. She simply fell asleep – there heard the call.

I cannot realise it even yet. We had planned such a lot for the New Year, but it was not to be. Who shall say it is not better so? The little baby is wonderful and has found her way right into my heart. I will not know how to part with her. Ethel is now lying in a beautiful part of the Omeo resting place. The funeral was conducted by the Presbyterian and Church of England ministers. It has been a shock to the whole town. Mother and father will be here tomorrow night.

There, mother dear, I can say no more now. After I have heard from you I will write again. This seems to have bound me all the closer to you – please write just as you can. May God give you strength and grace to see His Hand on all of us. I feel too stunned to realise it all – have not known how to write this – but I have tried to tell you all. If you have any wishes, anything at all, let me know and I will do my very best to fulfil them. Goodnight, dear mother –

you are still to me. Good night and God bless you all, Love from Ronald.

Gossip spread like a bush fire, reaching Constable McMillan, the local policeman, who sent a message to the superintendent at the county town of Sale, who dispatched a Detective Sergeant Mulfahey to investigate. Meanwhile, Griggs, unbelievably, had gone to stay at the Condons and on John Condon's advice had sent a letter to McMillan, 'I think it would be best if a full inquiry were made. It might effect a clearing up of any rumours.'

Mulfahey and McMillan went first to see Lottie Condon and to their surprise she gave them a full bed-by-bed account of her sexual relationship with the preacher. When they called on the reverend himself he denied that there had been any strained relations with his wife or intimacy with Miss Condon. Mulfahey handed him Lottie's statement.

The passionate parson paled and confessed. Asked if he had any poison in the house, he handed three bottles to the officers; one the medical prescription prepared by Mr Perry, the chemist, another labelled 'Bloom of Peaches' and a third marked 'Strychnine.' The last, said Griggs, he had found in the house when he moved in, but he did not know how it came there.

Police asked that the body of Ethel Griggs be exhumed. At the post-mortem, Dr C. H. Mollison, Coroner's Surgeon, Melbourne, ordered the stomach, small intestines, large intestine, spleen, liver, heart and kidneys to be removed for analysis. Mr C. A. Taylor, a government analyst, looked at each one of them, tested them and picked up the phone. 'Every one of those organs contains arsenic which I have removed. It totals fifteen and a half grains.' Answering questions, he said 'three grains would just about cover a sixpence and if you powdered two peas it would be about the same as fifteen and a half grains.' Dr Mollison raised his eyebrows. 'That is more than five times a lethal dose. Three grains is enough to kill. If arsenic is in each of those organs it must have been administered in two doses.'

Sergeant Mulfahey and Constable McMillan knew that Griggs was still staying at the Condon house, to which they returned and searched the premises. They found in the blacksmith's shop behind the property an opened kerosene tin labelled 'white arsenic'. Griggs admitted he had been in that part of the premises but he denied any knowledge of arsenic there. He was taken to the police station and charged with his wife's murder.

When the trial opened in the Supreme Court at Sale, close to Victoria's ninety-mile beach, on March 7 before Sir William 'Iceberg' Irvine, Chief Justice of Victoria, the first astonishment came when Mr Perry, the chemist, went into the witness box. 'In or about December last year, the Reverend Griggs came into my shop asking to be supplied with some sulphuric acid and some nitric acid. I asked him what he wanted them for. He did not answer very straight out but he mentioned that he thought of trying some experiments in assaying. I did not supply him with the acids.

'About a month later Griggs again called at the shop and asked for the same things with the addition of some arsenic and cyanate of potash. This time when I asked him what he wanted them for he said he was thinking of taking a course in minerology. I did not supply him with those substances but recommended him to an expert in minerals.

116

'The only substance I made up for the minister was Dr Matthews' prescription.'

Mr G. Maxwell, KC, the parson's counsel, nearly seventy and going blind, suggested that as it was New Year's Day the chemist may have been feeling below par and put arsenic into the medicine by mistake, but the chemist showed that this was impossible. Both John Condon and Henry Harman, the rich benefactors of the Methodist Church, told how they kept arsenic on their premises for legitimate purposes and had to admit that Griggs could have had access to it.

Worse was to follow. The minister's mother-in-law, Mrs White, told the court that when her daughter left home she was in splendid health, good spirits and was looking forward to the reunion with her husband. The stewardess on board the SS *Nairana* which had brought mother and baby home, testified that she was perfectly all right on the crossing from Tasmania to Melbourne. The car driver and his two other passengers who came with her from Bruthen railway station home to Omeo said the same.

The Reverend Ronald Griggs, unordained minister of Omeo Methodist Church, Victoria, Australia, went into the witness box and on his oath admitted that he was infatuated with Miss Condon, had committed adultery with her often over a long period of time, and had met her on the night before his wife returned. He denied, however, administering any arsenic or any other poison to his wife. As for asking the chemist for poisons, he said he had found a piece of quartz which he thought was filled with gold specks. There was an old gold-mining book in the parsonage which said that a certain acid – he could not remember its name – would eat other metals but would not eat gold. He had not gone to the expert recommended by the chemist, but thought he would try it himself.

That was the evidence. Griggs's counsel, Mr Maxwell, in his address to the jury, well aware he was defending a man of the cloth, used old-fashioned courtroom oratory and pulpit morality:

A powerful section of the Press has done everything possible to prejudice the public mind against Griggs and to inflame the community against him. Before he went into the witness box, he was practically condemned. I have no hesitation in saying that if the ordinary man in the street had been asked, prior to the commencement of the case, 'What about Griggs?' the answer would have been, 'He is as Guilty as can be. I would hang him without a trial.' That was the attitude of the public mind and that is why you are told, as no doubt you will be by His Honour [the judge], that you must base your finding entirely on what you have heard from the witness box.

I honestly confess, I dread the effect of what you gentlemen may know outside. I am sure not one of you would conscientiously allow anything but the evidence to weigh with you in determining the fate of this man. And here is also the idea that because he is a minister – because he has been with this woman and untrue to his wife – that must weigh against him in his trial.

Gentlemen, I implore you not to condemn him of murder, simply because of that. After all, many a man who has been all that one could wish in other respects, has been weak in that direction. Why, in that Book which you hold up in your hands (when you take the oath) one of the greatest scenes in literature is where a poor woman, taken in adultery, is thrust in the presence of the Master and left to be condemned by the rabble, the Scribes and the Pharisees. The Master says, 'Let him who is without sin among you cast the first stone,' and all the accusers slink out of the place. The Master asks, 'Where are now thine accusers? Does no man accuse thee?' And the woman answers 'None, Lord,' and the Master says, 'Neither do I condemn thee.'

I feel that, however strong may be the allegations against this man, founded on matters that are not evidence, you will feel it your bounden duty to return a verdict of Not Guilty.

The jury went out at 3.40 p.m., disagreed, were recalled at 9.47 p.m., locked up for the night as was the practice in those days, and returned to court at 10.25 next morning still hopelessly deadlocked. The judge ordered a new trial.

The second time round, the position of Lottie Condon was made clearer. The prosecution told the new jury that she had given evidence at the inquest, but had not gone into the witness box at the first trial, although she had been in court. The Crown, knowing that adultery was not an issue, had no intention of calling her. The defence, knowing that adultery was still an embarrassment, did not call her either.

Mr Justice 'Gentle James' McFarlan, who presided, still thought she may have been able to throw a light on the issue of murder without bringing adultery into the examination, so of his own volition he called Lottie to the witness box. To most of his questions she answered, 'I do not remember.' She was of no help to either side.

The jury went out at 3.27 p.m. and returned more than six hours later at 10 p.m. The jury answered the crucial question, 'Not guilty' and that was the verdict of them all. As the Reverend Ronald Griggs was led out of the dock to freedom, a woman's voice was heard crying, 'I want to see him!' She was led away and no one knows whether the adulterous couple ever saw each other again.

The passionate parson assumed another name and obtained the post of an assistant minister to a congregation in Southern Australia, but his secret was revealed and he was dismissed. He was last heard of in *Smith's Weekly*, a Sydney newspaper, in which he wrote, almost six months later, 'That month I spent awaiting trial was the longest month I have ever known in my life. During my wait I may say without hypocrisy that the New Testament opened itself to me as I have never seen it before. It was a comfort and a strength to me. I felt that the presence of Christ was very close and real to me there . . . Although I have done wrong I feel a better Christian for it.'

And he was still reading daily in the Good Book about lustful desire which is bad (Romans viii) and charity which helped save him from the gallows (Corinthians xiii).

## Chapter Seven

# A LATIN MYSTERY

'The question is not simply whether Mr Watson is an object of legitimate compassion, which is undoubted; but whether the claims of justice can fitly be permitted to yield to those of mercy.'

*The Times.*

The Reverend John Selby Watson was a very heavy, learned man, a classical scholar, head teacher and author. He lived and breathed reason. Then he ordered a large made-to-measure packing case, pistol-whipped his wife to death in a bloody frenzy in his library, and dragged her to a side-room where he kept her, huddled, cold and dead, for three days. On the third day, he reached for a glass of poison to destroy himself, failed and was arrested. Why he killed his wife was a classic mystery and the explanation he left truly baffling.

It consisted of seventeen words in a dead language: *Felix in omnibus fere rebus praeterquam quod ad sexum attinet foemineum. Saepe olim amanti amare semper nocuit.*

Latin scholars, as is their habit, could never agree the precise meaning of the words in English. The argument was fuelled for days in the correspondence columns of *The Times*. The lawyer called by the Crown to prosecute the unsuccessfully suicidal killer had the first word. He said it meant: 'To one who has often loved it has always been harmful to love.'

Surely, one critic wrote, it means: 'To one who has acquired the habit of loving, it has often been an injury to cease to love.' That, responded Lord Winchilsea, was how a fifth-former at Eton would have put it. It expressed the same sentiments as Shakespeare when he wrote, 'True love hath often been the lover's bane.' Or did it mean, as another letter writer said, 'It is often injurious or fatal to a man who once loved to go on for ever loving'?

If only Watson had written his explanation in English. Lawyers from Lincoln's Inn, with an uncharacteristic love of plain English, insisted that the inscription meant, 'Many men have found that it is a great mistake to be too true to the object of a boyish passion.' From the Athenaeum Club, that Pall Mall retreat of bishops and other members of the Establishment, the message was translated as, 'Often to one who loved a long time ago, has to love perseveringly proved detrimental.'

And a German who wrote a learned paper on the murder, *Watson, ein unglücklichher Ehemann*, [Watson, An Unfortunate Husband] said it meant: 'it generally happens when parties marry rather late in life that each partner is blind to the loveless qualities of others.' 'The whole case,' he said, 'is a hideous warning against the rigorous demands of clericalism in matters of divorce. Such a union as that of Watson and his wife is immoral; it sets at nought the ordinary principles of humanity.'

Countless scholars, lawyers and doctors offered their opinions about this holy killing, a pathetic murder if ever there was one, carried out by a man who had led an otherwise guiltless life.

Watson was baptised at Crayford, then in Kent, now in south-east London, in 1804, the son of very poor parents of Scots origin. His grandfather taught him the basics of much that he knew but because of poverty he was thirty-four years of age before he won the gold medal for classical scholarship and graduated, a Bachelor of Arts, from Trinity College Dublin.

During his student days he had met Anne Armstrong,

the one human love of his life, but it was seven years before they could marry. Love without cash or prospects at his social level in those far-off Victorian times was for characters of fiction rather than fact.

Meantime, Watson entered the Church of England. Advancement in that communion without either influence or wherewithal was desperately slow. He was ordained a deacon by the Bishop of Ely in Cambridgeshire when he was thirty-five, and inducted as a priest by the Bishop of Bath and Wells at Langport, on the River Parrett in Somerset, where he remained a curate until he was thirty-seven. Watson's career only seemed to change for the better when, at the age of forty, against stiff competition, he was appointed headmaster by the governors of Stockwell Grammar School in Surrey before that district was incorporated into south-west London.

With money in his pocket, it was time he married and he wrote to his intended bride, Anne Armstrong, in Dublin. The letters, formal and stilted in style, are appropriately a classic Victorian tale of the progress of a cleric in love.

December 4th, 1844. – Madam, I must entreat you to pardon the liberty which I take in addressing to you this note. You have known me only from having seen me some years ago at Mrs Curran's in Marlborough Street, where I was attending the College; you may perhaps have forgotten me, but I still recollect you. I am now in Orders, and headmaster of the Proprietary Grammar School here. When I know that you have received this I should wish to say something more, if you will allow me to write to you a second time. I need not beg of you to favour me with an immediate reply, for I am sure you will have the kindness and politeness to do so. I have the honour to be, madam, with the highest esteem and respect, your very obedient servant, J. S. Watson.

Miss Armstrong replied at once and drew the next message:

December 9th. – Madam, I have to thank you for your obliging letter. You were always regarded by me as a lady of great excellence. Had I been able, soon after leaving College, to establish myself as I wished, I had it in my mind to make you a proposal of marriage. It may now be too late. Nor should I, however you receive this intimation, wish you to consider that I have done so until we have again met. Believe me to be, madam, with the most perfect esteem, your very obedient servant. J. S. Watson.

She must have sent him an encouraging reply – alas, the lady's letters are not available for publication – for he replied:

December 13th. – Madam, I had the pleasure of receiving your very sensible letter just now. As you do not discourage me I will say that I think it possible that I may cross over to Dublin about Christmas for a few days. I am living in apartments because I cannot afford to take a house; and yet I cannot but think that, with a person of your (as I judge) staid, quiet, and domestic habits, there would be no fear. Believe me to be, madam, very faithfully and obediently yours, J. S. Watson.

In his fourth letter, Watson was generally non-commital, although he gave details of his income, 'more than £300 for a consort and myself', but he waxed human and almost boyish with the signing off note: 'I have not forgotten the game at draughts, in which you did me the honour of beating me.'

The fifth message still contains the 'Dear Madam' and 'yours I remain most sincerely' touches but includes the passage:

> Do not think that you need to say much about your family to me, who am of no family. What you say concerning taking lodgings makes me believe that you must have much of that independence of spirit which I always supposed you to possess.

Passion in his writing seemed in short supply, but in the sixth and last letter of the pre-marital romance he said:

> Dear Madam. As to being 'angry' with you, as your humour is to express it, that, I trust, can never happen. It is long since I saw you, certainly more than seven years, and I know not, at least know but imperfectly, how during that period your time has been passed. Forgive me, dear Miss Armstrong, that I write this; you have only to burn it, and give me an answer when I have the happiness of meeting you, for it will be a happiness to me, whatever you may say to me, to see once more that dear face which I once so much admired, and which I thought – and think now – far above anything to which I had or have any personal pretensions to aspire. Believe me all the

liberties which I have taken in writing thus to you have been taken with the warmest regard to yourself, a regard which, I hope, will never be diminished, but that I shall still be always yours sincerely, J.S.W.

P.S. – Will you accept my second offer, dearest? With love. This riband is exchanged for the other.

Within a year of his school appointment he had sailed for Dublin, collected his Master of Arts degree, married Anne Armstrong, his postal fiancée, at St Mark's Church in the Irish capital and brought her back to live in Stockwell. The district, between Brixton and Vauxhall, Kennington and Clapham, was genteel in those days. Even so, for a man of such knowledge in a well-bred society, the pay was comparatively poor. He received only £300 a year and he had to recruit seventy pupils before he could receive four guineas (£4.20) more per annum for every additional scholar over that figure.

The dozen or so local governors kept him out of their monthly meetings, but he still had to appoint or dismiss all other masters and employees of the school and listen to the petty complaints and imaginary grievances of boys, parents and others.

The clergyman-schoolmaster worked hard running the school and still found time to translate the works of Xenophon, the fourth-century BC Greek historian and writer, and the works of various first-century BC Romans, the statesman, orator and writer Cicero, poet Lucretius, rhetorician Quintilian, lawyer Justinian, the biographer Cornelius Nepos and historian Sallust. All these works were published by Bohn's Classical Library, the first venture of its kind in the English language. Sir

John Lubbock chose the Xenophon as one of his *Hundred Best Books*, and some were sufficiently popular to be reprinted in Everyman's Library and the Loeb Classical Library seventy years later.

The author was no abject toady to fashionable opinions. In a biography of the controversial William Warburton, the English critic and Bishop of Gloucester, he told how the prelate won at one swoop a wife, an estate and a bishopric to go with them. Watson's *Life Of George Fox*, the founder of the Society of Friends (the Quakers), thought the movement a freakish survival doomed to disappear in the rational and orderly era of nineteenth-century enlightenment:

> Human nature remains always the same and no large proportion of mankind has ever shown a disposition to make themselves resemble the Quakers. Men are not yet prepared to relinquish contention, to submit to spoilation and personal violence, to abstain from lawsuits, to abolish armies and navies, and to turn their spears into pruning hooks. The world was intended to be as it is; and if peace were spread throughout it, it would be but a waste of dullness and inactivity . . .

A life of the Scottish hero and patriot, Sir William Wallace, followed and then another of Richard Porson, one of the finest English classical scholars, who was born in similar impoverished circumstances to Watson. That work gave a curious clue to the killing of Mrs Watson ten years before it occurred. A woman had insulted Porson. The offence was not described in detail, but Watson wrote:

We may suppose that it was of a very gross character. She may have indeed fancied that she had reason for offering such an insult. But there are women who imagine that they may say, without censure, the most disagreeable things to any man, however great and good, of whom they conceive a dislike or wish to be rid. As they are safe from personal chastisement, they venture to utter all the bitterness that may arise in their minds.

Nothing is more disgraceful to the female sex than these cowardly attacks on men, often of great ability and merit, whom they know to be restrained by good sense and gentlemanly forbearance towards the sex from retaliation. No man can know who has not experienced it how much mischief may be produced by the impertinent intrusion of a wife between her husband and his friends.

The person who made the attack on Porson 'was a woman of violent and overbearing temper, presumptuous and inconsiderate, and having little respect or kindness for any human being'.

Porson's life 'is an example and an admonition. How much a man may injure himself by indulgence in one unhappy propensity, and how much an elevated mind may suffer by long association with those of an inferior order.'

Was Watson really thinking of his own wife and the domestic scene? That passage was written in 1861. He murdered his wife in 1871 and was to say, in passing, that she had provoked and insulted him, an insult 'so abominable that I shall never utter it to a living soul'.

Watson, apart from picking up a Master of Arts from

Oxford University and a fellowship of the Royal Society
of Literature, continued to produce a total of fifty learned
works including religious meditations on *Sons Of
Strength, Wisdom, Patience* . . . about Samson, the herculean 'judge' of Israel; Solomon, king of Israel; and Job,
the much-afflicted Old Testament hero.

He was popular with parents and pupils, and the school
flourished, yet he remained comparatively poor, for
neither the school nor writing brought him fortune. A
famous surgeon said 'the mercantile value of this man of
great learning was far less than that of a donkey-engine.'

Watson turned to another means of supplementing his
income. He and his wife moved to a bigger house at 28 St
Martin's Road, Stockwell, for which they paid the comparatively high rent of £60 a year. But they offset this by
letting out beds to day boys who had to travel long
distances and, with the gracious permission of the governors, making a small profit.

In a peak year, 1865, his school had 100 pupils, which
gave him an additional income, and parents and boys
subscribed to an address, a silver salver and a purse of
money for their popular Head. But when after twenty-
five years, ceaseless overwork affected his powers of
teaching, argument and persuasion and the number of
pupils fell to fifty-one, the governors sacked him with
three months' notice but without pension or compensation of any kind. He suggested that he should take over
the school. The governors were willing to study the
proposal, but the clergyman had no savings, no money
with which to invest and nothing came of the idea. The
governors even dismissed the Watsons' housekeeper, Mrs
Tully, and her husband, the drill-master, and warned of
further economies.

Watson worked on his next gargantuan manuscript, the history of popes from the formation of the Papacy to the Reformation. By then, the clerical writer was very depressed. According to some, Mrs Watson, no doubt disillusioned, had become bitter and quarrelsome. According to another source she was particularly critical about her husband's alleged impotence, for she had dearly wanted to bear him children. Was this enough reason for him, at sixty-six years of age, to kill her?

A year after his dismissal from the school, in September, 1871, he went, as he had in previous years, to Chelsfield, a village in Kent, to help the rector whose curate was absent on leave. The vicar, the Reverend Ffoliot Baugh, described Watson on this occasion as 'in a daze', 'completely listless', 'with no conversation whatsoever'. He was incapable of delivering the sermon he had prepared, was confined to reciting prayers in a barely audible voice, and sent back to Stockwell.

On Sunday, October 8, the ex-schoolmaster and his wife went to morning prayer at their local St Andrew's Church, on the other side of the main Stockwell Road, and heard from the lectern the dreadful Old Testament warnings of violence from Micah, the eighth-century BC Hebrew prophet. The lesson was about the cruelty of princes, the falsehoods of prophets and what would happen to those who 'hate the good and love the evil; who pluck off their skin from off them; and their flesh from off their bones. Who also eat the flesh of my people, and flay their skin from off them; and they break their bones, and chop them in pieces, as for the pot, and as flesh within the cauldron. Then shall they cry unto the Lord, but he will not hear them: he will even hide his face from them at that time, as they have behaved themselves ill in their doings.

'Thus said the Lord concerning the prophets that make my people err, that bite with their teeth, and cry, Peace; and he that putteth not into their mouths, they even prepare war against him. Therefore night shall be unto you, that ye shall not have a vision; and it shall be dark unto you, that ye shall not divine; and the sun shall go down over the prophets, and the day shall be dark over them.'

Could Watson have been mesmerised by the warning to those who 'judge for reward, and the priests thereof teach for hire, and the prophets thereof divine for money'? Did the Reverend John Selby Watson see the governors of the school, himself or, more important, his wife among those to be punished? Or was he chosen to mete out punishment to she who spoke falsely?

But then, he could have also registered the other lesson from the epistle from St Paul to the Philippians preaching love, unity and humility. Was Watson about to snap?

That afternoon at 5 p.m., Mr and Mrs Tully, the former drill-master and housekeeper of the school, paid a courtesy call to cheer up the Watsons. They rang the bell three times, and after much tramping and stamping on the doorstep, Mrs Watson could be heard complaining there must be someone at the door. Mr Watson emerged, looking very cross, and said, 'Oh, it's only Mrs Tully,' and let them in.

He was, according to the former school housekeeper, 'polite, but frigidly polite'. There was what they called 'an atmosphere'. Mrs Watson told Mrs Tully, 'I am so frightened. I am afraid of anybody getting into the house by the back, over the garden wall.' As she talked, Watson remained standing by the door, as if he expected the guests to leave, but eventually came to sit with them. Since Mr Tully now worked for a very successful printer he had come to suggest that the sacked headmaster might turn to them for work. Watson seemed interested for a moment or two but the Tullys left at 5.30 p.m. with her curtsey and Watson's stiff bow.

At 9 p.m., Ellen Mary Payne, the servant girl, returned from her one half-day-a-fortnight holiday – 'my Sunday out,' she said – and was told by the cleric that Mrs Watson had gone 'out of town' and would be staying elsewhere. 'Your mistress won't be home for two or three days,' he told her. She thought this odd as her mistress had not mentioned it to her when she had left that afternoon. As she was climbing the stairs to bed, Mr Watson held the candle and pointed to a dark patch near the library door. 'This stain on the floor; it is port wine which your mistress has spilt. I have told you in case you might wonder what it was.'

And he did tell her not to go into the room adjoining the library. That was the room Mrs Watson had occupied since she and her husband had ceased to sleep together some time before.

On the Monday evening Watson said he would be away that night and the servant tried to find someone to spend the time with her; but when she could not do so, he ordered her to remain in the house by herself. She sat in the kitchen wondering whether she should lock up the house for the night. Watson must have changed his mind, for he reappeared at 11 p.m., when he called down the stairs, 'If you find anything wrong with me in the morning, go for Dr Rugg.'

'Are you ill, sir?' Ellen asked.

'I may require medicine in the morning,' he replied.

Next morning, Mrs Watson had not returned. Watson went out before breakfast. He disappeared down the Clapham Road to the hardwear shop where he ordered a large packing case to be made to his measurements. He returned, went out again, and came back a second time, when Ellen again inquired about her mistress. All he told her was, 'If you find anything wrong with me before dinner time, send for the doctor.'

About noon, after hearing strange movements upstairs, she went to the master's room and found him undressed, apparently unconscious on the bed, with a glass and some letters by his side. One was addressed to her, with a £5 note, 'For the servant, Ellen Payne, exclusive of her wages. Let no suspicion fall upon the servant, whom I believe to be a good girl.'

Ellen, who thought he had had an epileptic fit, hurried to the Clapham Road surgery of Dr George Philip Rugg, and handed him a note, which said:

'To the Surgeon. I have killed my wife in a fit of rage. Often and often she has provoked me and I have endeavoured to restrain myself, but rage overcame me, and I struck her. Her body will be found in the little room off the library. The key is in a letter on the table. I hope she will be buried as becomes a lady of birth and position. She is an Irish lady, and her name is Anne.'

Dr Rugg took the key, unlocked the library door and found in the small room the body of Mrs Watson. Her head had been smashed in eight places by a heavy instrument, cleaving the skull from top to bottom. There were other wounds on the lower limbs. Her clothes were saturated with blood.

Dr Rugg sniffed the glass by Watson's bed and the

phial nearby and knew the now recovering man had taken prussic acid, a colourless liquid with an odour of bitter almonds. The doctor recognised it instantly, hurried to the chemists and returned with an antidote which revived the clergyman. He suspected that the suicide attempt had been half-hearted, or that the self-poisoner had taken one sip, changed his mind and had probably spat it out.

In the dressing table drawer were found five old, rusty pistols. Four had not been touched for years while the fifth, a brass-barrelled, wooden-stocked flintlock, bore reddish stains on the butt. The stock was split both lengthwise and across. In the library were a rope and a hammer, a bloodstained sponge and that curious message in Latin. There was no doubt that the broken pistol was the weapon which had battered Mrs Watson's skull. Watson, asked if he wanted to see a solicitor, replied, 'No, I do not want to see anyone. The deed is done, and it is no use now.'

Watson was taken to Newgate Prison and charged with murder. In the cells, he was heard to mutter, 'My brother is quite sane, but I would not answer for my father.' He was advised by his solicitors and Sergeant Parry – a title which preceded that of Queen's Counsel – that he should plead temporary insanity. Asked about the packing case, he said that it was not for his slain wife but for his many unpublished manuscripts and other belongings, and besides, he had never even bothered to collect it. Parry thought he had better forget about the packing case since the meticulous ordering of its measurements after Mrs Watson's death would not help his plea of insanity.

On January 10, 1872, John Selby Watson, a clerk in holy orders, a thick-set man with a stooping gait that went with his age, stood on trial for his life at the Old Bailey

136

before Mr Justice Byles. The Hon. George Denman, later a judge, who prosecuted, was noticeably sympathetic to this man in the dock with the broad, prominent forehead, sunken grey eyes and pensive look.

Was he mad? The court heard Dr Rugg tell how Watson remained perfectly lucid with an air of complete detachment and how, for his stay in prison, he calmly made a list of his requirements: mattress, bedding, hairbrush, collar and tie, boot-hooks, some slices of cold beef, and 'b.f.k.' (bread, knife and fork), the last two of which were refused on account of his attempted suicide. Dr Rugg also produced a long, detailed note Watson had written directing those interested to his brother in America – last heard of at 82 Grand Street, Williamsburg, Virginia – and particulars of all his remaining literary manuscripts. Could the man who penned all that so clearly be other than sane?

Mr Denman quoted the jury a famous definition of insanity from Mr Justice Mellor in the case of Queen v. Southey.

'By the law of England every man is presumed sane until the contrary is shown. It would be most dangerous if it were otherwise. And when a person is to be saved from the consequences of his acts by this defence [of insanity] it must be shown from circumstances or positive testimony that the person at the time of the act was in such a state of mind from disease as to be unable to comprehend the nature and quality of his acts, and to know whether he was committing right or wrong. Some medical men have theories about insanity which, if applied generally, would be fatal to society. Life could not go on if men who committed great crimes are to be deemed insane on these theories. The standard of sense and responsibility they set up is far too high for common life and human society.'

How could they square the insanity plea with the servant Ellen's version of household bliss? 'My master always behaved with great kindness to me. I never noticed any angry feelings between him and his wife. They appeared to live happily and comfortably together. My mistress had her own way. They kept no company. He was rather a reserved man. They used to sit together after meals in the library and there Mr Watson was always writing or reading. He was industrious and hard-working, and used to sit up until about eleven o'clock.' But then servants don't hear everything.

Dr Edgar Sheppard, superintendent of Colney Hatch Asylum, Barnet, visited Watson in Newgate Prison, and came to the conclusion that he suffered from melancholia but was sane. Dr Begley, medical superintendent of Hanwell Lunatic Asylum, Middlesex, had four interviews with the clergyman and changed his mind. On the first two occasions he thought the prisoner was sane, wavered at the third and at the fourth came to the conclusion that he was of unsound mind.

At Newgate, the resident surgeon, Dr John Gibson, who saw Watson daily said he always found him rational and self-possessed and his depression was no more than other prisoners suffered. Dr Henry Maudsley, Professor of Medical Jurisprudence at University College London, after whom the Maudsley psychiatric hospital in Camberwell, south-east London, is named, thought Watson was not of sound mind, but qualified it by saying he had always found some evidences of insanity before a crime.

Two other doctors supported Professor Maudsley; but the issue had to be left to the jury. Mr Justice Byles told them that Watson had killed his wife without provocation. (At least, no one had given reliable evidence of any such provocation.) The jury would have to say whether he knew what he was doing, or whether he knew what he was doing was wrong. If they thought he did not, they would acquit him, but they must state the reason why.

Most people thought the jury would be out for a few minutes and return a verdict of not guilty by reason of insanity. They took ninety minutes to find him guilty, with a recommendation to mercy on account of his advanced age and previous good character. All Watson said before he was sentenced was, 'I only wish to say that the defence which has been maintained in my favour is a just and honest one.'

The Reverend John Selby Watson was sentenced to be hanged. What had happened in the secrecy of the jury room was that the jurors could not agree. Five thought he was insane, seven thought he was not; but majority verdicts in those days were not allowed. So the jurors compromised: if they could find him guilty, recommend mercy and thereby hope to save him from the gallows someone else could carry the responsibility for his ultimate fate.

The illogical verdict was seized on by *The Times*. 'The question is not simply whether Mr Watson is an object of legitimate compassion, which is undoubted; but whether the claims of justice can fitly be permitted to yield to those of mercy. If the Home Secretary should see fit not to modify the sentence, the public will bear in mind that there are other murderers beside clergymen, and that if extremity of temptation be once admitted a bar to execution, a dangerous hope might be opened to criminals.'

The only thing ever said publicly about his wife without fear of contradiction came from the doctor who performed the post-mortem examination, and that was that she suffered from cirrhosis of the liver caused not by excessive bouts of drinking but too frequent sips of port wine.

The Cabinet were called on to decide Watson's future, but they too were divided. Some could not believe that a man who wrote that Latin explanation could be insane. Eventually they agreed to a reprieve and that the death sentence be commuted to life imprisonment.

HM Prison, Parkhurst, Isle of Wight, became Watson's home. Twelve years later he had a fall in his cell and died. His friends paid for an insertion in the *The Times* Deaths column:

'On the 6th inst. at Parkhurst, Isle of Wight, the Rev John Selby Watson, M.A., many years Head Master of the Stockwell Proprietary Grammar School, Surrey, aged 80. Interred in Carisbrooke Cemetery.'

He had achieved wider fame at last, the only murderer permitted to have his obituary paid for and advertised in *The Times*. But he died without telling why he killed his wife or what precisely he meant by his Latin message.

*Chapter Eight*

# UNHOLY COMMUNION
# AND CHLOROFORM

'Now that she has been quite properly acquitted she should, in the interests of science, tell us how she did it.'

Sir James Paget,
Sergeant-surgeon to Queen Victoria.

The lady walking along the Thames embankment at Pimlico, her petite figure muffled in a cloak against the post-Christmas cold, turned her lustrous eyes to her clergyman friend and, with her appealing French accent, asked the Reverend George Dyson to get her some chloroform.

That is not the start of a romantic novel. It is a conversation related by the parson himself in the witness box as he gave evidence on his Christian oath at the Old Bailey. His friend, Mrs Adelaide Bartlett, was in the dock on trial for her life for the murder of Edwin, her husband.

Mrs Bartlett, who had just turned thirty, had wanted the drug, she said, to soothe her husband, ten years her senior, to make him sleep. She meant that Edwin had just rediscovered the delights of her body and chloroform would dampen his sexual ardour. But then the words were spoken with the reticence peculiar to Victorian times.

Chloroform is a volatile drug and as Mrs Bartlett would use it on her handkerchief, wafting it below his nostrils, she knew she would need a lot of it, about as much as would fill a medicine bottle. She added that her husband suffered from an internal complaint which produced violent paroxysms and only chloroform would quieten him. The sovereign she handed the cleric would more than cover the cost.

The preacher had to go to three different chemists, two in Wimbledon, one in Putney, to obtain such a large quantity of the drug, explaining at each shop that he needed it to remove grease stains from clothing. When he had acquired about four ounces in three bottles he poured them into one six-ounce medicine bottle and hurried back to Pimlico to give it to Adelaide.

No wonder the almost immediate death of Mrs Bartlett's husband, the merry grocer, with his stomach full of chloroform, caused such a scandal.

Sex, financial gain and elimination of an unwanted partner were already recognised as common motives for murder in the annals of crime, though not all together in one killing. The introduction of liquid chloroform as an instrument of deliberate slaughter was quite unknown. The involvement of a priest turned the whole affair into a very odd case indeed.

He was the twenty-seven-year-old son of the Reverend George Dyson, senior, a Wesleyan minister first of Llanelly, Carmarthen, then the Dorset resort of Poole. George, junior, was also ordained in the Methodist Church and continued to study for his Bachelor of Arts degree from Trinity College Dublin. He preached with evangelical fervour in the newly-built Wesleyan chapel in the village street of Merton, some two miles from Wimbledon, Surrey, long before Merton became a bustling commuter suburb.

One Sunday, the Bartletts, who lived at The Cottage, Merton Abbey, began attending morning services at his chapel. Dyson's pulpit manner, promising salvation, threatening damnation, appealing directly to the hearts and minds of his congregation, particularly the women, made him very popular. The attendance of the Bartletts, and particularly Adelaide, demanded a courtesy call and after a decent interval, another. From such occasional, polite beginnings, there sprang up between them a remarkable intimacy.

Dyson was academically ambitious but not a particularly attractive-looking person. He had close-cropped whiskers, a full droopy moustache, a weak mouth, receding chin and mournful eyes like those of the prize St Bernard dogs the Bartletts bred and exhibited. On the other hand, Edwin, slight, muscular, blue-eyed, fair-haired and bearded was a commercially ambitious, hard-working middle-class grocer who apparently envied others their education.

He wanted that learning for his wife, Adelaide, who for understandable reasons had been deprived of proper English schooling. Mrs Bartlett, born Adelaide Blanche de la Tremoille, was illegitimate. She was conceived at Windsor, during the 1855 state visit of the Emperor Napoleon III to Britain. Her father was supposed to be Lord Alfred Paget, Queen Victoria's equerry; her mother Clara Chamberlain, younger daughter of a clerk in the Stock Exchange, and wife of the Comte de Thouars d'Escury. Adelaide was whisked away to a Roman Catholic boarding school in Orléans and left there.

Popular folk legends often ascribe illustrious forebears to those born on the wrong side of the blanket. But Adelaide was at least the unacknowledged daughter of an Englishman of good social position and he had her brought, at the age of nineteen, from the French boarding school to England where a husband would be found for her. She stayed by chance with Edwin's elder brother, Charles, an estate agent, and his well-to-do wife at Kingston-upon-Thames, Surrey, in a house where a good-looking but idle younger brother, Frederick Bartlett, also resided.

Edwin, ten years her senior, met Adelaide at that house just once and was smitten. She had short curly hair, an *avant-garde* style which did not become fashionable in Britain for several decades. She had an independence and pertness of manner which women found bold but men found becoming if not challenging. And that mouth was inviting.

Edwin Bartlett immediately called on his solicitor, who contacted the bride's guardians. Consent and conditions for marriage were laid down and accepted – her hand in marriage and a dowry to finance his partnership in the provisions and wines firm of Baxter and Bartlett in return for which Edwin must never inquire about Adelaide's parents and must undertake to complete her education. The anonymous good father was also in the background a decade later to instruct and pay an expensive legal team to defend his daughter on a charge of murdering her husband.

The marriage at Croydon on April 9, 1875, was witnessed only by Edwin's sister, Mrs Caroline James, and the bride's uncle, a Mr William Chamberlain. As soon as the couple were married the husband fulfilled part of his contract by sending the bride back to school, seeing her for any length of time only during the holidays.

'I married too young to even understand what marriage was about,' said Adelaide later. 'We entered into an agreement that it should be entirely platonic and that no sexual intercourse should occur. Except on one occasion, we abided by this agreement. The solitary exception was to enable me to have a child.'

Edwin enrolled Adelaide in Miss Dodd's boarding

146

school for girls in Stoke Newington, London, while he took lodgings opposite Clissold Park nearby. When she had completed the course there she went to a Protestant convent school in Belgium, where she wrote devoted letters to her husband across the Channel.

When the student returned, in her twenty-second year, she found her husband absorbed in his rapidly expanding partnership which by then comprised six shops, in Herne Hill, Dulwich, Brixton and other parts of south London, and a tea warehouse in the city.

While he worked long hours, Adelaide had to spend much lonely time with the dogs they bred, her embroidery and her piano lessons first above one of his shops in Station Road, Herne Hill, then above another in Lordship Lane, Dulwich, before moving to Merton.

Edwin, ostensibly concerned for her continued education, pressed the Reverend Dyson to return to their cottage to help Adelaide with her studies in Latin, history, geography and mathematics. No one, according to below-stairs gossip, recalled seeing a single book on such weighty subjects during the friendship which followed. The invitation sowed the seeds of tragedy to come.

Edwin's father, Mr Edwin Bartlett senior, a widower and not very successful builder, known as Old Bartlett, had lived with his son and daughter-in-law at Herne Hill. He disapproved of the marriage and Adelaide; she was a foreigner and a Roman Catholic. When she disappeared, not for the first time, 'to stay with my aunt' and could not be found, her father-in-law spread the story that Adelaide had been misbehaving with Frederick, his younger son.

Edwin demanded an apology from his father. Old

Bartlett confessed that the accusation was false, a document making the admission was drawn up by a solicitor, Bartlett senior signed it and an awkward peace was restored, although Old Bartlett was later to retract his apology. 'Adelaide ran away, and was away for a week or more,' he said, 'and Edwin and me thought she had gone along – we almost knew she had gone – with Fred Bartlett, the brother, and we were after her. Fred fled to America directly it was found out.'

Partly because of Adelaide's intense dislike of her father-in-law, the Bartletts moved first to a flat above another of his shops in Lordship Lane, Dulwich, then to Merton, where the cottage was too small or too far distant to admit the difficult in-law. But he continued to see Edwin almost daily in one or another of his son's business premises.

Both Edwin and Adelaide had another interest – in Dr Thomas Low Nichols' *Esoteric Anthropology, or the Mysteries of Man – A Comprehensive and Confidential Treatise on the Structure, Functions, Passional Attractions and Perversions, True and False Physical and Social Conditions and the Most Intimate Relations of Men and Women.*

Dr Nichols, an American, had no licence to practise medicine in Britain, but in his book he taught birth control 'as pure in morals as it is true in science'. It was, of course, only justified if a woman 'was compelled to submit to the embrace of her husband while her health or other conditions forbid her to have children'.

In the Bartlett household the tome was left lying open on a chair, on the bed or wherever it was last consulted. When Adelaide was expecting a child, she consulted the author's wife, Dr Mary Grove Nichols, who could practise medicine in this country. As a result of her counselling, the Bartletts called the London Association of Nurses in New Bond Street and hired Annie Walker, a nurse and midwife with fourteen years' experience.

When the pregnancy became difficult and the confinement painful, Nurse Walker asked the husband if he was apprehensive on his wife's account. When he was told that it was the life of the child that was in danger, Edwin asked her 'to take the case through' and not to call a doctor as 'I would rather not have any man interfering with her.'

The nurse at the last moment insisted on calling in a physician but by the time he arrived, as she had feared, Adelaide Bartlett's child was stillborn.

Nurse Walker became one of Adelaide's few female friends and confidants. She remained with her for four weeks before the delivery and three weeks afterwards. Both husband and wife had told her that the conception of that child was the result of a one and only single sexual act without contraception. After she lost the child, Adelaide swore she would never have any more children.

When the Reverend Mr Dyson arrived on the scene, he was pressed to stay for tea, or for supper, and came as often as he chose, even though the husband was away for long hours at his business. And although Victorian reticence even at the time of the trial kept the truth from the public, Sir Edward Clarke, QC, MP, who defended Mrs Bartlett, revealed many years later:

'It was not long before he (Dyson) made love to Mrs Bartlett and found her entirely responsive. He mentioned their mutual affection to the husband, and, so far from meeting any objection, found him quite willing to permit and even to encourage the intimacy.'

149

About the time the Bartletts' tenancy of the Merton cottage came to an end, Dyson had to go to Dublin to obtain his Bachelor of Arts degree. The Bartletts took a holiday in Dover and invited their clerical friend to share the vacation at their expense. He could not, he said, spare the time from his flock to take the full holiday but he did stay with them on two occasions, even though Edwin would get up in the middle of the night to catch the 3 a.m. train back to London to be at his shops long before they opened for business, leaving Dyson and Adelaide alone in Dover.

Since the parson had to exist on a stipend of £100 a year, Edwin gave him a cheque for his rail fares. This generosity was a sample of a much bigger gesture to come.

Edwin had made a will and his wife had complained more than once in his presence and that of Nurse Walker that he had left her the sole heiress on condition that she did not marry again. Now Edwin changed his will, leaving her everything unconditionally, appointing his solicitor and Mr Dyson as executors. His signature was witnessed by two clerks in his grocery business. Old Bartlett, when he heard, promptly filed a legal challenge to the will.

Edwin told Dyson verbally of the change and then wrote him a most odd, sentimental letter:

'Dear George, Would that I could find words to express my thankfulness to you for the very loving letter you sent to Adelaide today. It would have done anybody good to see her overflowing with joy as she read it whilst walking along the street, and afterwards she read it to me. I felt my heart going out to you. I long to tell you how proud I feel at the thought I should soon be able to clasp the hand of the man who from his heart could pen such noble thoughts. Who can help loving you? I felt that I must say two words, "Thank you," and my desire to do so is my excuse for troubling you with this. Looking towards the future with joyfulness, I am, Yours affectionately, Edwin.'

The letter from the Rev George to the joyful wife has not, alas, survived but the clergyman replied:

'My Dear Edwin, Thank you very much for the brotherly letter you sent me yesterday. I am sure I respond from my heart to your wish that our friendship may ripen with the lapse of time, and I do so with confidence, for I feel that our friendship is founded on a firm, abiding basis – trust and esteem. I have from a boy been ever longing for the trust and confidence of others. I have never been so perfectly happy as when in possession of this. It is in this respect, as in many others, that you have shown yourself a true friend. You have thanked me, and now I thank you, yet I ought to confess that I read your warm and generous letter with a kind of half fear – a fear lest you should ever be disappointed in me and find me a far more prosy and matter-of-fact creature than you expect. Thank you, moreover, for the telegram [containing the rail fares for the holiday]; it was very considerate to send it. I am looking forward with much pleasure to next week. Thus far I have been able to stave off any work, and trust to be able to keep it clear. Dear old Dover, it will ever possess a pleasant memory for me in my mind and a warm place in my heart. With very kind regards, Believe me, Yours affectionately, George.'

When the Bartletts left Dover, they moved to 85 Claverton Street, Pimlico, in the City of Westminster. Edwin bought George a season ticket so he could travel from his new, bigger chapel on the Upper Richmond

Road from Putney to Waterloo and visit them more frequently.

According to Alice Fulcher, a servant at Claverton Street, Dyson 'used to come once or twice a week and before Mr Bartlett's illness he came three or four times a week. As early as nine or half past nine and sometimes later. Mr Bartlett sometimes went to business at eight or half-past eight and returned between five and six in the evening. He sometimes went out again. Sometimes Mr Dyson stayed till dinner time and dined with Mr and Mrs Bartlett. The usual time for dinner was between five and six o'clock.'

There was a blue serge lounge coat and carpet slippers in the back room kept for Mr Dyson so that he could change out of his clerical garb. Fulcher noticed that sometimes when he was visiting 'window curtains were pulled together and then pinned. I have seen them [Mr Dyson and Mrs Bartlett] sitting on the sofa together and I have also seen them sitting on the floor together. I have seen Mr Dyson sitting on a low chair and Mrs Bartlett sitting on the floor with her head on Mr Dyson's knee.' She never saw any learning books.

Dyson was no doubt encouraged by the fact that in the event of Edwin's death, the grocer wished to 'give' Adelaide to the parson. 'If anything happens to me you two may come together.' After all Edwin had derived the keenest pleasure from watching the effects of his wife's charms upon other men. Bartlett had actually asked Dyson to kiss her and had been beside himself with pleasure as he watched them embracing again and again.

Old Bartlett did not know or at least would not admit that his son had 'any solid ideas' about married life which differed from those of other people, but he was 'a merry man' always chaffing and joking. He used to say, his father continued, that 'one ought to have two wives, one to take out and one to do the work.'

The Reverend Dyson had had conversations about the two-wife theory with Edwin Bartlett. Edwin had asked him if the Bible specifically ruled on the principle of one man, one wife for he thought that there might be 'a wife for companionship and one for service' or 'use' as some put it. Dyson told him there was no sanction in the Good Book for such an arrangement.

The discussion, according to the clergyman, was odd rather than immoral, and not unwholesome, coming as it did from Edwin. 'He was a man with strange ideas, speaking half-playfully the first time but more seriously on some later occasion.'

There was no secret understanding between them about a future marriage to Adelaide, he claimed. He swore that no impropriety had taken place. He had kissed Adelaide both when her husband was present and when he was absent. But he could not explain convincingly the reason for a conversation in which Edwin found some trifling fault with his wife and Dyson had countered, 'If ever she comes under my care, I shall have to teach her differently.'

Dyson claimed he had told Edwin that he was growing very attached to Mrs Bartlett, the attachment was disturbing his work, and he thought it best if he discontinued the friendship. Bartlett had said, 'Why should you discontinue it?' He thought the friendship had been 'a great benefit' to his wife, and that since she liked Dyson's preaching he might lead her back to the frame of mind and disposition of heart towards her husband she had shown when she wrote to him from the convent all those years ago.

At the beginning of December, 1885, Edwin became ill for the first time in his life. Only five years previously he had been passed by the British Equitable Insurance Company as a first-class life risk.

Dr Alfred Leach, a local doctor, now saw that he suffered from bad dental work; a plate had been fitted without removing the teeth stumps, which Dr Leach remedied by taking the patient to another dentist. But the doctor had seen traces of mercury poisoning in Edwin's mouth, and it occurred to him that Edwin may have taken mercury, used in those days to counter venereal disease.

That might have explained the Bartletts sleeping in separate beds at Claverton Street and Edwin's abstinence from the sexual act, for fear of passing the disease to his wife, but Edwin (out of Mrs Bartlett's hearing) denied either taking mercury or having had syphilis. Curiously, Mrs Bartlett said that she had in fact consulted the American Dr Nichol about her husband. Nichol, although he could not practise medicine in Britain, might well have passed himself off as a sexologist if not a venereologist.

Edwin Bartlett might, for one reason or another, have taken mercury medicinally and become addicted to it, but in such an atmosphere of falsehood and reticence, who could be sure?

He was suffering from severe pain in his left side, from sickness, diarrhoea and haemorrhage of the bowels, weak pulse, extreme nervousness and prostration. Nor could he look into the light for very long. The doctor diagnosed mercurialism or sub-acute gastritis. He should have known, as every doctor knows, that it is acute mercury poisoning which causes nausea and vomiting, pain in the abdomen and diarrhoea. Chronic mercury poisoning, on the other hand, from the inhalation of mercury vapour (a known addiction), causes brain damage with staggering, tunnel vision, garbled speech, severe tremor and emotional disturbances.

The doctor prescribed purgatives. The patient remained sleepless, depressed and lacking in energy. Another doctor said he was surprised that such a fit man should be lying in bed.

Adelaide Bartlett sent her husband's business partner, Mr Baxter, an order for New Year's Eve groceries – a nice fruit cake, a bottle of walnuts, a bottle of Colonel Skinner's Mango Chutney and a bottle of brandy called 'Lord's Extra' – although she confessed in the accompanying letter, 'I know these things are not fit for Edwin to eat but he fancies them.'

On New Year's Eve, at 3 p.m., the sick man ate a lunch of jugged hare. At 9 p.m. he enjoyed a supper of half a dozen oysters, bread and butter, some mango chutney, cake and tea, and ordered a haddock for breakfast.

Edwin Bartlett did not live to eat the haddock. Mrs Bartlett awoke Mr Doggett, her landlord – ironically, the registrar of deaths for the district – at 4 a.m. and said that she thought Mr Bartlett was dead. Mr Doggett found him in bed, lying on his back with his left hand on his breast.

On the mantelpiece, within reach of the bed, was a tumbler half-full of brandy, which also had about it a smell of chloroform and paregoric.

Mr Doggett thought he had been dead a couple of hours. The fire appeared to have been stoked up. And he was not the only person with the idea that the delay in raising the alarm and the stoking of the fire may have been to allow time to dispel the tell-tale smell of chloroform.

The doctor found an almost empty bottle of chlorodyne, but Mrs Bartlett said that Edwin had only used that to rinse his gums for his dental complaint. When doctors opened the body for a post-mortem examination the smell was such that they thought he had swallowed a whole bottle of chloroform. No one found the bottle which had contained it. A policeman did discover in Edwin's belongings some contraceptives 'of French manufacture', as he put it.

Twenty-four hours later, on January 2, the Reverend George Dyson arrived with condolences and worries. The moment he was alone with Adelaide he asked what had happened to the bottle he had brought her.

'I have not had occasion to use it,' she said. 'The bottle is just as you gave it me.'

Dyson was not satisfied. He persisted with his questions, to which she replied, 'You must not be worried about it' and 'You should dismiss it from your mind' for this 'is a very critical time for me'.

On Sunday, January 3, after preaching to the Putney faithful Dyson walked on Wandsworth Common where he threw away the three bottles which had originally contained the chloroform he had bought.

On the Monday the widow was very angry because Dyson was bothering her about a piece of paper which she tore up and handed to him. It was a rather pathetic poem he had written for her:

Who is it that hath burst the door
Unclosed the heart that shut before
And set her queenlike on its throne
And made its homage all her own – My Birdie.

Adelaide had earlier told Dyson, 'Edwin has not more than a year to live – and he knows it.' Now their conversation was overheard by Mrs Alice Matthews, a friend of Adelaide's. Dyson said, 'You did tell me that Edwin was going to die soon.'

Mrs Bartlett replied, 'I never said anything of the kind,' at which Dyson bowed his head on the piano and said, 'Oh, my God! I am a ruined man.'

When he returned in the evening she asked him to say nothing about the chloroform but he said, 'I shall make a clean breast of the affair.'

A friend of Mrs Bartlett's said that Dyson appeared to be 'panic-stricken'. He said he had been 'duped' by 'a wicked woman'. Edwin had deliberately thrown him into her company and he had been 'attacked on my weakest side'.

In between hearings by the coroner, Adelaide told the parson over tea, 'You are distressing yourself unnecessarily.'

'I have reason to be alarmed,' he retorted.

'If you do not incriminate yourself,' she told him, 'I shall not incriminate you.'

Two days later they had a final meeting. Dyson, considerably upset, said, 'My career is at an end. I shall be forced to resign my ministry. Supposing it was proved – that you–'

'Do not mince matters,' snapped Adelaide. 'Say, if you want to say it, that I gave him the chloroform.'

'I want to know what became of the chloroform.'

'I poured the chloroform from the railway carriage window and threw the bottle into Peckham Rye Pond.'

Doctors said that chloroform taken in that quantity would have seared Edwin's organs and caused him to vomit. There was no vomit. No one heard roars of agony echoing through the Claverton Street lodgings on New Year's Day, 1886. There was no trace of burns around the mouth or windpipe.

Nevertheless the coroner's jury returned a verdict that Edwin had been murdered by his wife and that the Reverend George Dyson was an accessory before the fact of that murder.

The Crown calculated that there would be more chance of an Old Bailey jury convicting Adelaide Bartlett if Dyson was not prosecuted but instead gave evidence against her. When the trial opened, Dyson appeared briefly in the dock, no evidence was offered against him, and he was formally declared not guilty.

Sir Edward Clarke, counsel for the defence, reasoned differently. 'The more I can associate Dyson's actions with those of Mrs Bartlett, the more I can strengthen the reluctance of the jury to send her to the hangman's cord while he passes unrebuked to freedom.'

The prosecutor, the Attorney-General, Sir Charles Russell, QC, MP, insisted that Mr Bartlett had been lulled into a doze by the external application of chloroform. Then, when he was semi-comatose, Mrs Bartlett had administered the fatal dose.

Sir Edward Clarke listed everything in his client's favour: how she had lived in friendship and affection with her husband for years; tended him by day; sacrificed her night's sleep, holding his toe; nursed him and talked about him taking a rest. The husband, though ill, had asked for another medical opinion lest his wife was wrongly accused of ill-treating him. She, in turn, had wished they were unmarried in order that she might have the happiness of marrying him again. Yet overnight she was said to have become a murderess.

And then came the most important question of the trial. Sir Edward asked the Crown's principal medical witness: 'If the post-mortem examination had been performed, as Mrs Bartlett wished it to be, on the very day on which death took place, there would have been still better opportunity of determining the cause of death?'

Dr Thomas Stevenson, Professor of Jurisprudence at Guy's Hospital: 'Yes.'

When the examination did take place there was no sign of burning. No traces of vomit had been found.

The role of the clergyman was not forgotten. Sir Edward, in his closing address, said, 'I think Mr Dyson will never in his life read the account of a trial for murder without thinking how heavily his own rash, unjustified conduct would have told against him if he had been put upon his trial.'

Mr Justice Wills, summing up for the jury, said, 'You cannot doubt that they (Mrs Bartlett and Dyson) got to that state of intimacy when in some fashion or other the possible death of the husband and the possibility of Dyson succeeding him were matters of familiar discussion.' And later, 'It is not a pleasant spectacle, that of a Christian minister steadily taking advantage of the husband's weakness, increasing the frequency of his visits under the guise of giving lessons (as to which, however, there is scarcely a trace of corroborative evidence) passing hour after hour – twice, three times or four times a week – with the woman.'

The foreman of the Old Bailey jury, asked if they found the prisoner guilty or not guilty, replied: 'We have well considered the evidence, and, although we think grave suspicion is attached to the prisoner, we do not think there is sufficient evidence to show how or by whom the chloroform was administered.'

The Clerk of the Court: 'Then you say that the prisoner is Not Guilty, gentlemen?'

Foreman: 'Not Guilty.'

No one could explain how Adelaide, or anyone else, could have put the chloroform down Edwin's throat without him protesting or vomiting or without it burning him. Sir James Paget, Sergeant-surgeon to Queen Victoria, and the joint founder of pathology, said, 'Now that she has been quite properly acquitted she should, in the interests of science, tell us how she did it.'

Adelaide wrote a letter of thanks to Sir Edward Clarke: 'I have heard many eloquent Jesuits preach but I never listened to anything finer than your speech.'

Beyond that she kept her silence. She returned to France, and thence to America, where rumour said she had again taken up with the younger Bartlett brother, Frederick. Dyson did not reveal anything. His name disappeared both from outside his Putney chapel and from the roll of Methodist ministers; and he went to Australia and, for him, fortunate oblivion.

*Chapter Nine*

# THE WAY OF A MAN
# WITH A MAID

'I was very much surprised to hear that there is some scandal going the round about you and me going into the Doctor's Chapel for immoral Purposes.'

Letter from William Gardiner
to Rose Harsent.

The Primitive Methodists sat round the pews, questioning William Gardiner, assistant steward, treasurer, Sunday School superintendent and choirmaster. How was it that he, married with six children, spent so much time alone in the chapel with Rose Harsent, the twenty-three-year-old village belle?

Two young men, George Wright and Alphonso Skinner, who were employed under foreman Gardiner at the same workshop, had followed him and Rose to the Doctor's Chapel, an isolated barn-like building in a village field, and listened from outside to the conversation.

'Did you see me reading my Bible last Sunday?' asked Rose.

'No, what were you reading about?' Gardiner replied.

'I was reading about like what we have been doing here tonight. I'll tell you where it is.'

Rose picked up the Good Book and pointed to Genesis, chapter thirty-eight, verses 8 and 9. 'And Judah said unto Onan, Go in unto thy brother's wife, and marry her, and raise up seed to thy brother. And Onan knew that the seed should not be his; and it came to pass, when he went in unto his brother's wife, that he spilled his seed on the ground, lest that he should give seed to his brother.'

The eavesdroppers had no doubt that they were going to 'hear something indecent' which accompanied an act of masturbation or *coitus interruptus*. The last was probably

163

the only kind of birth control the villagers knew. The listeners also heard laughing and rustling and a woman's voice calling out, 'Oh, oh!'

At last, according to the informers, who had hidden behind a hedge, Rose said, 'I shall be out tomorrow night at nine o'clock. You must let me go.'

That, and the subsequent village gossip, was not forgotten two years later when William Gardiner twice stood trial for the murder of Rose Harsent. Twice juries disagreed. And Gardiner walked free.

What took place on May 1, 1901, and in the early hours of Sunday, June 1, 1902, ruffled the peace of the countryside around Peasenhall, Suffolk. The South Folk, whence Suffolk gets its name, were hardy, earthy people, descended from the Angles. Their ancestors had found the sweeping coastline, with no natural harbours, backed by marshland constantly washed by the sea, and beyond the low hills the treacherous fens. Later Dutch immigrants, finding the geography similar to their homeland, drained the fens, built ports, planted bulbs and imported other native influences particularly in building gabled houses. Most of them accepted a traditional chapel-taught sexual morality, which was against fornication and upheld the seventh commandment, 'Thou shalt not commit adultery.' Not to mention the sixth commandment, 'Thou shalt do no murder.'

There is still a quaint smock mill, a reminder of earlier times, in Peasenhall, and among the Nonconformists, Dissenters, and chapel folk the unsolved mystery of Rose Harsent's death remains. Was it a holy killing, born out of sex and passion, and maybe revenge? Was it an accident? Or was it suicide? Whatever the truth, it carried with it a cautionary moral tale.

William Gardiner claimed that he had gone to the Doctor's Chapel with Rose Harsent only to help her move a stiff door. His behaviour towards her was of choirmaster to chorister, Sunday School teacher to pupil, elder to young person, and perfectly proper. He had written Rose two letters, the first of which read:

Dear Rose, I was very much surprised this morning to hear that there is some scandal going the round about you and me going into the Doctor's Chapel for immoral Purposes so that I shall put it into other hands at once as I have found out who it was that started it. Bill Wright and Skinner say they saw us there, but I shall summons them for defamation of character unless they withdraw what they have said and give me a written apology. I shall see Bob tonight, and we will come and see you together if possible. I shall at the same time see your father and tell him. Yours &c., William Gardiner.

The second letter said:

Dear Rose, I have broke the news to Mrs Gardiner this morning, she is awfully upset but she say she knows it is wrong, for I was home from ½ past 9 o'clock so I could not possibly be with you an hour so she wont believe anything about it. I have asked Mr Burgess [a local bricklayer who knew everyone concerned] to ask those two Chaps to come to the Chapel tonight and have it out with them there however they stand by such a tale I don't know but I don't think God will forsake me now and if we put our trust in Him it will end right but its awfully hard work to have to face people when they are all suspicious of you but by Gods help whether they believe me or not I shall try and live it down and prove by my future conduct that its all false, I only wish I could take it to Court but I don't see a shadow of a chance to get the case as I don't think you would be strong enough to face a trial. Trusting that God will direct us and make the way clear. I remains, yours in trouble, W. Gardiner.

Gardiner, whose jet black hair and beard gave him a Spanish appearance, had the kind of forbidding countenance to rebut the gossips – but was he innocent? The elders of the church thought the matter so important that Mr John Guy, superintendent of the Wangford circuit of the Primitive Methodists, was called to conduct the inquiry at Sibton, the adjacent hamlet to Peasenhall, where the misbehaviour was supposed to have occurred.

There they might be able to decide whether Gardiner's protestations were genuine or bluster. He challenged his two accusers face to face and demanded a withdrawal of their accusations. He went to a firm of solicitors in Ipswich, the county town, who threatened proceedings for slander unless an apology was forthcoming. But they did not get one.

Besides, there seemed no reason for the story to have been invented. There was no known antagonism between Gardiner and the two story-tellers until this time. At the factory where Gardiner was the master-carpenter one of the pair was reprimanded about his work but that was at a later date. The evidence of the two men was denied by the two accused – Rose was interviewed privately in the presence of her mother – and no conclusion could be reached by the twenty or so church members who heard the case. As a result, the scandal was not referred to a congregation of elders, which had power of punishment and could dismiss Gardiner from his church appointments. Instead, he was told by Mr Guy, 'You had better be very careful in the future, Mr Gardiner. I hope it will be a lesson for life for you.'

Gardiner promised to keep clear of Rose Harsent in future. But the following February, Henry Rouse, a local preacher, who had laid the original complaint against Gardiner, saw him walking again with Rose at night after dark, away from their homes towards Yaxford a mile or so away. He spoke to them, wishing them 'Goodnight', but they did not reply. Later the preacher took Gardiner aside and said, 'I am somewhat surprised that you should continue to walk about with that girl. There is so much talk, and it will do the chapel a great deal of harm.'

Gardiner told him, 'If you do not say anything about it, it shall never occur again.'

Yet later still, while he was preaching in the chapel, Rouse saw 'Gardiner have his feet in Rose Harsent's lap'. Worshippers close by could see them. The preacher later told a jury, 'You gentlemen know what I mean by the lap of a person. I ceased to speak, with the intention of telling one of them to walk out of the chapel, but something seemed to speak to me not to expose them there.'

Rouse got his wife to write an anonymous letter to Gardiner, at his dictation, and kept a copy of it. He thought it might have more influence on Gardiner, he said, than if he identified himself as the writer. The message said:

Dear Mr Gardiner, I write to warn you of your conduct with the girl Rose, as I find when she come into the chapel she must place herself next to you, which keep the people's minds still in the belief that you are a guilty man, and in that case you will drive many from the chapel, and those that would join the cause are kept away through it. We are told to shun the least appearance of evil. I do not wish you to leave God's house, but there must be a difference before God's cause can prosper, which I hope you will see to be right as people cannot hear when the enemy of souls bring this before them. I write to you as one that love your soul, and I hope you will have her sit in some other place, and remove such feeling which for sake (sic) she will do.

A year and a month after the incident in the Doctor's Chapel, Rose was dead. She had died horribly. She was found in her nightdress, her face towards the wall, at the bottom of the stairs of the house where she worked. A bloody gash crossed her throat, a jagged stab wound was visible on her breast, her nightdress was singed and her flesh charred. She was also six months pregnant.

William Gardiner was still master-carpenter and foreman of J. and J. Smyth, agricultural implement makers, at the Drill Works in the village. He was still only in his mid-thirties, married and the father of six children, and regarded by few as still a pillar of the Primitive Methodist faith. He was known behind his back, rather cheekily, as 'Holy Willie'.

He still lived in a cottage in the main street of Peasenhall. Not far away, on the same thoroughfare, Rose Harsent was retained in service as a maid to Deacon

William Crisp and his wife Georgina at Providence House, a picturesque gabled Dutch building with a walled garden.

On the night of May 31, 1902, June came busting out all over with a horrendous thunderstorm. Lightning, thunder, and torrential rain lit and deafened the village. At Providence House, Mrs Crisp was worried about Rose. She had tackled her about being pregnant but Rose had denied it. Soon after ten o'clock she said 'Goodnight' to the girl. Some time in the night she heard a scream and a thud as if someone had fallen. But thinking that she must have been mistaken and it was the noise of the storm, she went back to sleep.

Rose occupied a bedroom and a kitchen above the Crisps' bedroom which was reached separately by stairs from the main kitchen of the house. At some hour that night she left her bed in her nightgown and went downstairs with a lamp to light the way. Next morning, when the storm had abated, her father, William Harsent, called with fresh linen and found her dead at the foot of those stairs.

Before any investigation could take place the name of William Gardiner was on the lips of many villagers. Rose's throat had been cut, her windpipe severed, her body partly burned. The injury to her breast had been caused by a sharp implement thrust upwards. The fire had been started with the aid of the paraffin lamp which she had carried and which now lay shattered beside her in three pieces. There was also a broken medicine bottle containing traces of paraffin which bore a label marked, 'Two to three teaspoonfuls, a sixth part to be taken every four hours – Mrs Gardiner's children.'

Under Rose's body was a copy of the *East Anglian*

*Daily Times*, dated May 30, which was said by Gardiner's brother to have been delivered by him to William's house on that day. Upstairs in her bedroom, officers found letters and a note which had been delivered on the eve of the girl's death by Frederick Brewer, the local postman. 'D.R. [Dear Rose]' it said, 'I will try to see you tonight at 12 o'clock at your place if you put a light in your window at ten o'clock for about 10 minutes then you can take it out again. Don't have a light in your room at twelve, as I will come round to the back.' It was unsigned.

Outside the house were footprints which went to and from Gardiner's cottage. James Morris, a young gamekeeper, passed through the village at 5 a.m. on the day of the murder, before the body was discovered. With a detective's eye for poachers, he noticed the prints, which were of rubber soles with bars across their treads. At the inquest a juryman drew a picture of them at Morris's dictation. The shoe prints were matched and found identical to those made by shoes discovered in Gardiner's home.

In Gardiner's pockets was a knife with a blade bearing traces of blood.

The investigators put two and two together. The dead girl was six months pregnant. The motive for her death did not need much reasoning. Gardiner was arrested and put on trial at Ipswich Assizes in November 1902. Mrs Gardiner gave evidence that her husband had been with her all night, apart from a half-hour period at around 11.30 p.m. Gardiner denied writing the note.

Mr Burgess, the bricklayer, had stopped to talk to the master-carpenter at his door for fifteen minutes and after he left he had seen the light (which was supposed to be on for ten minutes) in Rose's room. Mrs Gardiner, asked about the incriminating medicine bottle, said it had contained camphorated oil which had been prescribed for her children, and she had lent it to Rose Harsent, as an act of charity, when she had a cold. As for the knife, William had been cutting up rabbits but forensic scientists in Britain in those days had not developed with certainty the means of telling human from animal blood.

As for the shoes which bore the same characteristics on the soles as the prints found outside the house, Gardiner insisted he had not worn them for many months.

According to the defence, when news of the death and knowledge of the girl's condition was first whispered around the village, many people thought it was suicide. Now the defence suggested that it could have been an accident. Imagine a girl in the dark, holding the hem of her nightgown in one hand, the oil lamp and temporary paraffin bottle high in the other. She could have tripped and fallen on the glass paraffin lamp she was carrying, shattering the bowl from which a shard of glass caused her fatal injuries. The flame from the lamp could have burnt her.

Mr Ernest Wild, later Sir Ernest, KC, Recorder of the City of London, appeared for the accused man and played on the fact that much of the chapel-goers' lives were spent spying, eavesdropping and criticising the morals and anti-social behaviour of others. They were not beyond exercising their imaginations. And village prejudice against Gardiner was heavily based on the suspicions of the previous year, in spite of the fact that on that occasion, when he had been questioned about his relationship with Rose, no conclusion had been reached. He had not been punished and had lost none of his offices in the chapel.

The first trial was conducted prejudicially against Gardiner by Mr Justice Grantham. It was long before majority verdicts and one man held out for an acquittal and thus robbed the hangman of another victim. The jury could not agree and there was no prospect of them doing so. The second time, after a more even-handed hearing by Mr Justice Lawrence, only one juryman voted to send him to the gallows. Again a hung jury.

The Crown abandoned the prosecution, and entered a *nolle prosequi*. It means 'unwilling to prosecute' and is an undertaking by the plaintiff to discontinue the action. In criminal cases, it stays the prosecution on indictment – the written or printed accusation of the crime – but it is not an acquittal. Fresh proceedings may be brought at another date. But they never were.

William Gardiner shaved off his black beard and black moustache, was freed from prison and, with his family, quit the joinery, left the village and opened a shop near London, where they lived out their lives in obscurity. The village went back to wondering.

*Chapter Ten*

# SUFFER THE LITTLE CHILDREN

'That baby farmer from Reading still haunts my dreams.'

The Chief Warder of Newgate Prison.

The sight of a black-bonneted girl in uniform, carrying a 'Blood and Fire' banner or beating a tambourine and marching with a brass band on a Sunday morning, is still one of the traditional sights of Christian Britain. It tells the beholders that there is still a Salvation Army which is ready to deploy its troops, men and women, across the battlefield of poverty and misery. For soldiers at war, alcoholics, derelicts, missing persons and above all abandoned children the Salvation Army has outlived most other voluntary agencies set up for their material benefit and spiritual gain.

Sister Amelia Elizabeth Dyer, who was born in the year Queen Victoria came to the throne, was one of the Army's banner-wavers. She could be seen touring the dockland pubs of Bristol on Saturday nights, seeking alms for the cause from sailors and dockers – and trying to persuade them to give up the demon drink – and marching with the Bristol citadel band on the Sabbath.

She separated from her husband, William, a sour man working in a Bristol vinegar factory, supposedly over the hours she spent looking after children whose single or married parents could not cope or who would rather they had never had children in the first place. At least that is the story her grown-up married daughter, MaryAnn Dyer, nicknamed Polly, put about. He had forbidden his wife to board or adopt any more babies, said Polly, because it brought the police and the parish officers to their door.

'Suffer the children to come unto me,' said the Lord, 'and forbid them not for theirs is the kingdom of heaven.' Amelia practised what the Lord preached. When she appeared years later in the dock at the Old Bailey, a slight woman, only five feet tall, with white hair worn in a bun, she had an air of godliness of which General Booth, founder of the Salvation Army, who was then sixty-seven, would have been proud – until he knew the truth.

For many years the homes where Amelia lived seemed full of very young children, mostly newly born, for whom a poor parent would pay a few shillings a month boarding fee or a few pounds to have them permanently adopted. Her Salvation Army reference was sufficient for her to be trusted. Some sharp-eyed parish guardian, however, thought she was taking in more children than she could handle and in 1880 at Long Ashton, Bristol, a police court sentenced her to six months' imprisonment for being a non-registered baby farmer.

There followed a series of apparent attempts to kill herself. Some thought she was mad, some that her suicide attempts were not genuine. In those days attempted suicide was an offence. In November 1891 she was taken into Gloucester Asylum with a self-inflicted superficial throat wound. She was allowed out after a month. Wells Asylum opened its doors to her in December, 1893, when her daughter claimed she had thrown herself into the River Severn. Another month later she was shown out again. Unspecified 'attempted suicide' was written on another docket at Gloucester Asylum when they gave her a bed again in December, 1894.

While she was being looked after there, the parish officer found in her home four children who were imme-diately sent to the Barton Regis Workhouse where two of their mothers – 'ladies in a good position', said the master – reclaimed them. They said that they had paid Mrs Dyer £80 and £40, respectively, to adopt them. Mothers who dumped their babies on others tended to exaggerate the payments they made, to salve their consciences and in order not to give the impression that they had merely dumped unwanted possessions.

Amelia Dyer was transferred from her last asylum to that same workhouse where she stayed until June, 1895. If anyone had looked down the workhouse register they would have found that on June 13 another inmate, Granny Smith, left its protection for a day's leave and never returned. She later turned up as Mrs Dyer's friend, companion and lodger.

That same month, June, 1895, Mrs Dyer quit Bristol for Cardiff, where her son-in-law, Arthur Ernest Palmer, a twenty-five-year-old unemployed Mr-Fixit-if-it-will-earn, and her daughter Polly lived.

But her troubles were by no means over. Polly gave birth to a baby which died. The death certificate put the cause as 'convulsions and diarrhoea' although the family doctor expressed none too quietly the suspicion that neglect had had a hand in the baby's demise. Within weeks, the Palmers were so in debt that they fled Wales along with Mrs Dyer and her recently acquired assistant, Granny Smith. After a night in a temperance hotel in Reading, the family moved to Caversham on the banks of the River Thames, first to Elm Road, then to Piggott's Road and later to Kensington Road, all in the same district.

Women who were burdened with children were attracted by the advertisement Mrs Dyer placed in a Reading newspaper, offering to board them for a modest charge. Mrs Dyer posed as the wife of a wealthy farmer, which was sometimes believed by her clients and sometimes not.

On March 30, 1896, bargemen working the Caversham section of the Thames at Reading took from the river a brown paper parcel in which they found newspapers, and inside them, the corpse of a baby girl. She had been strangled by tape, wrapped in a parcel, tied to a brick and dumped in the water. A constable who was called noticed that some of the newspapers were still dry and calculated the package had not been in the water long. Better still, on the brown paper was a decipherable address, 'Mrs Thomas, Piggott's Road, Lower Caversham.'

When police called there no Mrs Thomas could be found and the last occupant, Mrs Dyer, had vanished. But the brick tied to the package matched other bricks around the house, marked with the same red-hot-iron mark. The fact that Mrs Dyer was also Mrs Harding, Mrs Smith, Mrs Stanfield, Mrs Thomas, Mrs Wathen, Mrs Weymouth and maybe more made the task of finding her more difficult.

By the time police made it known that they wanted to interview Mrs Dyer, two more babies had been found dead in the Thames. She was eventually arrested at Reading railway station, presumably embarking on another board or adoption enterprise, and held on a charge of murdering a nameless infant. Her daughter was charged with being an accessory before the fact of murder, her son-in-law with being an accessory after the fact.

Today, when a child dies of neglect or cruelty which could have been anticipated, the social services often blame the tragedy on a breakdown of communication. A hundred years ago little or no communication existed between the responsible parish authorities and police in one district and those in another. When the recently founded National Society for the Prevention of Cruelty to Children sent an inspector to the Dyer household in Reading, he did not know of Mrs Dyer's previous conviction in Gloucestershire. The call, as a result, produced little more than the advice that in view of the number of children being boarded she should register as a baby farmer.

After she was arrested in April, 1896, her history became known to all. By the end of that month police had compiled an appalling diary of the activities of the 'Baby Farmer of Reading', as the newspaper headlines dubbed her.

September 23, 1895: Mrs Dyer's daughter, Polly, went to Gloucester to collect the ten-month-old baby of barmaid Elizabeth Goulding and a payment of £10.

November (day uncertain): Willie Thornton, aged nine, arrived. His parents were never traced. There was a girl in the house at the time, probably the Goulding baby.

January, 1896: A small baby girl arrived, but the mother did not believe Mrs Dyer was the wife of a wealthy farmer and left with her child.

March 29: Mrs Dyer threw into the river the brown paper parcel containing the baby.

March 30: The baby was found and later identified as Helena Fry. A man told police he had seen Mrs Dyer on the river tow-path looking into the water at the place where the body was discovered.

March 31: The day after the baby was found in the Thames, Mrs Dyer took a train to Cheltenham, Gloucestershire, where an unmarried mother, Eleanor Marmon, handed over her baby, Doris, aged four months.

April 1: Mrs Dyer collected her daughter, then living in Willesden, Middlesex, and travelled to Paddington, the London terminus of the Great Western Railway. Under the railway station clock, they met by appointment Mrs Sergeant, a lady who said that her maid, Miss Simmons, had been 'in trouble'. The girl had seen Mrs Dyer's advertisement in the *Weekly Dispatch*: 'Couple having no child would like the care of one or would adopt one. Terms £10.' The lady explained that Simmons had gone to another job but would be very grateful if Mrs Dyer would take her child, Harry. She handed over the baby and £5 on account.

April 2: Two babies in a carpet bag were thrown into the Thames at Reading, not far from the point where the previous baby in the brown paper parcel had been found.

April 4: Mrs Dyer was arrested. While waiting to be charged at Reading police station she took a pair of scissors from her pocket. A policeman, believing she was about to stab herself, took them from her. A little later she untied a boot-lace and put it round her neck but was prevented from knotting it. Told that her son-in-law had been brought in, she asked, 'What's Arthur here for? He's done nothing.'

April 8: The body of a boy aged two or three months, badly decomposed, was found but never identified.

April 10: The body of another boy, also not identified, was discovered. On the same day the carpet bag containing two corpses was dragged from the river and the bodies identified as those of Doris Marmon, taken from her mother on March 31, and Harry Simmons, collected at Paddington on April 1.

The total number of dead children found was seven.

Five more could not be found, two were returned to their mothers, and Granny Smith refused to accept another child who was brought to the door. Granny then disappeared, obviously fearful of the consequences.

While on remand in Reading Gaol awaiting a court hearing, Mrs Dyer wrote to the police superintendent in charge of the case:

> Dear Sir,
>
> Will you kindly grant me the favour of presenting this to the Magistrate on Saturday the 18th inst. I must relieve my mind. I do not know, and I feel my days are numbered, but I do feel it an awful thing, drawing innocent people into trouble. I do know I shall have to answer before my Maker in Heaven for the awful crimes I have committed, but as God Almighty is my Judge in Heaven as on Earth, neither my daughter, Mary Ann Palmer, nor her husband, Alfred Ernest Palmer, I do most solemnly swear that neither of them had anything at all to do with it. They never knew I contemplated doing such a wicked thing until too late. I am speaking the truth and nothing but the truth as I hope to be forgiven. I myself and I alone must stand before my Maker in Heaven to give an answer for it all.
>
> Witness my hand, Amelia Dyer.

She turned to the prison matron and said, 'Now I've eased my mind.'

Matron read it and pointed out to her that 'By this letter you have pleaded guilty to everything.'

'I wish to. They can't charge me with anything worse than I've done.'

Police had assembled a mass of evidence. There was insufficient to convict her son-in-law, Alfred Palmer, but he was taken to Devonport, where he was charged with abandoning four-year-old Queenie Baker. Mrs Dyer had been in an asylum at the time, and presumably there was no one to look after the child. Palmer was brought before the magistrates and jailed for six months.

Polly, his wife, had to undergo two ordeals. First she was required to give evidence against her mother, then to face charges of being an accessory before the fact because she had gone to bring barmaid Elizabeth Goulding's baby from Gloucester to Reading, where the infant was murdered.

Mrs Dyer appeared at the Old Bailey on May 21, 1896. She was charged with the one offence of killing Doris Marmon, the child she took from an unmarried mother at Cheltenham. The second charge of killing Harry Simmons, the child brought from Paddington railway station, was not proceeded with. Her counsel did not deny her guilt but sought a verdict of insanity.

Dr Logan of Gloucester Asylum went into the witness box and testified that two years previously, she had suffered from delusions and claimed she heard voices which told her to kill herself, and that the birds talked to her. She was also violent. On one occasion she rushed at him with a poker, threatening to break his skull.

Dr Forbes Winslow, called by the defence, said he had examined Mrs Dyer in Holloway Prison, London, where she was held pending trial. He thought she was suffering from melancholia and delusional insanity. She told him that her bed was sinking through the floor. She also had visions. In one of them, she said, 'the sights and sounds were so horrible that I prefer to keep them to myself. I thought I was handling my mother's bones out of her coffin.' Asked about her feelings of guilt or remorse, she said she thought she had the right to take the lives of others because she had been ill-treated at Gloucester Asylum and put in a padded cell. Who else but a mad person would tell police, so early in their enquiries, 'You'll know all mine by the tape round their necks.'

The prosecution maintained that Dyer's insanity was a sham. Two doctors who had committed her to asylums admitted that they may have been mistaken as to her mental condition at the time. Holloway's medical officer testified that her memory of events was perfect except for the deaths of the babies. She told him that she could not have committed the crimes when she was sane for she loved babies so much.

Dyer had said that her own mother had died in a mental asylum, but a brother, who had not seen his sister for thirty years, was found, brought to court and said that the story was quite untrue. Their mother had died in her own bed.

Polly proved a fascinating witness: a misunderstood, misled daughter or a vicious copy-cat of her evil mother? It is still difficult to believe that she had not been a key figure in the baby farming activities of her mother for fifteen years or more. She must have been a party to the collecting, lodging, boarding, profiteering or even the deaths of at least one of the seven children who certainly died while under her mother's care.

Both in her cell and at the Old Bailey Mrs Dyer did everything to exonerate her daughter from any blame. More than one person present must have thought about St John's Gospel (xv: 13) 'Greater love hath no man than this, that a man lay down his life for his friends.' In this

183

case it was a mother's love for her daughter and, by extension, her son-in-law.

The daughter, who had to be accompanied by a wardress, for she was still in custody awaiting trial as an accessory, took her mother's cue. She went into the witness box and 'with the utmost composure', as one commentator remarked, swore away the life of her mother. It is difficult to calculate the workings of the mind of a daughter who would give such evidence.

Polly recalled how her mother had called at her new home at Willesden, Middlesex, on March 31, holding a carpet bag in one hand and in other arm a baby, which she later identified as Doris Marmon. 'My mother told me that she was holding the baby for a neighbour, Mrs Harris, who had just gone out to do some shopping. I went out to fetch some coal for the fire and when I came back in mother was putting the carpet bag under the sofa.

'My mother opened a parcel and gave me a child's dress and a fur-lined coat to go with it. She had brought Ernest [Alfred Palmer's middle name, presumably the one he preferred to be known by] and me a ham which I thought must have been bought with the £10 she got from Eleanor Marmon.'

Despite rigorous questioning, Polly maintained that the clothes came from the Marmon baby, which 'must have been strangled and put in the carpet bag while I was out fetching the coal'. That night, Mrs Dyer slept on the sofa with the carpet bag tucked safely underneath.

Next morning, Mrs Dyer must have been thinking of dumping the carpet bag with its contents in the river. She asked her daughter to fetch her a brick. When Polly refused her mother went outside and found one herself.

Mrs Dyer and her daughter headed for Paddington to

meet Mrs Sergeant and the new adoptee, Harry Simmons. They were no sooner on the train than the child became restless. According to Polly, her mother complained, 'The little devil! If it keeps on like this much longer I shan't stick it for long.'

Only a few hours later, in the evening, Mrs Dyer was in the living room and called to her daughter, 'Don't come in for a minute.' When she did enter the room, the child was motionless on the sofa with a white cloth over his face. Polly said on oath that she believed the child was sleeping.

When Ernest came home and asked, 'Is that the little nipper?' Mrs Dyer refused to let him even look at the child. Nor would she let her daughter prepare food for the baby. She locked the room before she, her daughter and son-in-law went to the music-hall. That night she again slept on the sofa.

By morning the baby had disappeared, although Polly kept staring at the strangely shaped parcel under the sofa.

'What will the neighbours think, seeing you come in with a baby and go out without it?' asked Polly.

'You can very well think of something,' Mrs Dyer retorted.

Polly also remembered her husband going with her to the station. She carried a parcel of clothes while her mother carried the bulging, half-open carpet bag. Her husband had to hold the bag while Mrs Dyer went into a shop to buy some cakes to eat on the journey. And still the court was expected to believe that Mrs Polly Palmer had nothing to do with the deaths of the nurslings in her mother's care.

Mrs Dyer was sentenced to death. Her daughter was

taken to Berkshire Assizes to face trial as an accessory before the fact of the murder of the baby she had collected from barmaid Elizabeth Goulding. Her reward for giving evidence against her mother was that the Crown offered no evidence against her; she was found not guilty and discharged. Her mother was executed at Newgate on June 10, 1896. She was fifty-seven, the oldest woman in Britain to be hanged for more than half a century. The Chief Warder of Newgate, who had been unconcerned at seeing so many evil people go to their fate, nevertheless complained, 'That baby farmer from Reading still haunts my dreams.'

A Glasgow police likeness of Bible John, the ballroom-dancing killer who preached to lonely women, sexually assaulted and murdered them (*Caledonian Newspapers Ltd*)

Police search the alley where the body of the first victim, Patricia Docker, was found (*Syndication International Ltd*)

Patricia Docker. She left a four-year-old son and a broken five-year-old marriage (*Caledonian Newspapers Ltd*)

Jemima 'Mina' MacDonald nursing one of her three children before she went dancing and became victim number two (*Caledonian Newspapers Ltd*)

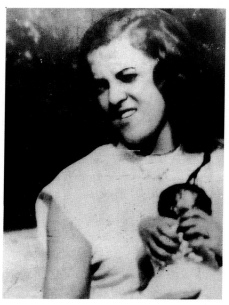

Mary Hackett, aged six, of Halifax, Yorkshire, went out to play for ten minutes and was never seen alive again (*Syndication International Ltd*)

Mary's father, Martin Hackett (*left*) watches water diviner Jack Quain try to find her (*Syndication International Ltd*)

Mary was found battered to death in the church crypt a stone's throw from her home. Caretaker Albert Hall (*above*) before he was arrested, tried and anged for her murder (*Syndication International Ltd*)

The Holy Bible is a formidable weapon in the hands of an evil man and with the Good Book, as Shakespeare said, 'the Devil can cite scripture for his purpose.'

Bible John, just one of Satan's aliases, took it with him for his Friday and Saturday night killings. His first call to the Barrowland Ballroom, to the east of Glasgow's main shopping centre, on Friday, February 23, 1968, started a pattern, an almost rhythmic style which suited the venue where he found his victims. And he became the only known holy serial killer in history.

He was described as having film-star good looks, 6ft 2in tall (although his acknowledged height was later reduced), with a neat suit, and a short back and sides haircut that suggested he was in the armed services, the police or the prison service. His field Bible, the kind that soldiers carry, fitted in an ordinary coat pocket without noticeable bulging.

As the queue to join the nightly hop stretched down the street, Bible John would attach himself to a group, a pair of girls or better still, a lass on her own. In any case he had a gift for separating any girl who would listen to him from her companions. His kind of talk – warning the lasses against walking home alone, against the promiscuity of bad men and the shame of being seduced and then abandoned – seemed to convince them that he was safe, respectable and harmless. And he was a very good dancer, possibly even a ballroom champion or at least a contender at some time.

That was most probably how he met twenty-five-year-old Patricia Docker, a nursing auxiliary at Mearnskirk Hospital. He talked to her about morality. He could deftly find the right pages of his black Book for the appropriate quotation. In his refined Scottish voice he would condemn lax morals, using words like 'fornication' and citing the behaviour of Jezebel, a favourite wanton, in his conversation.

Patricia's five-year-old marriage to a Royal Air Force corporal had broken up, and she and her four-year-old son were living with her parents. But Patricia never reached home. After the strains of the last waltz faded away in the morning air she was never seen alive again. Later that day her naked body was found in the entrance to a back lane garage 200 yards from her home in Langside Place. She had been strangled with her own tights.

There was no sign of her clothing, but nearby was a used sanitary towel, and during the post-mortem it was found she had been menstruating at the time of her death.

Plain-clothes Glasgow policemen took up ballroom dancing and included the Barrowland on their nightly patrols. They also brushed up on their scriptures. But they were too late. Bible John had moved on and did not return for eighteen months.

Jemima MacDonald was, according to those who knew her, 'tapping mad'. She would do anything for a dance. She had brought up three children without the advantage of a husband and she liked to show her independence. Whenever she could get away from the bairns she was off to her local hop, the Barrowland Ballroom, with her dancing shoes wrapped in a neat brown paper parcel. Sometime during the evening or the early hours she had met Bible John and listened to him denouncing the whoremongers who played on the kindnesses and fears of the likes of Jemima.

She, like Patricia Docker, had nearly reached home. Twenty yards from her bed she was strangled and dumped in a derelict tenement. She too had been menstruating at the time of her death.

This time there was a bonus. Police had more details of the man they wanted to interview. Jemima had been seen dancing with a man 6ft 2in tall, slim, clean and markedly well-mannered, aged between twenty-five and thirty-five, with short reddish hair, blue suit, and white shirt.

There was enough detail to produce an Identikit picture. The Scots, always protective of the right of suspects to be innocent until proven guilty, had never before in their criminal history published a 'wanted' picture prior to conviction. Alas, in the twirling coloured lights of the ballroom, the view of John may not have been as clear as those who described him imagined. No one came forward to identify him; but Bible John just had to take the floor again.

Within a month, Helen Puttock, twenty-nine and married with two children, went dancing at the Barrowland with her sister, Jeannie. Her husband, George, stayed at home minding the baby. Soon Helen was being whirled around the floor by her twinkle-toed escort. And like his previous partners she too was found strangled and dead, this time in a back area close to her home at Earl Street, Scotstoun.

Detective Chief Superintendent Joe Beattie had even more clues. Her body had been found by her sister,

Jeannie, who had also met Bible John. They had all travelled in the same taxi together. He was sandy-haired, she said, and she had the impression that he was a 'mummy's boy' who was annoyed at her presence as he concentrated on her sister. The conversation was stilted, until he told the sisters that his parents were strictly religious, absolute teetotallers, who had brought him and his sister up in the ways of the Lord. He could still recite whole verses of the Bible from memory to prove his upbringing.

As they passed the rebuilt site of a foster home he had quoted from Exodus (ii: 3 and 4): 'And when she could not longer hide him, she took for him an ark of bulrushes and daubed it with slime and with pitch, and put the child therein. And she lay it in the flags by the river's brink; and his sister stood afar off, to wit what would be done to him.'

Jeannie shuddered as she remembered the lines. She recalled that he had said he played golf, and his cousin had recently holed in one, although he had never managed the feat. When she asked him what he did at New Year, the traditional Scots celebration of Hogmanay, he had repeated that he did not drink, but prayed. The taxi dropped Jeannie off first. Helen continued her journey with Bible John.

It seemed from that description it would only be a matter of time before he would be in a police station being asked if he knew the quotation, 'Thou shalt do no murder.' But the investigation dragged on. Millions must have seen the police 'wanted' poster:

'Do you know this man? He's Bible John! Glasgow police have issued this picture of a man they wish to interview in connection with the death of Mrs Helen

Puttock, Glasgow, last October. His name is not known but he regularly quotes from the Bible.

'Description: Aged between 26 and 30 years, is between 5ft 10ins and 6ft tall, has fair-reddish or auburn hair, speaks with a polite Glasgow accent and has an erect posture. If you think you know him, phone Glasgow murder inquiry HQ – 041-339 1113. or any police station in your area.'

The Identikit pictures were sent to Interpol at St Cloud in Paris and relayed to police forces round the world. West Germany, Hong Kong and even Zanzibar responded to the appeal but the promising leads led nowhere. Dutchman Gerard Croiset, self-styled psychic detective, flew from Amsterdam to Glasgow to offer his help. Croiset had travelled to Scotland before to assist in murder investigations with some success, but this time his help was of no avail. Then a Scot who had been working in Australia came home and told police that years before he used to go dancing with red-haired Bible John. Police were pointed in the direction of Amsterdam, where they found a Bible-punching John, only there was no positive evidence to show that he had ever been in or anywhere near Glasgow at the time of the killings.

Detectives thought that the holy killer intended to enjoy a sexual dalliance with his victims, but was prevented, for one reason or another from achieving fulfilment and so, in fury, battered them to death. There were other unsolved murders of a similar nature in Scotland, but Bible John had gone to ground. No trace of Glasgow's Bible-punching killer was ever found.

Of course, there is not just one Bible John but many. He is even an international figure. In Hollywood he was Mr

Bible Johns. According to police he had put the whole of Los Angeles in a state of fear. In the short space of two years he may have been responsible for as many as a hundred rapes and just one murder.

One block south of Santa Monica Boulevard a tall attractive blonde from the Midwest lived in a first-floor apartment. She was making her way in show business, always writing home that something big was 'just round the corner'.

She always kept her doors and windows locked at night, but one night in January, 1982, she heard her bedroom door creak open and before she could scream or switch on her light, a hand was clamped over her mouth, and a tall, thick-set man by her bed warned her, 'We are going to have some fun together.'

All the time, he kept a sharp-tipped weapon against her neck, as he ordered her to take off her nightgown. Twice he lost his erection and ordered her to make him 'hard again'. The rapist told her to keep her eyes shut and not to look at him, and after two hours said, 'You're a nice piece of ass, but killing you wouldn't mean anything to me. Just keep your eyes shut for ten minutes and don't be calling anyone.'

The victim said he spoke with a southern or eastern accent, and while she could not describe his colour or features he wore a knit watchman's cap, a light windbreaker-type coat and blue jeans which he did not remove during the rape.

Within a month a forty-six-year-old widowed schoolteacher in the same neighbourhood was raped by a man she described as black, about 5ft 10in tall, weighing around 200 pounds, sporting medium length sideburns and a moustache. And he wore light blue pants, a windbreaker and a knit hat. He did not remove his gloves or his trousers when he committed the rape. She too was raped twice in two hours with a screwdriver held tightly against her neck.

There was another, then another, and another. The police had a *modus operandi* on the rapist. He always operated between 2 and 5 a.m., always in the district of singles and professional people, always chose a woman who lived on her own and broke into her apartment; always wore similar clothes, blue pants and grey or blue windcheater which he did not remove; carried the same weapon, raped twice in two hours, and uttered the same threat, 'Don't call anyone for ten minutes or I'll kill you.'

Flyers bearing a likeness of the assailant were handed to beat officers and, when the rapes continued in a comparatively localised area, investigators wondered why the rapist had not been caught. They extended their search of records to include burglars and cat burglars, since this rapist had always forced an entry but never disturbed a single neighbour nor anyone except his victim.

On Friday, December 10, thirty-seven-year-old Sandra Trine returned to her Hollywood apartment with her flat-mate. They stayed up to watch a 1 a.m. television movie, then fell asleep. At about 2.30 a.m. the flat-mate was awakened by a noise. She thought it might be a neighbour in the hallway returning home, but the noise was coming from inside the apartment.

Sandra woke up and said, 'What was that?' A male voice answered, 'Don't say nothing or you're dead.' He repeatedly raped both of them, threatening each with his screwdriver to their throats that he would kill the other if they resisted or raised their voices. Each tried to save the life of her room-mate by consenting to the brutal sexual attacks which included oral sex.

At 3.15 a.m. paramedics called to the apartment fought for Sandra Trine's life. They managed to clear her throat then worked to restart her heart. She was taken to the Hollywood Presbyterian Hospital but found to be dead on arrival. She had choked to death on her own vomit, caused by her being forced to have oral sex with her attacker. The hunt for a serial rapist turned into a hunt for a killer. Nothing happened for two months until the rapist reappeared elsewhere, breaking into apartments, raping a sixty-nine-year-old woman, then a twenty-nine-year-old health counsellor, then a thirty-six-year-old pharmacist.

By then, police discovered he only operated in a square of ten blocks. His victims, aged between twenty-four and seventy-one, were white, with the sole exception of the murder victim, and he only operated in the early hours of Friday and Saturday mornings. Detectives calculated that he was a night shift worker, that his rape escapades were in pairs, then adjourned, then two more, then another break. Could it be, the police asked themselves, that here was a rapist driven by an abnormal sexual urge, who, after two rapes, was satisfied and then perhaps remorseful, until the urge took hold again.

If this was so, it could explain why he always wore the same clothes. It could be a subconscious wish to be arrested and to be cured. The theory was not far from the truth.

A few minutes before midnight on June 4, 1984, a police officer driving a cruising patrol car with his head-lights switched off turned out of Santa Monica Boulevard into an alley where he saw by a parked car a black man just as the rape victims had described. Jerald Curtis Johns, aged thirty-two, a night clerk at the Kiplinger Retirement Hotel in Hollywood, was arrested.

Why had they not been able to pick him up before? Police Lieutenant Edward Hocking explained, 'Mr Bible Johns was a Jekyll and Hyde character. He was a popular group leader in the Church of the Open Door, a staunch Christian group dedicated to helping the down and out.

'When I checked with the church, officials found it impossible to believe that their good friend did the things we said he did. He was so into Jesus you wouldn't believe it. And he carried the Bible with him all the time.'

At the church, a spokesman said, 'Mr Bible Johns spent most of his free days doing charity work for his church and volunteering for other Christian duties. He was an absolutely selfless individual who believed in following the teachings of the Lord Jesus Christ and helping others. He knew his Bible and was always quoting from it.'

Psychiatrists and others tried to explain Johns's behaviour. There was the Jekyll and Hyde theory, the argument that he was a victim of racism and tried to get his own back by raping only white women – but that could not explain the rape and murder of Sandra Trine, who was black – and a theory, advanced by his sister, who flew from the east coast for his trial, that he had been possessed by Satan. 'It was Satan,' she said. 'He only attacks the strong ones.'

Then officials delved into Johns's background. After following a twenty-four-year-old Hollywood dancer home from a nightclub and raping her he had served six months in jail and was then ordered to seek psychiatric help. That was in 1973. Two years later he followed another twenty-four-year-old home from her job at the Bank of America and attacked her. He was declared a mentally disordered sex offender and was committed to the Patton State Hospital. When doctors freed him two years later, he was placed on probation and ordered to continue out-patient psychotherapy. But within a month he was arrested again for trying to rape two Hollywood women.

At that time, he wrote to the judge, 'After having failed in my third attempt to live a wholesome and constructive life, I wanted to do nothing but die. I wanted desperately to succeed in making my life count. I looked for work, but in applying for jobs I refused to lie about my past and was often flatly rejected. A mentally disordered sex offender is not exactly welcomed.

'But I discovered Christ after being paroled and adopted a daily life-style that included daily readings from the Bible.'

Many observers believed the Jekyll and Hyde theory that Johns was a sincere Christian except when he was driven by an abnormal sexual urge to rape, but the law did not. Superior Court Judge Everett E. Ricks could not understand why the prosecution had not demanded the death penalty as they were entitled to do in a case of murder in furtherance of rape.

Johns pleaded not guilty to murder and eighty-nine other offences stemming from assaults on eleven Hollywood women. He then agreed to a plea bargain and changed his plea to guilty to avoid the death penalty. A deputy District Attorney explained that her office held that the death penalty was inappropriate because, despite his extensive criminal record, the murder he committed was not intentional but an 'accident' during a rape.

'We're satisfied that Mr Johns spends the rest of his natural life in prison. He has no known mental problems other than he has a propensity to rape.'

Superior Court Judge Ricks rejected a plea to return Johns to the Patton State Hospital for the mentally ill and said, 'This is one of the worst cases I've seen in twenty-five years.' He sentenced Johns to one of the longest jail terms ever imposed in Californian legal history, 142 years, which means he must serve seventy-one years, half the sentence, before being eligible for parole.

## Chapter Twelve

# FOR WHOM
# THE BELLS TOLL

'I received an instruction from on high to kill
her and cut her up.'

Father Hans Schmidt.

From Hull, Hell and Halifax
Good Lord, deliver us.

That old prayer of beggars and vagabonds was quoted by
Taylor, the Water Poet (1580–1653) and when things go
wrong in those northerly towns, losers still utter it. The
original reason for the supplication to the Almighty was
that vagabonds knew they could be sent to prison with
hard labour for idling in Hull whilst in Halifax cloth
thieves could expect to be beheaded – literally, by an
early model of the guillotine.

Halifax residents would have wished more than that on
whoever murdered six-year-old Mary Hackett; but no
one thought for a moment it could have anything to do
with the local church or church folk.

Mary was one of four children of Martin Hackett, a
gardener who kept the flower beds neat in the local
cemetery, and his wife, Anastasia. They lived in Cemetery Lodge down Lister Lane. At 12.55 p.m. on
Wednesday, August 12, 1953, Mary hopped out of the
door. Her mother had been shopping. Her father was
mending a lawnmower. Her mother told her not to be
long, for she was preparing her dinner. She did not have
to tell her not to talk to strangers. There were seldom if
ever any strangers about in Lister Lane.

'I'll only be ten minutes,' said the girl as she made for
the pile of builder's sand just ten yards from her own

front door. And they were the last words heard from her. When her mother and an aunt who was staying with the Hacketts went to look for her, the parks and playgrounds which bordered the lane were deserted. The cemetery was silent. Summer sun could be seen through the smoke from the economically declining mills. But no Mary; no little girl with a pigtail, green dress, white socks, blue shoes.

It was so unlike the child to stray. When her mother knocked on the neighbours' doors, they looked out through the lace curtains before answering. No one usually knocked at their doors at that hour. No mother around there ever lost her children. No children around there ever disappeared. But Mary had.

Police brought along a dog and 300 yards away it sat on the kerb of a busy road and stared at the passing traffic. A BBC radio appeal produced no response. The search, without clue or scent, had to be extended house to house. Five hundred buildings were combed for signs of the lass. The constables moved on to the roads that extend out of Halifax to the wild and desolate hills that surround the mill town. They beat the fern and heather, dragged the reservoir, even dug up old tombstones in the cemetery which had shifted in case the child might have fallen or been put into a premature grave there.

After two weeks, Chief Constable G. Goodman called in Scotland Yard. The Murder Squad officers from London were two veterans in the field of homicide, Detective Superintendent John Ball and Detective Sergeant Dennis Hawkins. They went over the same ground covered by the local police and handed out 2,000 questionnaires.

Halifax police had already searched the Park Congregational Church just across the road from the Hackett home. Ball would have it examined again. Someone mentioned that it had a vast underground crypt honey-combed with tunnels which during World War Two had been used as an air raid shelter. A thousand people could be reasonably safe in there. Ball and Hawkins wondered whether little Mary Hackett could have gone there.

They met the silver-haired caretaker, Albert George Hall, who was forty-eight years of age and lived in Church House in Francis Street. He was only too anxious to help. He immediately offered the information that on the day the girl disappeared he had heard whisperings coming from the direction of the crypt. He had thought nothing of it at the time, putting it down to imagination.

When the detectives returned next day, Hall mentioned something that had slipped his memory. He had seen a strange man about the building a fortnight previously. When asked if he could describe the stranger he gave a detailed word picture including height, build, clothes, and even that the man wore a blue tie.

Ball thought it rather odd that the caretaker had not mentioned such an important matter before – a stranger in an area where no strangers trod. But then laymen do not think like policemen and Hall was always willing to talk. He referred to the officers as 'my friends'.

The superintendent asked for a watch to be kept on caretaker Hall, preferably by different officers each day, so that the man would not suspect he was being observed. When this was done, the officers noticed something decidedly odd. All the chairs in the crypt had been piled up against one wall without apparent reason.

The Murder Squad officers took turns to call on the church caretaker, accept his kind invitation to tea and sample his wife's home-baked cakes. As he had been so helpful, they even invited him to the police station to show him how a murder investigation was conducted. During this visit, Hall suddenly remembered that when he had described the stranger he had seen he had said that the man had worn a blue tie. Now he remembered it was a blue scarf.

'Sorry, I must have got it wrong the first time. You know how it is. When you're busy you don't always see things too clearly.'

Busy? The policemen then understood why the chairs had been moved in the crypt. Hall had decided to do a bit of decorating. Two paint tins stood opened with brushes ready on the floor. When they mentioned it, he commented seriously, 'Certainly needs it. You know how shabby these places can get. But you've got a more difficult job, trying to find a missing person.'

On September 21, the fortieth day after Mary Hackett disappeared, Superintendent Ball and Sergeant Hawkins led a squad of police and firemen into the vault. They carried picks, shovels and arc lights, for the previous search had been conducted by torchlight. Hall, the caretaker, stared in horror. He even protested, 'You have no right to come in here digging. This is a sacred place. I'm not going to allow you in, digging. It's sacrilege.'

Ball removed from his pocket a piece of paper and said, 'Read that!' It was a search warrant.

The searchers wasted no time. The tallest had to stoop, for the roof was barely six feet high and festooned with cobwebs. They moved the piled-up chairs and began digging. Then they saw an area of flesh, the back of a child's leg. Ball called on them to stop. 'Get the pathologist,' he ordered. Ninety minutes later, Dr David Price supervised the continuing search as the body of the little girl was carefully lifted from the temporary grave. Mary had been buried face down. Bloodstains were clearly visible on the soil and on the wall. The wall did need repainting.

Her face was unrecognisable. Injuries to her head were horrible. Her sobbing mother could only identify her body from the three-inch hand-stitched lace hem of her green dress and a single shoe. The other was missing. At the post-mortem, the doctor said, 'There is a big hole on the back of her skull on the left side measuring about six inches by four inches. Her skull has been beaten so much that the bones have been broken into thirty-two fragments. She was killed by repeated blows to the back of the skull with a blunt instrument or was beaten against a solid wall or floor with great force. There has been no sexual interference.'

Ball and Hawkins talked it over and came to the conclusion that the killer had lured her into the crypt; threatened or frightened her; she screamed in fear and to silence her he had caused those injuries.

They invited the caretaker to the police station for more tea and cakes. Ball told him, 'You know how much we all want to catch this fellow before he commits another crime like that. Can you think of anything you may have possibly overlooked? You know what a dreadful crime it was.'

Hall shook his head and said, 'Bashing the back of her head in like that. I should think so.'

Ball: 'Who said anything about bashing her head in?'

Hall: 'Your sergeant told me.'

But Detective Sergeant Hawkins had not been in the crypt at the time the body was found. He had been sent on another inquiry. He had not spoken to Hall since the body was found, nor had any other police officer.

Hall refused to say any more. Detectives went through thirty voluntary statements he had made. And they included the words, 'Kids are always shrieking and screaming as they play in the streets.'

Next day, a plain-clothes officer followed Hall, who led him to a mental hospital at Scalebor Park at Burley-in-Wharfedale. The resident medical superintendent told the police that Hall had been a patient there. He had called to tell the doctor that he had nothing to do with the murder. His mind was quite clear about the day Mary Hackett disappeared and he repeated his story that Detective Sergeant Hawkins had told him about her injuries.

Told later that he would be charged with murder, Hall said, 'Very well. I've been expecting this. But I didn't do it. You'll see.'

At Leeds Assizes, before Mr Justice Pearson, he protested his innocence to the end of the four-day trial. The jury of ten men and two women found him guilty. Asked if he had anything to say before sentence was passed on him, Hall said, 'I am not guilty of this terrible crime. It is a terrible crime, I admit, but I am not guilty of it. I just thank you, my lord, for conducting this trial in the best of . . .' And for once words failed him.

Hall was sentenced to death and hanged at Leeds Prison in April, 1954.

Detective Superintendent Ball, recalling the case, said, 'The longer we were in Halifax the more Hall wanted to be near us. That in itself is strange. It made me suspicious because most people with no direct connection with the investigation would rather distance themselves from officers from Scotland Yard or the local police. I have no positive idea of the motive . . .'

Who knows why the devout worshipper, the cassocked priest, the attentive sidesman, the scrupulous caretaker, all of whom demonstrate at least every Sunday their goodly, peaceful characteristics to their fellow men, should suddenly kill.

Statistically, no one knows how many holy killers are schizophrenics. One per cent of western populations have an apparent personality disorder, with delusions, dissociation and emotional deterioration. Schizophrenia is the most common major psychiatric illness known to medicine. Sometimes it has a genetic origin, but equally it can be triggered by environmental factors, among them the church. Certainly a number of those who have killed in a religious setting have exhibited behaviour consistent with a diagnosis of schizophrenia.

Religious belief, and religious observance, can turn the minds of susceptible people from normal reasoning, and exacerbate the tendencies of the schizophrenics among them to confuse literal and metaphorical meaning. The saying of prayers, the chanting of psalms, the singing of hymns, the genuflecting on one knee, the kneeling on hassocks or stone floors, the repeated crossing of oneself all concentrate the brain on patterns that differ from normal everyday behaviour.

Albert George Hall was to all intents and purposes a diligent church employee, until his sudden explosion of inexplicable violence with its tragic consequences. A remarkably similar pattern was shown by another caretaker, this time on the other side of the Atlantic, at the yellow-brick North Hill Methodist Church in Akron, Ohio.

Ruth Zwicker, the pianist there, was a beautiful, well-groomed brunette and at twenty-three still a hard-working student. She had graduated with a music teacher's degree and was working for further honours. Because there was no piano at her home, she practised and played on the instrument in the Sunday School at North Hill, Akron, Ohio, the home of the American airships which pioneered that mode of travel between the wars.

On Easter Saturday, April 12, 1941, she left her home on Wall Street to practise for the Paschal festival the following day. It is an important event for Christians, who are required to attend church at least once a year, one of which occasions shall be Easter in celebration of our Lord's crucifixion and resurrection. Ruth left home early in her Ford coupé, dropped off her younger sister, Carol, at dancing classes and went on to the church. She would play through the hymns for tomorrow's services and then go shopping with her mother. No one saw her alive again.

Saturday passed and no Ruth returned home. Her parents, five sisters and two brothers could not understand it. It was so unlike her not to be there.

As the large congregation gathered for the Easter Sunday morning service, detectives arrived. One asked the family, 'Are you sure that Ruth got to the church?'

Ruth's father, manager of a local cemetery, replied, 'Sure. She was seen there by Lukens, the janitor. He said he still could hear her playing the piano in the Sunday School rooms as late as 10.30 a.m. But he didn't see her going out.'

Her father had found her car still parked opposite the church, but could find no sign of his daughter. 'The janitor helped me search the building, but we couldn't even find her music or her metronome. She must have taken them with her when she left, but her car was still outside. It doesn't make sense.'

Asked if she had money with her, Mr Zwicker said, 'less than a dollar. I had her shopping money with me.'

Mrs Lukens, the janitor's wife, later telephoned the Zwickers to tell them she had again searched the church from top to bottom but found no trace of Ruth. Detectives decided to look yet again.

They talked to Albert Lukens, the caretaker. 'I heard her but I didn't see her,' he confirmed. 'The playing stopped around 10.30 a.m. I know she's a pretty thing but other than nodding to her occasionally when I saw her I've had nothing to do with her.'

Mrs Lukens said she went to the church at 11 a.m. to remind Albert to get dressed for lunch because they were expecting guests. 'But I didn't see the Zwicker girl or anybody else there at the time.'

Mr Lukens suggested the officers speak to Jack Bates, a lanky ginger-haired teenager, who sometimes helped around the church. The detectives remembered that Bates and two other teenagers had been accused of molesting a fifteen-year-old girl in a hut on the local golf course, but the evidence was not strong enough to justify charges and the boys had been released.

Detectives questioned Bates closely for a long time but all he could tell them was that he had heard Ruth playing a little after 9 a.m., he had sat and listened for an hour and then went to neighbours at 10 o'clock. She was still there playing when he left, and the neighbours confirmed his account.

As the officers were about to leave they noticed that the heat within the church was oppressive. Sweat moistened their brows. The windows were sealed. They asked Lukens how long he intended to keep the fire at full blast. He replied that the church needed drying out, and reckoned it would be done by Friday.

Friday, the officers returned to the church and the boiler room, where they complained that someone had already sifted the ashes. They took off their coats and went to the dustbins where they found ashes filled with clinker, a human bone, a zip-fastener that could have come from a music case and 100 other 'foreign objects'.

Lukens, fifty-eight years of age, a big, heavy man with a long, sullen face, told he was being taken to police headquarters, protested, 'You have no cause to arrest me. Anybody could have placed her body in the firebox. The church is always open.'

Then they asked him about the time, years before, that he was charged with beating a young woman to death with a poker, for which he was sentenced to life imprisonment. And the time he was paroled and killed a twenty-two-year-old woman with a hammer. A grand jury had refused to indict him on circumstantial evidence, but he was convicted of breaching his parole and sent back to jail for five years. Was Ruth Zwicker, the pianist, his third victim?

The janitor mopped his brow, asked to see his wife first and then confessed, 'I was collecting waste-paper baskets when I passed the room where she was playing the piano. She was getting ready to quit and I stopped to talk to her. I suddenly couldn't help myself. I took her in my arms and tried to kiss her. She slapped my face and started to struggle. She fell and her head hit the piano bench. She lay still and I thought she was dead.

'Then I remembered my past life. You guys would find

out about it. Nobody would believe it was an accident, even though that's the truth. I picked up the girl's body and took it down to the coal cellar where I put it on the coal pile. Next morning—'

An officer interrupted, 'You mean Easter Sunday.'

Lukens hesitated. He looked at the ceiling. It was as if he could hear the hymn-singing upstairs. 'Easter morning I got up early and found the body still there. I had hoped she might have revived and walked away. I wasn't at all sure she was dead but she sure looked like it. So I built a big fire and stuffed her body in the furnace.

'No, I did not rape her . . .'

There was no way of disproving anything he said. There was not enough of Ruth Zwicker left to tell. Lukens was charged with first degree murder, convicted and sentenced to life imprisonment.

How many more unbalanced killers are there lurking behind the sanctity of holy ground? One particularly weird and theatrical occupant of the role, with his long black moustache and his black cape, was Thomas W. Piper. Piper was sexton of the Warren Avenue Baptist Church, Boston, Massachusetts. He was an archetypal church guardian, performing his duties by rote, greeting the congregation pleasantly. On Sundays he tolled the bell summoning Baptists to prayer with one hand and waved to the arriving worshippers with the other.

Those who were not concentrating on their devotions might have seen him lolling in the last pew swigging from a bottle containing a home-made brew of whiskey and laudanum. (Laudanum, nowadays refined for use in specific drugs, was once prescribed as a natural tincture for a variety of conditions.)

213

Charity demanded that if Piper appeared eccentric, he was forgiven by the Christians around him, even when he was seen theatrically twisting his black moustache at women and leering and winking at the girls in church. A bachelor, a lonely man; the churchgoing folk understood.

When Bridget Landregan, a local servant girl, was found murdered at Dorchester on the outskirts of town on December 5, 1873, no one looked to the church or the belfry. A resident hearing a disturbance in a thicket at Upham's Corner saw in the falling light a figure whooping like someone demented, his black cape on his shoulders flying in the breeze, a prototype for Batman. He vanished over an embankment, and the alarmed resident tramped into the thicket, where he came upon the naked body of Bridget, her head bashed in.

Then another girl, Mary Sullivan, was attacked, her head also battered; the victim, said a witness, of a crying, barking human being, dressed all in black.

A third outcry was heard when Mary Tynam, described as 'a girl of the town' was attacked as she slept. Although fiendishly mutilated she survived for a year in an asylum, but never regained her senses sufficiently to identify her assailant.

Sexton Piper continued to welcome the devout. The attacks continued. Then, nearer to home, he invited five-year-old Mabel H. Young into the belfry of Warren Avenue Baptist Church to see his pet pigeons. The girl eagerly followed him. Once inside the belfry he hit Mabel a number of heavy blows to the head. As he went to leave the bell tower, the girl's aunt, Augusta Hobbs, led a search party for the child up the stairs. Piper swiftly dropped out of an upstairs window and casually walked back into the church.

Several men broke down the belfry door and Piper was apparently genuinely astonished to hear the screams which followed. However, when Piper's baseball bat was found leaning against the church wall covered in blood, the sexton was arrested.

Piper was ordered to touch the body of Mabel Young, a practice based on the superstition that if the corpse bled at the touch of a suspect then that person was the killer. The sexton's touch was inconclusive.

From his prison cell, Piper shouted his innocence. At his trial, he admitted that he had been drunk the day of the girl's death but insisted he knew nothing about the belfry attack. The jury found him guilty and sentenced him to be hanged.

A few days before his execution, Piper summoned his lawyers to his cell, confessed to all four murders, hung his head and said, 'I am a very bad man.' The psychiatric evaluation came too late.

Church belfries had a fascination for more than one holy killer. They are remote, lonely places. Not all people will venture the heights to reach them. Some cannot cope with the noise of the bells when standing next to them. Medical student William Henry Theodore Durrant had no such reservations.

He was, moreover, in those stricter times, the kind of young man to whom most mothers would like their daughters introduced. He did wear his hair too long, but he kissed his mother whenever they met and whenever they said farewell. Besides, he was studying medicine, which in itself was a mark of respectability. In addition, he was the Sunday School deputy superintendent at San Francisco's Emmanuel Baptist Church.

So proper and polite at church meetings, according to those who knew him he was obsessed with religion and sex. He understood the one but feared the other. He confided to a fellow student, 'I have no knowledge of women.' Nevertheless, he pursued them.

This tall, slim young man with the pale face and luminous blue eyes was in turn attractive to women. The current admirer was eighteen-year-old Blanche Lamont, an active member of the Emmanuel Baptist Church, who lived with her uncle and aunt.

Blanche was dark, with curly hair and long curling eyelashes, and a figure that would make any warm-blooded male look twice. That morning of April 3, 1895, she walked out in a fashionable figure-hugging basque jacket over a full black skirt, a floppy-brimmed hat, adorned with feathers, tied under her chin with pink ribbon. To anyone who saw her she looked sweet, innocent, and desirable, and was obviously on a date.

Blanche was neither naïve nor innocent. She knew that Theo Durrant was not interested in platonic love, if there was such a thing. She must have known about the sexual encounters that took place in the cloistered library and vestry rooms in the church building during the day and early evening, before the janitor locked up for the night. There had been stories of 'strange actions on the part of some of the young people of the church'.

Theo and Blanche were an attractive couple, so good-looking that everybody could remember seeing them. At 8.15 a.m. they were on the corner of 21st and Mission Streets where, with his arm around her shoulder, he steered her on to an electric street-car. Passengers admired and envied them. Car conductor Henry Shell-mont recalled, 'He was fooling with her gloves which she had removed. He seemed to be talking very sweetly to her.'

At Polk Street, they alighted from the car and went their own ways, he to the Cooper Medical College, she to the Normal School, where she was training to be a teacher. At 2 p.m. they were back, watched by Mrs Mary Vogel who kept a constant weather-eye for loiterers whom she suspected of being burglars. 'He ran like an eager boy when he spotted her on the corner by the Normal School,' she remembered.

One of Blanche's fellow students, May Lannigan, noticed them board the cable car: 'It was the man's hair that attracted my attention. It struck me as unusual to see a gentleman with such long hair.'

The wind had turned gusty and as the couple strode purposefully towards the towering Emmanuel Baptist Church on Bartlett Street, Mrs Elizabeth Crosset, a middle-aged lady of propriety, noticed, 'Her clothes blew considerably around her limbs – her form – her dress.' Theo must have noticed, too.

Mrs Caroline Leak saw Blanche enter the church, followed by Durrant, and that was the last time anyone admitted seeing Miss Lamont alive.

Five o'clock was approaching when George King, the nineteen-year-old organist at Emmanuel, took his seat at the keyboard and played a few introductory bars to Handel's *Messiah* in preparation for the forthcoming Easter Service. He was interrupted by footsteps and turned to see Theo Durrant coming, to his surprise, from the stairs which led up to the belfry tower. The organist must have looked puzzled, because Theo said hastily, 'I've been fixing a gas jet upstairs and breathed some escaping gas. Would you go to the corner drug store and

217

fetch me some Bromo-Seltzer?'

When King returned, Durrant looked much better and, after listening to the organ practice, he left with the musician, returning for the evening service a few hours later. As he entered the church porch the first person he met was Blanche's aunt, Mrs Triphena Noble.

'Is Blanche here tonight?' he asked boldly.

'No,' she replied. 'She has not returned home for dinner, and it is most worrying.'

'I'm sorry she is not with us for I have a book – *The Newcomers* by Thackeray – for her, but I will send it to the house.'

Strangely, Mrs Noble, despite her worries, did not report Blanche's absence to the police for several days. It certainly suggested that she might be a wayward girl. When Theo was asked, along with other friends of the missing student, he actually suggested that she might have 'gone astray'.

Meanwhile, Durrant had tried to pawn Blanche's rings but when he could not raise money on them he sent them, wrapped in newspaper, to Mrs Noble with the name of the organist, George King, written on the envelope.

By then jealousy had entered the drama. Twenty-one-year-old Minnie Williams, another member of the Baptist congregation, told a friend, 'I know too much about the disappearance of Blanche. I think she has met with foul play.' How she knew she did not say. But at 8 p.m. on Good Friday, April 12, nine days after Blanche vanished, Theo and Minnie were seen outside the Baptist Church. They were arguing. Durrant was being aggressive.

A passer-by, Mr Hodgkins, a claims adjuster for an insurance company, the kind of witness whose reliability cannot be denied, said Durrant's behaviour 'was unbecoming to a gentleman', so he had intervened to restore peace. When he looked back he saw Minnie take Theo's arm and, like any other affectionate couple, they entered the church.

Ninety minutes later, a tired, dishevelled and distracted Theo arrived at the home of one of the church members to take part in a Christian Endeavour group meeting. He asked first to be excused to wash his hands but by two hours later he seemed composed, his usual, polished self. He did however say that he had to return to the church, where he had 'left something behind'.

Next morning, the Saturday, the members of the Ladies' Society, one of those groups indispensable to churches for many duties, arrived to decorate the church for the Easter services the following day. One of them opened a cupboard and screamed. Other ladies clamoured around to see the ghastly scene: the mutilated body of Minnie Williams, half naked, stabbed in each breast, her wrists slashed and underclothes stuffed in her mouth. Blood from her wounds had spurted down the cupboard walls.

That Sunday morning, the newspapers reminded the police that Blanche Lamont, another member of the Baptist community, had not been seen for ten days. The church's Easter schedule was disturbed as policemen insisted on searching the whole of the 120-foot-high building. The belfry tower was never used. The church had no bell, and no church official could remember ever having been in there. The door to the belfry, thought to have been boarded up, was found to have been forced.

Inside they faced another horror. On the dust-covered floor lay the naked body of Blanche Lamont. Her clothes had been stuffed behind the belfry beams. Deep bruises on her throat showed that she had been strangled. And a doctor called to the scene muttered, 'Someone knows something about medicine.' Two wooden blocks had been placed to hold the dead girl's head in position. 'Looks as if it has been prepared for an autopsy,' said the doctor. 'Then somebody has decided she is ready for burial so they have crossed her hands across her breast.'

Further examination showed that while Minnie had been a willing party to sexual intercourse before she was murdered, Blanche had 'not parted with life and honour without a struggle'. The case of Miss Lamont looked like that of a girl who had changed her mind about sex, had been strangled, and her body then violated. The case of Miss Williams was a matter of murder in the furtherance of consensual sex.

The army of witnesses from a wide area around San Francisco hastened to tell what they knew. Durrant, who had not attempted to hide his associations with the two women, was horrified that such allegations should be made against such an ardent churchgoer.

Because most of the witnesses had seen him with Blanche the prosecution decided to proceed with the indictment of her murder. Each day the 'sweet-pea' flower girl of San Francisco arrived at the court to supply the defendant with a posy. The jury were out for a mere five minutes and he was sentenced to death by hanging, a record for any major murder trial. 'I shall die like a Durrant,' he declared stoutly. Legal wrangling put off his execution for almost three years. In the meantime he made sure that he was not forgotten. His views were widely quoted on a variety of subjects:

'It is not so awful to go to such a death. Such a death as

mine may be a means of abolishing capital punishment in this state,' were early words in a campaign that were still being heard more than half a century later.

When the Baptist minister urged him to confess and purge his conscience in this world so he would be ready for the next, he cried, 'No! No! I will not confess the murders because I am not guilty.' He kept asking why they had not found bloodstains on his clothing if he was the murderer. The answer was that he had stripped himself naked before performing the sex act and the murders. One woman came forward and claimed she had seen Theodore Durrant in the church in his 'birthday suit' but did not elaborate on the circumstances.

While in San Quentin prison, he became a convert to the Roman Catholic faith because his Baptist minister stated, 'I have not been successful in concealing my conviction of his guilt.'

Medically, the pastor thought Durrant was 'a psychological monster'. Doctors tended to the view he was a schizophrenic, suffering from nightmares and hallucinations, unable to distinguish between the real and imaginary world. He could be outwardly normal, but inwardly abnormal, beyond human control.

The Supreme Court finally confirmed that the death sentence would be carried out on April 3, 1897. Durrant used this last chance for publicity by telling Amos Lunt, the hangman, 'Don't put that rope on, my boy, until after I talk . . .

'To those who wish me to say something, I wish to say this: I have no animosity against anyone but to those who have persecuted me and hounded me to my grave, innocent as I am. I forgive them all. They will receive their justice from the Holy God above, to whom I now go to receive my justice, which will be the justice given to an innocent boy who has not stained his hands with the crimes that have been put upon him by the Press of San Francisco. I forgive them all, for I do not hold anything against them for it.

'I do not look upon people now as enemies. I forgive them as I expect to be forgiven for anything I have done, but the fair name of California will forever be blackened with the crime of taking innocent blood, and whether or not they ever discover the committors of these crimes matters little to me . . .'

By this time Amos, the hangman, was getting tired of the harangue, and began to finger the hood.

Durrant continued, 'They must consider for themselves who wished to start up a sensation that I am innocent. I say now this day before God, to whom I now go to meet my dues, I am innocent . . .' Suddenly, the executioner had had enough. He quickly pulled the hood over Durrant's head, adjusted the noose and pulled the lever.

It was all over except for the bizarre scene in which the 'refreshment boy', a convict detailed to look after the bereaved on such occasions, offered Mr and Mrs Durrant a beverage, accompanied by a substantial lunch of roast beef and vegetables. As the body of their son, with blackened face and protruding tongue, lay in an open coffin barely six feet away, Mrs Durrant was heard to say, 'Please, papa, give me a little more of the roast.'

Sixteen years later, on the opposite coast of America, yet another holy killer was at work. Like all murder stories it began with a body – of sorts. On Wednesday, September 6, 1913, eighteen-year-old Mary Bann was walking the shore of Woodcliff, New Jersey, when she saw a curiously-shaped parcel floating in the Hudson River between the Jersey coastline and Long Island, New York.

Mary got a pole and prodded the bobbing flotsam and after lifting it by its rope binding on to a jetty she lost all interest in the matter and went home. Two boys who arrived on the scene later were more inquisitive, picked the knots and found what was left of a young woman.

Her body had been reduced to an upper portion of the torso. She had been decapitated; the body had been severed at the waist; her arms amputated. All possible means of identification, face, teeth, fingerprints, and footprints had been removed. The flesh had been subject to buffeting tides.

The New York coroner, Dr Israel Feinburg, did his best. She was between twenty and thirty years of age, and had been dead less than a week. Police took away a pillowcase in which what remained of the body had been wrapped. The manufacturer's label was still attached.

Whence the body had come, and therefore which authority should investigate the death, was to raise questions. The following Sunday, September 7, the lower part of the torso, showing that the legs had also been amputated, was washed ashore three miles downstream at Weehawken, New Jersey. A New Jersey case? Not quite. This part of the torso was wrapped first in another piece of the pillowcase, this part embroidered with a letter 'A', and then in a newspaper and a piece of tar-paper which bore unmistakable traces of crystalline rock from the Manhattan, New York, shore. The newspaper was dated August 13.

Parcel number three contained a leg and was taken out of the water at Keansburg, New Jersey. By then the police had come to the conclusion, after consulting the dockers and waterfront experts and studying the times of the tides and the earthy residue on the parcels, that the body belonged to New York. There was little that medical science could do to help with the identification. There were a couple of small matters: her skin was amazingly smooth, with a creamy white complexion and she had a very small pink birthmark under the left shoulder. Other than that, the inspector and three officers were left with a pillowcase in two pieces.

It was not an ordinary pillowcase, but was made of a strong cotton fabric, oddly patterned and rather expensive, so while the newspaper headlines cried, 'The Ghastly Catch' and 'The Mystery of the Dismembered Woman', detectives laundered the rag-trade district for clues. Their reward was the information that the pillowcase was an expensive experiment which had not sold well, and rather than let it take up space on drapers' shelves the manufacturers had sold the linen cheaply. The agent had, in fact, a complete list of the destinations of every pillow that had left his warehouse.

From the river tides the detectives managed to calculate that the shops most likely to have sold the pillow-slips would be northwards in upper Manhattan and close to the Hudson River. Mr George Sachs of no. 2762 Eighth Avenue, close to 137th Street, looked at his books and remembered:

'August 25. I have a note of it. A young couple. She was quite attractive but he was peculiar, thin, pale-faced with very bright brown eyes. They bought a chair, bed springs, an enamelled bed, two pillows and pillow-slips.'

Indeed, the note showed that the purchases had been delivered to a four-roomed apartment on the third floor of no. 68 Bradhurst Avenue. On the way to that address, the officers called on two shops which had on the same day sold tar-paper and medicated manila paper, presumably to stifle any unpleasant smells from whatever was wrapped within it. And the landlord of 68 Bradhurst Avenue confirmed that a Mr H. Schmidt had rented the flat on August 25 'for a young relative of mine who is getting married'.

On Saturday morning, September 13, ten days after the first parcel had been discovered, officers entered the flat. It looked like a butcher's shop. Dried blood was on a knife, and there were bloodstains on the floors and in the bath. Two gaudy pillows but only one pillow-slip told what had happened. There was a bonus. In a handbag – and what woman leaves her handbag at home for so many days? – were letters from Hungary addressed to Miss Anna Aumüller, c/o The Rectory, St Boniface's Church, Second Avenue, New York; a marriage licence issued in that city dated February 26, 1913, and a marriage licence stating that Anna Aumüller had been married six months previously to Hans Schmidt by the Reverend Hans Schmidt.

A curious habit that, not entirely confined to the 'Big Apple'; but in those days when bearing children out of wedlock was not considered proper, officials at the hatch, match and dispatch registry were often sufficiently obliging to predate a marriage certificate. When a priest made the request the process was all the more straightforward.

The detectives headed for St Boniface's, where they found the rector Father John S. Braun and his sister, the housekeeper, more than somewhat reluctant to discuss Anna. The housekeeper identified her from the description of her skin and the tiny pink birthmark. She had worked at the rectory for three years.

225

Then there was the matter of the young man who arrived about the same time as Anna and came to live in the rectory. Father Braun could not bring himself to think there was anything improper in their relationship, but he had to admit that he had dismissed Anna on August 31 because he was 'not satisfied with her way of life'.

Who was the young man? The answers came slowly. Hans Schmidt, yes; Father Hans Schmidt, yes, a Roman Catholic priest, in fact Father Braun's assistant. And where was he now? In Harlem, at St Joseph's Church on the corner of West 125th Street and Morningside Avenue.

Even then, and it was approaching midnight, the detectives called at St Joseph's, and faced the deathly pale priest with the bright brown eyes.

'Did you kill her?' they asked him.

'Yes. I loved her.'

Roman Catholic priests with girlfriends with whom they have intimate relations were not exactly commonplace. Priests who then kill and butcher their lady companions are still rarer. The story that Father Schmidt had to tell was perhaps unique in the annals of the Roman Catholic Church.

For a long time he slumped in a chair, his head on the table, his shoulders shaking, his body racked with sobs. Then the officers took the pathetic figure in the Roman collar and soutane to the bloody rented apartment with all its memories where he told the following macabre tale:

'I received an instruction from on high to kill her and cut her up. Anna will be a sacrifice of blood and atonement, I was told by the voice. Acting on that instruction I cut her throat while she slept, then took her body to pieces in the bath.

'I drank her blood and had intercourse with her after I had killed her. I then wrapped up the parts of her in several bundles – I think there were seven altogether – and took them to the river. I took several trips on the crosstown car along 125th Street to the Fort Lee Ferry. I always waited until she was in midstream before I dropped off each parcel from the end of a boat.'

Asked if he felt any regret, he asked if he could change out of his clerical garb and don the clothing of a layman. He was unworthy of anything. Even before he was taken to the Tombs prison house he tried to cut his throat with a razor blade, but was unsuccessful.

More remarkable evidence was to come at his trial. The defence offered evidence of insanity. Schmidt's sister said that he had had visions at the age of ten. Back in his cell, the prison chaplain asked him about these apparitions. 'I was directed to kill Anna Aumüller by Saint Elizabeth. Saint Elizabeth is my patron and she directed me to make the sacrifice of the girl I loved. The sacrifice was to be consummated in blood as was the sacrifice of Abraham.'

According to his sister, Schmidt also offered animals in similar bloody ceremonies. He had a liking for cutting off the heads of geese. 'He would get quite excited as a child of about ten when he could be taken to the slaughter-house,' she added.

The prosecution thought this was a ploy to save him from the death penalty. They argued that the murder had a simpler and more mercenary motive. Anna was expensive. She had been pregnant by him. He offered the suggestion that he had arranged for her to have an abortion, which had gone wrong, and she had died by accident. But he did not know that the post-mortem on the body had revealed no evidence either of pregnancy or of abortion. He had tried to insure her life for $5,000 but gave the insurance company no reason, possibly thinking a pregnant single woman insured by a poverty-sworn priest was no recommendation that the premiums would be paid.

Further searches through the cleric's papers at the rectory revealed receipts for the rent of an apartment at 516 West 134th Street. There police found a printing plant for the production of forged ten- and twenty-dollar bills.

Father Schmidt was sent to the electric chair and in his final confession insisted that he was going to die not because he had murdered his beloved Anna but because he had borne false witness against his neighbour. Lying was obviously a much more heinous crime to him than murder.

## Chapter Thirteen

# HOLY KILLERS,
# FRENCH STYLE

'Would it not be better to leave a village priestless than give it to priests of such a character? They preach morality and bring the clergy into contempt.'

Dr Emile Laurent, *L'année Criminelle*.

In most countries, deference to the church and the priesthood has for centuries ensured that references to their part in many horrendous crimes have been censored and historical records either glossed over or completely ignored. Not so in France. Dr Emile Laurent in *L'année Criminelle* (1889–1900) greeted the twentieth century with these words:

Owing to the difficulty in the last fifty years in recruiting priests, the clergy have been compelled to admit into their ranks persons in every way deplorable in character. I am able to instance a small village which, during thirty years, has furnished four priests whom I will describe as A, B, C and D. A is the son of a prostitute who had married as her second husband a man who had been two or three times imprisoned for theft and fraud. B is the son of a peasant who has undergone fifteen days' imprisonment for theft. C comes of a family enjoying the worst possible reputation, and repudiated by the whole village. His father, an incorrigible drunkard, has many times appeared before the Correctional Tribunal. D is the son of peasants in comfortable circumstances. Being greedy, idle and unfit for any occupation, his father thought the best way to get rid of him was to make him a priest. Whilst still at the seminary he was often found in houses of ill-fame.

Would it not be better to leave a village priestless than give it to priests of such a character? They preach morality and bring the clergy into contempt.

Has it really changed? Father Guy Desnoyers, village priest of Uruffe, in eastern France, was sentenced to life imprisonment for murdering his pregnant girlfriend. He was the Don Juan of the châteaux, the cottages, the vineyards and many beds in between.

His passions overruled his religious prudence. One of his girlfriends, nineteen-year-old Regine Faye, became pregnant by him. She carried his baby for eight months until one day, in 1956, he took her for a drive into the countryside in his car. He had bought the vehicle with money borrowed from another woman friend.

Out of earshot, he put a gun to the back of her head, fired and killed her. At his trial, he said that he had offered her the last rites and final absolution. Then he mutilated her and killed the unborn baby in her womb because it was, he said, 'the fruit of sin'. He killed her because she refused to have an abortion or leave the area to avoid a scandal.

The Roman Catholic hierarchy behaved with quite astonishing compassion. Desnoyers' offence in those days was punishable by the guillotine but the bishops wielded their influence and the priest was sentenced to life imprisonment. From his cell he let it be known that on his eventual release he would enter a Trappist monastery – at the original La Trappe in Normandy – where strict austerity and the vows of silence are rigidly maintained. To everybody's surprise, President Pompidou reduced his life sentence to enable him to take up his new calling.

Curiously, the rakish padre had never been excommunicated. He had been barred from priestly duties but allowed to perform other church functions in the prison. Then suddenly, no one mentioned the Trappist monastery any more. The jaunty libertine had been entertaining a woman prison visitor in his cell, a divorcee with two children, whom he said he wanted to marry.

The woman, who asked for her identity to be kept secret, said, 'I was eighteen when the crime took place. I remember everyone discussing the murder. I started visiting him when I heard that no one else ever did so. I have still not definitely made up my mind about marriage. My only fear is for him when he comes out of prison. I do not think he has any idea of what awaits him outside.' After escaping the guillotine, a longer prison sentence, and the full wrath of the church, maybe even the anger of other women may not hold for him too much fear.

At Laval, the chief town in the department of Mayenne, on the road eastwards to Le Mans car racing track, parishioners still talk about the day one hundred years ago, January 2, 1894, when the Abbé Fricot of the nearby parish of Entrammes was making up his accounts with the help of his curate, Abbé Bruneau. At 6.30 p.m., choristers waiting at the rectory door were told their choir practice had been cancelled without prior notice. At 7 p.m., when the servant girl came to tell the priests that supper was ready, Abbé Fricot was not there.

Bruneau began playing the harmonium before eating his evening meal alone. When asked about Abbé Fricot, he said that the priest had gone out. He did not know where. He did not know when Fricot would return.

Later, when Abbé Fricot had still not returned, a search of the premises and the surrounding grounds was started, with neighbours summoned to help.

The search continued all night. In the morning, when he still had not been found, Bruneau told one parishioner, 'The Abbé has been very odd for some time; he is worried about family affairs. I should never be astonished to hear that he had committed suicide. If, as I very much fear, he has destroyed himself, there must be no scandal, for religion's sake. We will take him up and lay him on his bed without saying any more about it.'

They found Abbé Fricot in the well beneath two feet of water, under a pile of logs and poles. The poles had been used to push him under the surface. Bloodied finger- and boot-prints showed where he had tried to cling to the wall of the well. Logs had been heaped on top of him to keep him down. His head had been smashed in, his nose pulped, his face and hands covered with bruises. A doctor calculated that he had been beaten for up to two hours and then after a delay someone had returned to finish the task of killing him.

When a nun visited the rectory, Bruneau confided in her, 'Sister, I saw Monsieur le Curé close to the well last night. There can be no doubt that he committed suicide, but to save his memory we have thrown logs over him so that people may think he has been murdered.' But suicides do not rifle their own belongings, take all the money, the deeds, the repair fund and even the money for poor relief. Nor do they tie 1,500 missing francs in a handkerchief and bury the loot in the granary.

The whole story was told when Bruneau, aged thirty-three, was brought before the *Cour d'Assises* at Laval. His income was never more than 1,500 francs a year yet he regularly drew sums of 1,000 francs from the bank. The abbé claimed he had been left 16,000 francs by a nun (which was in fact intended for charity) while his other riches came from swindles, breaches of trust, thefts and murder. He had previously served in the parish of Astillé. When the vicarage there burned down and insurance money was paid out on a policy arranged by Bruneau, he accused his senior priest, Abbé Pointeau, of being responsible. Both were moved to different parishes.

Abbé Bruneau had no sooner arrived at Entrammes than 550 francs disappeared from a chest in the vestry and the Abbé Fricot confided to his servant girl, Jeanette, that he suspected the curate. On the night of Fricot's murder, Bruneau (according to Jeanette) tried to push her in the well. Worse had already occurred.

Almost six months previously, neighbours of Madame Bourdais, a widowed florist of Laval, were alarmed at 10 p.m. by cries of help and hurried footsteps on the stairs. When they went to investigate they found her shop door wide open, the flower seller lying on the floor, her throat opened by a gaping wound extending to the spine. One eyelid had been torn off, one eye put out: just two of the forty-three cuts to which she had been subjected. The knife blade had been bent in the violence. Upstairs, furniture had been ransacked, two purses were found empty in a cupboard, a number of bank shares the florist was known to own had vanished, as had a number of 40-franc pieces.

There had been no break-in. The killer must have been known to the florist or had his own keys. When they later searched Bruneau's belongings, they found hand-filed skeleton keys. But half an hour after the florist's murder, a cabman saw the abbé walk from the direction of the florist's shop, picked him up and was asked to take him to the outskirts of Entrammes. He said he would 'walk up the hill', the cabbie recalled.

When a neighbour expressed surprise that police had not arrested anyone for the crime, Bruneau said, 'There's nothing wonderful about that. For instance I could murder you in your chimney corner with your wife and children without anyone suspecting me of it.' Bruneau also made the mistake of using a lot of 40-franc pieces to buy a railway ticket and that too was remembered.

Many tourists have expressed amazement that this story should be remembered and talked about a century after it happened. Alas, it is not about the crime that the locals go into detail, but about the Abbé Bruneau's frequent visits to the local cat-house. A bordello madame who maintained a record recited at Bruneau's trial his visits, his favourite girls and his sexual preferences. When he did not turn up at the local bawdy-houses, the girls sent taxi-cabs to the presbytery to remind and collect him. When it seemed that the judge had heard enough of these side issues, she revealed that he was by no means the only priest to habituate the whorehouse and that they usually wore their black cassocks, too.

Bruneau was found guilty, sentenced to death and 16,000 turned up at the guillotine to hear him still declare his innocence. *Avec dignité*, they said.

Before Bruneau, there grew up in a remote village in the Pyrénées, close to the Spanish Mediterranean border, an orphan peasant boy, Joseph Auriol, whose father was going to be in jail for a long time. His uncle intended him to be a schoolteacher. Joseph was bright but inattentive. One day he heard a famous preacher and decided he could become a priest with less effort than it would take to teach or till the soil. His superficial education admitted him to the seminary at Prades, but he flunked his exams and returned to the village. There his uncle threatened to throw him out if he did not become a priest.

This time he succeeded. He became the abbé at Prats-de-Mollo in the mountains, where for five years he survived the gossip about his late-night calls on young ladies of the parish. Next came the priesthood at Noh-édes, an even more remote valley in the mountains, where he was looked after by two elderly well-to-do sisters, Rose and Marie Fonda. Rose, the elder, was overweight and suffered from heart trouble. Marie was pale, thin and anaemic. They mothered the priest, deco-rated his church, tended his flock, mended his linen and made his lonely existence more bearable.

He repaid them by gathering from the mountainside poisonous herbs, like the root of hellebore, which he had learnt about in his youth. The herbs were of two types, he told the sisters, one for cardiac complaints, the other for anaemia, and he prayed they would improve the ladies' health.

At the same time, Auriol was paying court to the village schoolteacher, an alluring twenty-two-year-old, Alexandrine Vernet. She wrote bad poetry, had a taste for dirty books, and she captivated the priest. They became so close that the cleric had to arrange for Alexandrine to become the teacher in Taurynia, a sequestered village miles away. The distance meant noth-ing to him, since he had written, 'I am appalled at the passion which the sight of you inspires in my breast.'

Abbé Auriol, dressed as a smuggler, an acceptable kind of night worker in the region, climbed the mountain paths to be with his lover whenever he could. Taurynia was too small to keep their secret. When he could spend more time with her, they boarded the train for Prades. The priest would stand in the compartment window to repel would-be boarders, crying, 'Full up!' When the train left the station, he would change from his religious robes, don a false beard and when the train reached its destination, a bearded swain and his lover would disembark for the nearest hotel for more hours of enjoyment.

So intense was this love affair that the padre wrote to his uncle and pleaded for help. He wanted to quit the priesthood, cross the border into Spain and marry Alexandrine, and if he could have a portion of his inheritance immediately he could start a new life and a new profession. His uncle was adamant. He must remain a priest or become a beggar.

In July, 1870, Mlle Marie Fonda, after taking breakfast with her sister, was seized with a violent sickness and died within the hour. Anaemia seemed a sufficient reason for her to die. Burial was prompt. Her property was left to her surviving sister.

Within a week, Abbé Auriol accompanied Mlle Rose Fonda to the office of a notary in Perpignan, the chief town of the department of Pyrénées-Orientales, where she swore a will leaving all her possessions to the priest. Auriol was so excited he wrote on August 28 to Alexandrine, who was going away for a few days.

My Love, my Beloved – Rose has made her will in my favour. She has been ill for some time, the least exertion brings on a fever. Write to me before you leave, and mind and don't fret about anything. Take care of yourself at all times for the sake of your beloved. Since yesterday a lot of my people have been ill, some kind of epidemic. Adieu to the moment of your starting. Ever yours, Joseph.

The epidemic, of a form of cholera, was no fiction. The tea he gave Rose on August 30 was corrupt. After twelve hours of pain and sickness, Rose died. Her death was not unexpected. The shock of her sister's demise, her obesity, her faulty heart and the epidemic which had struck the town were thought responsible.

Abbé Auriol was her sole beneficiary. He lost no time, sold up her lands, property and possessions, and told his superiors and parishioners that because of overwork and grief at the loss of so many friends, he was taking a month's holiday. He had 15,000 francs in his pocket and went to Perpignan to consult his lawyer with one nagging problem. Marie had left her estate in writing to Rose. Rose had left her estate verbally to the priest in the confessional. Without referring to the actual people involved he put to his lawyer the question: Are testamentary dispositions made by a penitent in favour of her confessor legal and valid?

Before the attorney could answer, gendarmes, alerted by an anonymous letter, walked in and arrested Auriol. He was searched; eleven thousand francs and a phial of prussic acid, which he tried to pour out, were taken from him. Next day, while on his way to the *Juge d'Instruction* or magistrate he slipped his guard but after a chase over two miles was recaptured.

He had made a rendezvous with Alexandrine at Carcassonne, the picturesque town a few miles north in the Aude department. He did not arrive. She did not know of his arrest. In desperation, she wrote to him:

I am still at the Hôtel St Pierre, where I am ready to wait for ever, but come quickly or I shall die of despair. Unkind and ungrateful that you are, what have I done? Have I loved you too well? Is that my fault? Are these your promises, the oaths you have sworn to me?

You mean to desert me? Then why did you allow me to leave my poor parents? Why have you dragged me away from their loving care to leave me to misery and the contempt of all men?

Adieu for ever.

God will punish you as you deserve. I go to tell all to a priest.

Alexandrine.

When she still did not hear from her lover, she confessed to a priest, was admitted to a convent, and when she learned of his arrest she vanished from Carcassonne without trace.

The bodies of both Rose and Marie were exhumed. Doctors were told to look for poisonous hellebore root in the case of Marie, but they said it must have been rapidly absorbed into her system; and for prussic acid in the body of Rose, but they said that left no trace at all.

Many attacks have been made and many defences mounted on behalf of the French *Juges d'Instructions* but in this case the examining magistrate exercised his undoubted powers to extract a confession from the Abbé Auriol. He was put in solitary confinement until further notice. On the thirty-seventh day, he called for the *Procurateur de la République* and his assistant the *Juge* and acknowledged his guilt:

To set my conscience at rest with God and man, and that my repentance may accord with the magnitude of my crimes, in full submission to human justice and the will of God, I confess myself guilty of having put to death by poison two holy ladies to whom I owed nothing but gratitude. I committed this sin in the sole hope of thereby acquiring a fortune that would have enabled me to gratify a guilty passion. I only pray that my present state may serve as an example to all my brethren in the priesthood, and that, above all, this declaration and my sincere confession may serve to efface the great scandal which my recent conduct has provoked and my ultimate condemnation will provoke yet further.

When almost a year later Auriol came before the *Cour d'Assises* at Perpignan, he recanted his confession. The tenor of his argument with the hostile President of the Court can be judged by this exchange:

Auriol: 'I am innocent of the deaths of these two women. If I accepted the inheritance of Rose Fonda it was only because I wished to administer it for the benefit of her infant nephews.'

President: 'And you proceeded to administer the property by selling the land as cheap as dirt, and leaving the country?'

Auriol: 'In accusing myself falsely I was prompted by a mistaken form of reasoning. I believed that these lies against myself would serve to expiate in the sight of God the immoralities I had committed.'

There were more bitter exchanges, accompanied by protests from counsel, but more remarkable was the allegation from a doctor in the witness box that Alexandrine

Vernet, Auriol's lover, had had an earlier suitor. The young man had fallen ill. The doctor had refused to bleed him because it would be very injurious to his health. When the doctor had departed, Abbé Auriol bled the patient and he died.

Auriol was found guilty of the murders of the two sisters but with extenuating circumstances. He had desperately sought to quit the priesthood before committing the crimes. Such reservations deprived the court of the power of sentencing the guilty to death. The abbé was sentenced to penal servitude for life.

The French, of course, had many more holy killers but few, perhaps, could equal the appalling record of the Abbé Boudes of the departments of Aveyron and Tarn close to the Pyrénées. He was born in 1830, expelled at the age of twenty-five from the Perigueux seminary for stealing a cassock and candlesticks, and at twenty-six thrown out of an ecclesiastical college for immorality. He then vanished to Italy where he was consecrated a priest, after which the French church had no option but to admit him.

The Bishop of Rodez in the Massif Central appointed him a curate at Lagarde, where he robbed his parishioners on their deathbeds. He would listen to the secrets of the confessional and persuade those who had not long to live to channel their wills to his benefit. He extorted money from the dying by frightening them with the prospect of eternal damnation. And he was guilty of all sorts of immorality.

Having previously been found guilty of dishonesty by the church educational authorities he feared exposure of his guilt again. His priest knew all about his financial crimes, and thinking the reverend father would report him to the bishop, Boudes devised an ingenious plan to kill the clergyman. He poisoned the chalice from which the cleric would drink at Mass. At the last moment before the Mass, a choirboy noticed something wrong with the wine and reported it.

An investigation traced some of the poison to Abbé Boudes but the priest was too forgiving to pursue the complaint and the curate accepted a transfer to Viviers. There he procured an abortion for a young girl, lent money at extortionate rates of interest, forged bills of exchange, obtained clerical garments without paying for them, robbed another priest and offered a young man a certificate confirming that he had heart disease to enable him to avoid military service.

Again he transferred parishes, this time to Taurines where he was promoted to the rank of priest. There he continued his old habits; forgery, abortion, money-lending, stealing a plough and sacred ornaments from a neighbouring church. One night, during a burglary at the next-door church of Saint-Cirq, the parish priest, Abbé Alvar, was found dead in his bed. Money had been stolen; the priest's body was covered with knife wounds and scratches made by a human nail, and there was a bloody hand-print on his shoulder. The cleric's sister said two men with blackened faces had broken into the house, killed her brother, and chased her until she fell down a ravine to safety. The ordeal had robbed her of some of her reason.

Boudes fled to Taurines, was arrested in the Ardèche, and charged with the murder of the priest. With the compassion of the church and the connivance of the judiciary he was allowed to plead mental disability. This enabled him to be held in an asylum at Montpelier until the legal period of atonement for his crimes had been served.

That, however, would have meant serving many years, and the criminal cleric had no intention of remaining in a mental institution all that time. After about ten years he confided to a warder, 'They think I am mad because I have committed some trifling breaches of the sixth commandment [Thou shalt do no murder]. But I am not. And I mean to get out of this.' The asylum warder helped him escape and he reappeared in the Department of Tarn as an Alsatian priest, Father Jean Mary. Soon he was appointed Professor of Religious Studies at the Ste Marie School at Albi, chief town of the *département*.

There he ingratiated himself with a pupil called Calmels, who lived with his grandmother, a lady of considerable wealth, at the Château of Pendaries. Professor Boudes, made tutor to the boy, persuaded the grandmother to sell him land valued at 80,000 francs for a fraction of that figure. Unfortunately for him, a girl from his home town of Perigueux recognised the priest, who was almost entirely bald but for two tufts of hair behind each ear. His identity revealed, the old lady's relatives, anxious about her property, told the authorities and after a chase the priest was arrested. 'Kill me,' he cried. 'Empty your revolvers into my head. You will be doing me a service.' This time he was ruled perfectly sane.

Boudes had the cheek to write to his Bishop:

Monseigneur, Behold me in the Rodez prison and about to appear before the *Cour d'Assises*. I am none the less innocent of the crimes laid to my charge. It is not I, I swear before God, who killed the Curé of Saint-Cirq, and, if I did, I cannot be convicted, or even accused of the crime, since it is covered by prescription [a legal waiver]. They can then accuse me of nothing, save a few trifling peccadilloes which I hardly remember.

I should be extremely obliged and grateful, Monseigneur, if you would come and see me, or at least send your secretary.

When I have been acquitted by my judges, and I am absolutely certain that I shall be, my one and only desire is to withdraw myself into the privacy of a monastery, forgotten of all men, and where I may for my part forget them.

The reply from the Bishop of Rodez should remove any doubt about how indulgent the Roman Catholic Church could be towards their sinful sermonisers:

Monsieur Le Curé, My poor Monsieur le Curé, if there are faults in your parishioners, have you not given them good cause to observe yours? And whilst they are in their right expecting guidance from their shepherd, have they not also the right to acquaint the lawful authority, their bishop, with behaviour which is contrary not only to the priestly character but to the absolute rules of a priestly life. They have, my good Curé, not only the right but it is their duty to do so, leaving to me the task of weighing and judging their allegations. And now what are these allegations which you ask to know? You are accused –

1. Of having often, if not habitually, neglected to recite your breviary. Certain of your parishioners who have travelled with you and had you continually

in their sight declare that they have not seen you once open your book of prayer.

2. You are accused of theft and embezzlement, and these charges you cannot well deny. It has been ascertained by the inspection of registers and accounts that you have in many cases embezzled sums that did not belong to you. Of this there can be no doubt. With regard to the fees for special masses, you know better than I do, my poor curé, what traffic you have made in these and the liability you have incurred in this respect.

3. You are accused of not confessing yourself, and it would be impossible for anyone to say to what priest, in case of serious illness, one ought to send to assist you. You know as well as I do whether this is the case or not.

4. You are accused of shocking immorality, and without dwelling on the past, I need only cite one fact brought to my notice. That is the attempted violation of a little girl aged thirteen, of which you have allowed yourself quite recently to be guilty. I have no actual proof of this, but it could be easily established, and you know well that, if it were so, it would be a matter for the *Cour d'Assises*.

5. By your reckless language, threats and sinister prophecies, a number of fires have broken out in your parish and have been laid to your charge, and many of your parishioners, I am told, keep guard over their houses and intend to inform the authorities of the threats you have addressed to them.

6. During your residence at Lagarde your conduct has given rise to more awful rumours still, which I

refrain from alluding to, as there are limits even to crime, and by the blessing of God you have not yet passed beyond them.

You ask me for facts my good curé. Here are some which in all conscience are grave enough. I do not judge you, nor is it my wish to ruin you. I would rather save you. But if you think my action can be of any avail, you must follow my directions and not offer me yours.

[The Bishop here suggested that Boudes should resign his office and leave the district.]

I repeat, my dear Monsieur le Curé, the expression of my feelings of devotion towards you.

P.S. It is no use you coming to discuss your matters with me. I could not say any more to you than what I have written. Burn this letter that it may not one day be found in your possession and become for you a *chirographum mortis* [a deathly autograph].

Abbé Boudes did not resign his living, did not leave the district, and his neighbour, the Abbé Alvar, was burgled, robbed and murdered in his bed. Even the President of the *Cour d'Assises* which tried the priest for murder remarked, 'If your superiors had shown greater severity towards you, those who have a regard for religion would have been spared the shame of seeing you in the dock today.'

Abbé Boudes was sentenced for various crimes to penal servitude for life.

## Chapter Fourteen

# FIRE AND BRIMSTONE

'The people who sent him are responsible for his death. Whenever it becomes necessary for me to defend my life I will. It was the hand of God that killed him.'

The Reverend Frank Norris.

On a quiet Saturday afternoon in the town of Fort Worth, Texas, Elliott Chipps called on the Reverend J. Frank Norris, pastor of the First Baptist Church, to complain about the parson's pulpit attacks on his friends, the mayor and city council. If Norris didn't stop, Chipps said, he would kill the clergyman. Norris grabbed a .38 calibre Smith and Wesson revolver and shot Chipps dead. Self-defence, you may suppose. But Chipps was not even armed. And the Reverend Norris fired four times, hitting his target thrice.

Next day, before his victim had been buried, the clergyman returned to his packed church to preach as usual against the mayor and city council.

The Reverend Norris, forty-eight, married with a daughter and three sons, had been a pastor of the Church for seventeen years when the killing took place on July 17, 1926. He was six feet tall, aggressive and intense and a powerful Bible-punching fundamentalist preacher. He railed against card and pool playing, dancing and the theatre. The Baptist authorities disapproved of his unorthodox style, which had turned a staid church into a Barnum and Bailey circus, whipping up churchgoers' emotions to sing, sway and applaud sermons and campaigns.

When the Baptist Church disbarred him from their conventions, he cried, 'Should the Devil have all the best tunes? Should Beelzebub have all the applause? Why shouldn't people applaud in church? It proves that they are alive. What's the difference between a lot of deacons and preachers in the Amen corner shouting their "Amens" and allowing the congregation to express their "Amens" by clapping their hands?

'They don't like my sensational methods. They want a nice quiet mealy-mouthed preacher who hasn't the guts to hit sin hard and fight the gang. Join my church. We've got a great fight on here now. But we've got the enemy on the run. They're licked but they're still kicking.

'They talk about dignity and solemnity. Poppycock! Too many preachers think that a church should be like a graveyard. By all means, go to the graveyard if you want dignity and solemnity. I prefer life! Sensation is life. Lack of sensation is stagnation! A lot of preachers are so dignified they are petrified.

'J. Frank Norris will never preach to empty benches. I'll have a crowd if I have to start a dog fight.'

Norris attracted congregations of 6,000 and more, many from other churches. He greeted newcomers and converts at the platform with a handshake. He used the Church newspaper, the *Searchlight*, with a circulation of 65,000, and the Church radio station to spread his own brand of religion and keep up his attacks on local figures and what he regarded as their corrupt practices. He alleged that opponents had tried to wreck the radio station, and hired armed security guards to protect it with 'shoot to kill' orders.

Elliott Chipps, his victim, was forty-nine and in the lumber business. Divorced, with a fourteen-year-old son, on the eve of his death he had dined with his wife to talk about re-marriage. Chipps was a hedonist, one of the boys, a poker player, a whiskey drinker, a member of the town club, the country club, and the Shiners. When he was sober he was courteous, when he was drunk he was bad. A freemason, he was a close friend of powerful interests in Fort Worth, Texas, particularly H. E. Meacham, the mayor, who owned the dry goods store which bore his name.

That Saturday afternoon Chipps had called on Meacham and discussed the Reverend Norris's latest attack on the city fathers and big business interests. He had even left his spectacles on Meacham's desk while he went about his fatal task.

The issues between the reverend gunman and the friends of the victim were fierce. The First Baptist Church earned more than $1,000 a month income from the J. C. Penney store and at least one other, the Moore Rubber Company, through rental of buildings. As a result, the city levied taxes on income from those parts of their property that were not used exclusively for religious, educational or charitable purposes. Norris refused to pay the taxes. He also objected to paying taxes on water for his church, some of which, admittedly, was used in baptism; but gallons were also used in the church swimming pool.

From pulpit and radio he railed against 'graft, Romanism and taxation'. When the victims of his tongue were asked why they did not sue, one of them replied, 'Sue a beggar, you get a louse. Sue a preacher and you get the enmity of the whole congregation.'

The city authorities wanted to widen a thirty-foot alley into a ninety-foot street. To do so they needed to purchase the Roman Catholic academy of St Ignatius, for which they paid $62,000, and some other property which they bought for $90,000. Norris claimed that the deal was corrupt and that the city was pandering to Roman Catholicism. The officials whom Norris had accused of graft were incensed. They were properly elected or appointed. There had been no misconduct. They would, they said, have behaved in the same way whatever their religion in any city where they may have held office.

Mayor Meacham was a Roman Catholic. According to Pastor Norris, L. B. Haughey, a Catholic and manager of Meacham's department store, had offered those of his staff who belonged to the First Baptist Church the choice of withdrawing from membership or being sacked. The store countered by saying that employees had not been asked to abandon their faith but merely to desert the pastor, who was a vicious and open enemy of their employer.

Meacham himself later said that it was his 'duty and pleasure' to have paid $15,000 towards the fees of the lawyers who appeared for the prosecution of the murder charge against Norris.

The Baptist minister also waged a war against vice in Fort Worth, particularly in 'Hell's half-acre', the old tenderloin, three blocks by two between Main Street and the Santa Fe railway station. He claimed that the city sanctioned what went on there and benefited from the taxes paid by the property owners. But what city with a red-light district does not have the same embarrassment?

Norris was charged with the murder of Elliott Chipps, but the first issue was whether he could receive a fair trial in that county. His lawyers said he could not. The State replied that there were thousands of qualified electors who had no prejudice against him, and that the few who did had suffered unwarranted attacks made by Norris upon them. Powerful witnesses were called for both sides in the argument, but ninety per cent of the potential jurors empanelled said when asked that they had already made up their minds what their verdict would be.

Judge George E. Hosey ruled that there was a very real risk of an unfair trial if it was held in Fort Worth and he ruled that it be moved to Austin, the state capital.

When the case came for trial in Austin, Norris, who pleaded not guilty, gave his version of events. At about 3.30 p.m. on the Saturday in question he had received a telephone call from a stranger who threatened in very abusive and profane language to come round and kill him. 'We are coming over there to settle with you on that sermon.'

'Who is this?' asked Norris.

'It don't matter. I am not going to stand it any longer. I am coming over there to kill you, you—'

'Who is this?'

'Never mind my name. You'll find out when I get there.'

When Norris insisted on having the caller's name, the voice said, 'D. E. Chipps'.

Norris replied, 'I don't want you coming over here. You are mad. I don't want any trouble.'

'By God, I am coming anyway.'

About that time, the cleric asked his stenographer to make a note of the conversation.

Norris always claimed that he had been threatened before and even placated the caller and sent him away peacefully. On this occasion when Norris tried to pacify the caller, the only reply was 'Well, I'm coming up there.'

Witnesses were found who said that Chipps had made the call from the Westbrook Hotel, where he lived, and

255

where, a short time previously, he had arrived with 'an oblong package', no doubt bootleg whiskey, and asked for iced water to go with it.

After the telephone call, Norris sat discussing Sunday School business with his greying and balding aide, Mr L. M. Nutt, member of the Board of Deacons and superintendent of the Young Persons Department. Norris asked him if he knew a Mr Chipps. 'I think he does business down at the Bank,' replied Nutt, referring to the Farmers' and Mechanics' Bank, where he was the auditor.

Fifteen minutes later the large and belligerent Chipps rushed in without knocking, shook hands with Nutt and took a seat on the end of the settee. Norris claimed that he had employed a private detective to investigate his enemies who had warned him against this man Chipps. The intruder, he said, was in an angry mood, and Norris claimed that he had threatened his life, not only over the phone, but two nights previously. He had also been warned that Chipps was sometimes drunk, sometimes dangerous and sometimes armed.

Norris recalled, 'I looked at him and I saw he was so mad. I said, "I do not want any trouble with you." '

Chipps replied, 'You have got to retract that sermon on Meacham or I will kill you.'

Norris insisted, 'That sermon is already published. You are making an impossible demand. I do not want to discuss the matter with you. There is the door and I want you to go.'

The clergyman continued: 'He stood there, looked at me, hesitated, and as I reached and opened the door he said, "I do not want to have another word with you."

'And he turned and walked towards the door and went into the anteroom. And as he went out, just as he got to the door, he said, "Remember what I have told you. I mean every word of it."

'I said to him, "I repeat what I have said to you. I do not want any trouble with you." I then turned back to my desk and just as I got practically to my desk I heard him say, "I will kill you." I looked over my shoulder and saw him coming.

'He made a motion with his right arm so that his coat flared back. I could see his chest. With the other arm he made some motion over his shoulder. I cannot describe it exactly. Then shots rang out.'

According to Mr Nutt, Chipps said, 'I have something to say to you and I mean it. If you make another statement about my friends I am going to kill you.'

Nutt said to him, 'Dr Norris has had men say things like this to him before.'

Norris asked Chipps who his friends were and he told him they were Meacham, the mayor; O. E. Carr, the city manager, who fixed the taxes; and two others.

According to Nutt, the minister also invited him to the church to 'come out and hear me' [preach].

Chipps got up from the settee and was about to leave when he said, 'If you do [preach] I'll kill you.'

Chipps then, according to Nutt, made an unmistakable move to his hip-pocket as if to go for a gun.

If the clergyman is to be believed, the visitor went out but as he (Norris) returned to his desk Chipps came back. There was a difference of opinion from the defence as to what was said. Chipps either said, 'I'll come back,' 'All right, let's go to it,' or 'I'll kill you, let's go to it.'

That was when Norris grabbed the gun and fired four times. One shot went into the ceiling; a second into the arm Chipps put up to protect himself and then into the breast; a third entered the breast; a fourth entered the heart.

Norris said, 'I notified the police and had the ambulance summoned.'

Elliott Chipps died on the office floor, according to the ambulanceman. Police found he was unarmed. Lee, the Chief of Police, recovered the cleric's gun, escorted the pastor to the police station and recalled, 'He was just as cool as a cucumber. He was the coolest fellow you ever saw. And I have been in this game eighteen years and have answered many a murder call.'

Norris said, 'The people who sent him are responsible for his death. Whenever it becomes necessary for me to defend my life I will. It was the hand of God that killed him. Do you know the line from Kipling's poem, *If*? "If you can keep your head when all about you are losing theirs . . ." '

Lee charged the minister with murder but in view of his clerical position he didn't keep him in custody. Norris went to the city hall to talk to the District Attorney, which he thought would settle the matter. It didn't. The charge would have to be answered in court.

In the end a jury would have to decide whether Norris had reason to believe that Chipps was about to draw a gun, or thought he was going to get beaten up and shot his would-be attacker rather than suffer assault. Nutt and many others thought so. Or had Norris shot Chipps down in cold blood?

Judge James R. Hamilton would have to explain Texan law to the jury. If the State could prove to their satisfaction that Norris 'provoked the difficulty' by making a statement which started trouble that led to a serious result, then Norris was to blame. If Norris deliberately provoked the difficulty for the purpose of giving him an opportunity to shoot his victim it would be murder. If it was unpremeditated it would be manslaughter.

By chance, Mrs Roxie Parker, sixty-year-old widow of Judge W. R. Parker who used to preside over courts in Fort Worth, happened to be calling on the Reverend Norris that July afternoon to see if he would like to buy her eighty-acre county estate for a summer camp. Instead she became an eye-witness to a killing.

As she entered the anteroom to the parson's study, 'a man came through the door. His left side was towards me, his right hand was still on the door knob. Suddenly, it seemed to me, the door opened wide into the study. I'm not certain whether it was pulled open or swung open. I saw the man turn and face the open door. He raised his right hand like this [she held hers out to the level of her eyes] and I heard the man say "I'll come back." Then I saw Dr Norris. He had a gun. There was a shot. The man staggered and I turned and went back downstairs.'

Mrs Parker fled in terror, ran into the street and was nearly knocked down by a passing car which just braked in time. The prosecution, realising the effect the old lady had on the jury, decided to call no more witnesses.

The judge summed up evenly. The jury was out only forty-five minutes. They found the Reverend J. Frank Norris not guilty. The pastor, who had in the past few days lost much of his confidence, wept and said:

'But for the crusades I have made there never would have been an indictment. At the time of the tragedy we had evidence of the deep-laid conspiracy to assassinate me, and now it has been proven in open court. The conspirators, failing in this, sought to destroy me in the court house. Their testimony fell of its own weight. May God pity and forgive them.

'Mine is a sorrow – a Gethsemane – that will go with me to the end of my days.'

He added that the listeners could read in Romans ii 'those who condemn sin in others and sin themselves are inexcusable' and in Jeremiah xviii, 5–10 of 'God's power over nations' to build a new life. Others may well have thought there were scriptures which would condemn the Reverend Norris; but it was his day of victory.

Norris and the First Baptist Church, with their bigotry, attracted another kind of hatred, the white, Anglo-Saxon Protestants (WASPS) and the Ku Klux Klan, which used the church for both spiritual and political purposes. Two Sundays after the shooting, Lloyd P. Bloodworth, Grand Dragon of the Ku Klux Klan in Texas, mounted the rostrum of Norris's church, shook hands with the parson, prayed for him, and thanked God for his life, his boldness and his preaching of God's Word. The great Amens from the congregation would have done credit to Handel's *Messiah*, and the congregation put everything they had into the next hymn, 'Walking in footsteps of gentle forbearance, footsteps of faithfulness, mercy and love.' Norris then announced his next two sermons, one on Faith, one on The Present Menace of Roman Catholicism.

The menace of the Klan went back a long way. After the American Civil War a small organisation was set up to suppress the newly acquired rights of the emancipated slaves and was responsible for many violent crimes including murder. Founded in Pulaski, Tennessee, on Christmas Eve, 1865, by six veterans of the Southern

Confederate army, members met in secret, wearing grotesque uniforms of white cloaks and hoods with slits for their eyes. Within two years, the Ku Klux Klan was formally inaugurated in Nashville, Tennessee. Like so many secret student fraternities the members took their name partly from the Greek *kýklos* and for the sake of euphony partly from the Gaelic *clan*, not, as Arthur Conan Doyle's Sherlock Holmes supposed, from the sound of the cocking of a rifle.

The Invisible Empire of the South, as it was nicknamed, was divided into state realms, county provinces and local dens or Klaverns. A Grand Wizard ruled over an organisation of Grand Dragons, Grand Titans, and Grand Cyclopses; Kleagles and Exalted Cyclopses over hydras, furies, goblins, and nighthawks. General Nathan B. Forrest, a cavalry veteran, led Klansmen on a campaign of terror and death against ex-slaves, sympathisers – the original scalawags or scallywags – and the carpetbaggers who went to the South with few belongings to cash in on the end of slavery. Congress passed laws to suppress the Klan and it virtually died out.

But in 1915, the Reverend William J. Simmons, preacher, self-styled colonel, promoter of fraternal orders and travelling salesman, revived the Ku Klux Klan. At the top of Stone Mountain, near Atlanta, Georgia, he placed on a rock altar the US flag, an open Bible, a canteen of water and a naked sword. Fifteen fanatical supporters in white robes and hoods burned a cross, an act which was to become the hallmark of many future persecutions. They called themselves the Knights of the Ku Klux Klan, admitting nobody except native-born, white, Gentile, Protestant Americans. They protested their sole aim was Americanism, the promotion of

America and everything American, which meant perse-
cuting blacks, Jews, Roman Catholics, other ethnic
minorities, and even organised labour unions.

They even had their own language, called klanversa-
tions. Whenever they met, and particularly as they
entered churches, a sidesman would ask, 'A.Y.A.K?'
(Are you a Klansman?) To which the hoped for answer
was, 'A.K.I.A.' (A Klansman I am.) Each member was
bound by an oath, referred to as 'Itsub' (In the sacred
unfailing bond) and if non-members were approaching or
attempting to listen to their conversations, the warning
was given, 'Sanbog' (Strangers are near. Be on guard.)

The Reverend Simmons, spell-binding pulpit orator,
saw membership rise to five million. He was estimated to
earn $50,000 a month as a shareholder in the firm which
manufactured the robes and regalia. In support of their
beliefs, the Klan appointed chaplains drawn from sympathetic churches which provided the bulk of their members
and which they hired for their meetings.

Whenever KKK-inspired murders were committed,
there was usually to hand a KKK chaplain ready to give
spiritual comfort and other help to the perpetrators. The
role of these chaplains and their churches in a number of
Klan crimes is worthy of a separate investigation. State
governors, mayors, police chiefs, district attorneys and
occupants of virtually every position of power across the
United States held important Klan offices and were
eventually exposed. Only the clergy appear to have been
untouchable in the investigations which followed.

On March 15, 1925, the Grand Dragon of Indiana, D.
C. Stephenson, a follower of Simmons, abducted a
twenty-eight-year-old government worker, Madge Ober-
holtzer, drugged her, took her aboard a Chicago-bound

train and raped her. She was bruised, lacerated and bitten all over her body. Shattered and frightened by the unbelievable brutality the Grand Dragon had used, she took six mercury tablets and died a slow, agonising death thirty days later. Stephenson called for help from the Klan chaplains, but institutionalised churches were already sounding grave warnings to their clergy and laity about the dangers of the Klan.

It was one kind of transgression to pray disguised in a white cloak and hood and burn crosses to put the fear of God into black people, but a totally different sin to openly help and defend rapists and murderers of white victims in non-political crimes. Klansmen came out from behind their cloaks and hoods and denounced Stephenson. Despite the defence evidence that the victim had committed suicide Stephenson was sentenced to life imprisonment for murder. He was paroled after twenty-five years, but broke the terms of his freedom and was returned to jail where he spent the rest of his natural life. Two accomplices in the abduction were acquitted, although one of them was later shot dead by a jealous husband.

The power of the Klan was seriously damaged. World War Two revelations that they had links with the Nazi German-American Volksbund further reduced its numbers and support. A resurgence took place during the 1960s campaign for black civil rights when crosses were again burned in the Deep South. President Lyndon Johnson, who succeeded the assassinated President John F. Kennedy, went on nationwide television to appeal to Klan members to quit 'before it is too late'.

Perhaps the Klan will never completely die. Police caught up with some of their local activities on Tuesday,

September 22, 1981, when two men fishing the Mississippi at Blytheville, Arkansas, caught the body of a man
naked except for his jockey shorts, anchored to a rock on
the river bottom. He had been shot at close range by a
16-gauge shotgun on the right hand side, stabbed in the
body and slashed on the side of the head. He had been
dead about twenty-four hours.

Police scanned the most recent bulletins of missing
and wanted persons and seized on the one that fitted
the description of the dead man; twenty-five years of
age, almost six foot tall; slim build, brown hair.
Gregory Snodgrass, married and the father of three
children aged two, four and six, had vanished from his
home on a farm in Ottumwa, Iowa, four hundred miles
away on Sunday, September 20, two days before the
body had been found.

The father of the dead man said his son, a farmworker,
had drug and marriage problems and had recently moved
from Bolivar, Missouri, to Ottumwa, Iowa. Sheriff 'Bud'
Erwin and his men went to the farm, where they found a
device for sniffing cocaine containing traces of that drug,
marijuana and other narcotics available without prescription from chemists. The house was empty and had
recently been cleaned, probably with a mechanical sham-
poo device. Police were still wondering how Snodgrass
had travelled the four hundred miles and whether he had
been alive or dead when a couple told them that a man
and a woman had asked their help to transport a dead
body in a car.

The two seeking help were the dead man's wife, Mrs
Sheryl Snodgrass, and Michael Hood, a newcomer and
temporary chaplain to the Ku Klux Klan. Only a few
months before, Hood had asked a bartender about

joining the Klan and as a result of the conversation had swapped a flashlight and a tape recorder for a 16-gauge sawn-off double-barrelled shotgun. Then he had been appointed chaplain to say prayers for the KKK den. Sheryl had gone to Hood for counselling at the Bolivar Church of God and they had become close friends.

On the Sunday the body was found Hood, the temporary chaplain, Sheryl and the three children went to the home of the bartender Klansman where Hood said, 'I've been in a fight with a man. The man's dog got killed. It's in the trunk of the car. I want to get rid of it. I came to you because I thought as a Klansman you might be able to help me as I believe you have experience in this sort of thing.'

When Hood offered the barman a .30-.30 deer rifle, a valuable weapon, as a gift if he would help dispose of the dead dog, the bartender said he became suspicious. When they reached the Mississippi and Hood opened the boot of the car revealing the body of a dead man, the Klansman bartender ran away. Hood caught up with him, put a revolver to his face and threatened to kill him if he spoke to anyone about the corpse.

Interviewed by police, both Sheryl and Hood told a similar story. Sheryl arrived at Ottumwa to pick up her things to start a new life with Hood, dropping her counsellor-boyfriend half a mile down the road. She found one of her children playing with a shotgun her husband had bought that afternoon. She knew the Klan chaplain had the .30-.30 calibre deer rifle and the sawn-off 16-gauge shotgun as well as a blackjack and a can of Mace. When she reached the house and saw her husband, she told him she was going to leave him. He laughed and told her she was not going to take the children anywhere. There was shouting and screaming and Hood, alerted by the noise, came to the house and had an angry confrontation with Gregory.

Hood said he had only got the guns in order to sell them to build a new home for Sheryl and her children. He told officers, 'Greg Snodgrass and I scuffled over a knife. Snodgrass started to load his shotgun. I told him not to. "If you load another shell, I'll have to shoot you." He continued to load his shotgun so I shot him.'

On Friday, September 25, five days after the body was found, Hood arrived at the county sheriff's department with his own counsellor, James O. Friend, bus driver and part-time pastor of the Church of God. Friend, who held counselling sessions in bus shelters, had advised Hood to talk to the officers. As a result, both he and Sheryl Snodgrass were charged with first degree murder and remanded, Hood in custody, she on bail.

At their trial, Hood repudiated a tape-recorded confession he had made, said he had walked into the kitchen, seen Gregory levelling a shotgun at him and heard a shotgun blast. A wound in Snodgrass's chest opened up and blood came out, but he still walked towards Hood, who grabbed a kitchen knife and stabbed him five times. Mrs Snodgrass, even though she was beginning to tire of her Ku Klux Klan chaplain lover, said that she and not Hood had shot her husband dead.

The jury were instructed that they did not have to decide which one killed Gregory Snodgrass if they believed that one or the other had aided and abetted the murderer. The jury took four hours to find both defendants guilty and they were sentenced to life imprisonment without hope of parole.

Michael Hood, the newly joined Ku Klux Klan chaplain, who sought help from a fellow Klansman after the murder, was only twenty-two years of age: an indication of how short of members the Klan had become and how low in public and churchgoers' esteem they had fallen.

*Chapter Fifteen*

# BLACK SLAVE,
# WHITEST WITNESS

'Let them live: but let them be hewers of wood and drawers of water unto all the congregation.'

*Joshua ix, 21.*

The big Bible-belter had told his whites-only congregation often enough: 'Hear ye, brothers and sisters. We have it on the authority of the Good Book. "Let them live; but let them be hewers of wood and drawers of water unto all the congregation." ' Then one chilly Monday morning in November, almost a century and a half ago, three people walked into the woods beyond Lake Muttamuskeet near the coast of North Carolina, two shots rang out, and only two people returned.

Fortunately for the law, one of the Lord's hewers of wood and drawers of water was not far away. That was how Seth, a black slave, became an instrument of justice.

Seth was the personal servant of the Bible-belting Reverend George Washington Carawan, minister of the Baptist Church in Goose Creek. Named after the statesman, general and first president of the United States, who had recently died and for whom the whole nation was in mourning, this Washington was six feet tall, broad, clean-shaven – an unfashionably open-faced appearance for one in authority – and a hard-shell Baptist. His father had died while he was still a toddler, and he was one of four brought up by a rigid, unsmiling mother who talked more of hell than heaven.

He began life as a rebel. He went to all the Methodist and Baptist rallies, listened carefully to the Bible-punching preachers, learned to imitate their voices and gestures and then mimicked them to the amusement of his young friends. It was never too late for a sarcastic and profane sinner to mend his ways. He was twenty-seven before he saw the light and was plunged into the cleansing waters by none other than the paragon of Baptist preachers, Elder Enoch Brighouse.

That powerful patron expressed the fervent wish that Carawan would himself follow in his footsteps. Soon after his immersion the newcomer responded to the challenge, revealing that he had another, more important reason: the Lord Jesus Christ had come to him in a vision, haloed in glory, and handed him personally a scroll of parchment, commanding him to go forth and preach the gospel. Thus he entered the ministry, selling hymns and hell-fire.

His flock was spread among the islands and mainland between Albemarle and Pamlico sounds, two of several virtually tideless waters between the Atlantic Ocean and the river inlets of the Carolina coast. Carawan founded new churches, preached around an increasingly large circuit, and eventually succeeded his brother, Green Carawan, as minister of Goose Creek Island Church on the River Pungo.

In a quarter of a century, the bright-eyed Washington baptised more than 500 men and women, making sure they were made members of Christ, children of God and inheritors of the kingdom of heaven; and more than two dozen of them were raised to become preachers. He ruled his flock with a rod of iron and heavy-handed chastisement, cleansing, purifying and forgiving. In addition, he acquired two sizeable plantations, scores of slaves, a gun with which to threaten them and a whip to ensure there was no shirking in the fields.

Long before his entry into the church, at the age of

twenty-one, Washington married Elizabeth Carow and exhibited a remarkable display of jealousy. He first quarrelled noisily and publicly with his reverend brother, Green, accusing him of trying to have sex with his wife. Whether or not anyone took him seriously no one can be sure, but he certainly moved away from his brother to cultivate a farm further up the coast at Rose Bay. After eighteen years of marriage, Elizabeth died and within three weeks he had married Mary Bell, his housekeeper. The two wives bore him twenty children, of whom only three young sons survived.

At the age of fifty-three, he had survived much gossip. He was still a big man, a white-haired patrician loved by those who benefited from his Christian charity; but whispers about his darker side were growing into open conversation. At first, his defenders blamed the jealousy of the Reverend Albin R. Swindell, who preached in the same county and was as much a belter of the Bible and preacher of the Baptist faith as was Carawan. He gave public voice to what others thought was emotive speculation. Swindell told a public meeting of church members that the death of Carawan's first wife had not been above suspicion and that there had been found in the parson's travelling trunk a mysterious quantity of arsenic which he had bought just before Elizabeth's death.

Carawan's jealousy had singled out a youth called Hudson, accusing him of an unhealthy sexual interest in his wife, Mary, just as he had accused his brother, Green, of fancying his first wife, Elizabeth. The Reverend Swindell accused the Reverend Carawan of precisely the same crime, an unpreacherly interest in other female members of his church who were too frightened of him to complain. Moreover, he had seduced a naïve sixteen-year-old from his church and fathered her child. That accusation could not be ignored and Carawan was dismissed by the elders of the Baptist Church from his religious duties.

The lay recipients of his Christian charity in the form of farm produce and other benefits soon noticed a dearth of earthly manna and protested at the removal of their generous parson, and before long the Reverend Carawan was back in his pulpit, Bible-punching with fervour. He did not forgive, nor did he forget. Immediately, he went in search of Swindell.

With his gun loaded with buckshot, he found the rival preacher on his way to conduct a chapel meeting, jumped down from his cart and approached Swindell's buggy. Suddenly he stopped short and drew back, having noticed his accuser was with another man, and rather than risk a witness to assault or worse, stammered, 'Oh, I'm sorry, I'm having some trouble with runaway slaves. You haven't seen any about, have you?'

The two men cold-eyed Carawan, shook their heads and suggested the slaves may have gone in the opposite direction.

Whatever was said about Washington Carawan, he was in North Carolinan fashion a generous host and among the more regular visitors to his double-chimneyed farm-house was Clement H. Lassiter, a master at a local school. Still in his twenties, Lassiter was reserved and preoccupied, as befits a teacher, and overweight. He had been a guest at the Carawan table and on more than one occasion had been invited to spend the night at the parsonage rather than walk back to his lodgings.

One chill Monday morning in November, 1852, Lassiter, dressed in his Sunday best, quit his rented room, left his carpet bag of belongings with a neighbour and set off to look for another job at a school on the shores of Lake Mattamuskeet, a stretch of water separated from Pamlico Sound only by a narrow strip of land. He called on old friends along the route and they were later to recall that his mind seemed full of misgivings. All he would say was that 'anybody that would try to get his wife to swear my life away would take my life any way he could.' He did not name the 'anybody,' nor the wife, nor the reason for the strange remark.

Locals, however, attributed the teacher's unease to a strange altercation in the Carawan home. The minister had accused the master of making lecherous advances towards his wife. In addition, while Mrs Carawan had been labouring to move some heavy furniture, Lassiter had (said the preacher) stood about whittling a piece of wood and smirking inanely. When the clergyman had accused him of being an ingrate, the teacher had 'swiped at me with a knife, twice across my bowels'.

According to his own story, the reverend then took a rifle from above the mantelshelf and drove the ingrate from his house, although Lassiter had stood in the roadway for some time cursing the preacher before ambling away. Carawan had then taken his wife before a justice of the peace, ordering her to swear out a warrant charging Lassiter with attempted rape.

Mary later confided to neighbours that the charges were without foundation and that the young teacher had always behaved properly towards her. But Mrs Carawan feared that her husband might kill her, so she did exactly as she was told. Lassiter sued for slander and was quickly awarded $2,000 damages.

Only a few days afterwards, Clement Lassiter, master of geography, had to pass Carawan's house on his way to the lakeside school where he hoped to get work. He was never seen alive again. Monday and Tuesday passed. A friend with whom he had left his carpet bag became anxious and informed neighbours, but no one in the community around Lake Mattamuskeet had seen the missing teacher. Despite heavy rain, they decided to search the edge of the lake, Rose Bay and the overgrown land in between, cutting their way through briers, bushes, reeds and saplings.

Wednesday, Thursday and Friday the hunt continued. Then on the Saturday a cry rose from the woods. A searcher had found disturbed land, scraped the surface and stood up with a coat lapel in his hand. Clement Lassiter had been found, spreadeagled, dead and buried. Others mounted guard all night while the alarm was raised and word sent to the coroner of Hyde County.

The coroner, Dr Bryan Griffin, and a medical assistant arrived on the Sunday and, after taking the body hog-tied to a nearby house, carried out a post-mortem examination, concluding from the injuries on his body that Lassiter had been hit by a shotgun held by a taller person behind him and slightly to the right. Shot had entered the teacher's right arm; two pellets had penetrated his heart, others were lodged in the lungs and liver. The schoolmaster had died instantly, but the medicos could not say how long he had been dead.

One man had been missing from the search and the discovery; Washington Carawan. At eleven o'clock on the Saturday night the minister had called out a ferryman to launch his canoe and take him across the Pungo River from Hyde County to Beaufort County where, he said, he wanted to buy some land. No, the deal could not wait, he said; letters had been sent on ahead and he wanted to close the contract. On landing he disappeared into the woods. By the time the Hyde County sheriff arrived next day with a warrant for his arrest the clergyman was outside his jurisdiction.

With the pastor out of the way, witnesses came forward. One was Carawan Sawyer, a great-nephew, the orphaned son of the clergyman's own niece. He helped at the Rose Bay farm and he claimed that on the Monday, Lassiter had passed the parsonage door. Soon afterwards the reverend had followed him on a parallel route to his right. Soon after that, Mrs Carawan hurried after her husband. Her apron, said Sawyer, partly covered a shotgun she was carrying.

That was the signal for Seth, the hewer of wood and drawer of water, to come forward. Seth told the sheriff how his 'massah' had ambushed Lassiter and shot him in the back. Then, just before darkness fell, Carawan had led him across fields to the woodland road near where the schoolmaster lay dead. He had ordered Seth to help him carry the body further into the woods, where they had buried it.

The State of North Carolina did not accept the testimony of slaves as evidence in court, but the strict Baptists had no such scruples. They believed Seth, and struck Carawan from membership of the church and all offices. They even apologised to the Reverend Swindell for mistrusting his judgment. The flock came forward declaring that Carawan had not only cruelly beaten both his wives, Elizabeth and Mary, but had demanded and obtained sex with threats of damnation from other men's wives and their daughters. Other slaves alleged that before the parson left he had said to them, 'Boys, they have found Lassiter's body and I must leave or stay and be hanged.' And Mrs Mary Carawan pleaded for protection claiming that she feared her husband would kill her.

There was little left of the Bible-belter's reputation when he returned the following January to Goose Creek, as if nothing had happened, announcing that he was to sell some more land. Seth saw him first, and told a neighbour, who told another, until thirty of them stealthily surrounded the Carawan home, all armed and watchful. At a signal they all advanced, entered the house, and found the reverend gentleman in his nightshirt talking to his wife.

Carawan had breakfast and was then taken to a dungeon jail where he had ten months to help his team of lawyers plan his defence. He wrote some 400 pages by candlelight in the windowless room, successfully pleading that the case be removed from Hyde County because of prejudice and be tried in Washington in Beaufort County.

The trial was thorough, the prosecution bringing thirty witnesses who told of the search and the finding of the body, Carawan's flight and subsequent arrest. Occasionally, the prisoner would jump to his feet, protesting against 'falsehoods'. One witness admitted that he was drunk but claimed he could still tell the truth, and was imprisoned overnight for contempt of court.

Telling evidence came from one of the searchers, who told the preacher he had not seen Lassiter, to which Carawan allegedly replied, 'I think it's likely that you never will.' His great-nephew Carawan Sawyer swore that the defendant had said to him, 'If you say I was home all day on Monday, I'll give you the best Negro fellow I have got.'

The preacher also condemned himself with his own

pen. The prosecution, despite strenuous defence objections, produced in evidence two letters from the prisoner which they had intercepted. One wanted the great-nephew removed by bribery or failing that by violence. He had written: 'Dear Friend . . . Whether you can get a rogue to leave or not, deliver me. You understand me. You said you had boys that would do thus and thus. Are you going to let them falsely swear me out of my life? You can fix it. I know you can . . . If he will not leave, have done otherwise; for God's sake let it be done before the court in February . . . And don't delay, for delays breed dangers. You don't live in the neighbourhood, therefore you will not be thought of. Oh, deliver me, and never more will I forget you in this life, and I hope the Lord will not in the world to come.'

The other letter asked that his wife be warned not to give evidence and both were signed, in mock disguise, 'The Old Horse in the Stable'.

The defence called six witnesses and attacked the circumstantial evidence on which the prosecution case had been based. There was much eloquence and rhetoric on both sides, as fitted the times, but Edward J. Warren, the prosecution lawyer, summed up the argument: 'What is circumstantial evidence . . . ? If a man commits theft, he does it not in the presence of his fellows. If he commits arson, or burglary, or robbery, he takes no witness with him to testify to the act. If he commits murder, if he coolly and deliberately plots the crime of blood, he seeks to perpetrate the crime where no eye can see him, and where no human sagacity can follow his footsteps. How can he be detected, or brought to answer to justice and the violated law, except by administering the rules of circumstantial evidence?'

Judge John L. Bailey warned the jury so strongly that they must set aside the evidence of tainted, perjured or corrupt witnesses that Carawan confided to his wife and three small sons, who sat through the proceedings, 'The jury will acquit me and I will go home to Hyde County on the steamboat tomorrow.'

But the jury remained out a long time and were called back to have part of the proceedings clarified. Carawan changed his mind and told his wife, 'They will hang me.' He got permission for his wife and children to spend the night with him, then next morning told them and his fellow prisoners, 'Goodbye, you will never see me again.'

The preacher-turned-prophet wept, dried his tears, returned to the courtroom at 8.30 a.m. and stood as first the foreman and then each juror returned a verdict of guilty. The judge adjourned the hearing for an hour but he had barely left the courtroom when the Reverend George Washington Carawan, sitting between his lawyers, was on his feet, undid his coat and from inside his shirt pulled a single-shot pistol, aimed it at Warren, the prosecutor, and fired. The shot hit a locket Warren wore under his clothes and bounced off.

Confusion replaced law and order. Before a deputy could wrestle Carawan to the ground, he drew another single-shot pistol, put it to his head above the right ear, and fired again, shooting himself through the brain. No one asked how a closely guarded prisoner was in possession of not merely one firearm but two.

They were content to bury the Baptist minister at the site of the Beaufort gallows he had cheated. Later his relatives had the body dug up for reburial at Rose Bay, but the neighbours objected and his earthly remains were later laid in a grave in another bay even further away from his place of preaching.

At least they found another parson to sprinkle earth on the coffin and say, 'Unless one is born of water and the Spirit, he cannot enter the kingdom of God.' No one mentioned the hewers of wood and drawers of water.

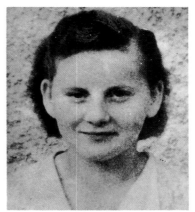

Regine Faye, aged nineteen, carried the French parish priest's baby for eight months (*Popperfoto*)

Father Guy Desnoyers demonstrates how he shot Regine dead. The church saved him from the guillotine (*Popperfoto*)

David Koresh, a High School drop-out, led the weird, sexually oriented Branch Davidian cult in Waco, Texas. Eighty-six followers, including seventeen children died in an apocalypse of fire (*Popperfoto*)

Koresh had turned the spartan former Methodist home for children into an armed ranch. This was all that remained after the fire (*Popperfoto*)

He repelled lawmen at first, but when they returned the fortress was transformed into a blazing inferno of suicide and murder (*Popperfoto*)

Jim Jones founded a People's Temple 'utopia' in Guyana (*Popperfoto*)

Hundreds of his followers died after drinking cyanide-laced soft drinks in a much-rehearsed mass suicide (*Popperfoto*)

## Chapter Sixteen

# A TABLEAU OF DEATH

'My heart is his, my life is his, all I have is his, poor as my body is . . . I am his for ever.'

Love letter from Mrs Eleanor Mills
to the Reverend Edward Wheeler Hall,
torn up and scattered around their bodies.

The couple lying under the crab-apple tree in Lovers'
Lane on the outskirts of town, he flat on his back, she
nestling in the crook of his arm with his hand on her knee,
should not have merited a second look. Lovers will be
lovers the world over and this Romeo and Juliet were no
different and not particularly attractive. He was bald,
overweight and forty-one; she was plain and uninterest-
ing at thirty-four.

What made younger flirts Raymond Schneider and his
fifteen-year-old girlfriend Pearl Bahmer look twice was
that the stretched out figures did not move. Under the
Panama hat which covered the man's face a .32 calibre
bullet had entered his brain. Under the brown scarf which
shielded the woman's countenance three .32 bullets had
entered her forehead and her throat was so badly cut she
was almost decapitated.

The dark double-breasted clerical grey suit and the
dog-collar were enough to identify the man as a parson
and the helpful murderer had left the clergyman's visiting
card at his feet. He was the Reverend Edward Wheeler
Hall, pastor of St John the Evangelist Protestant Episco-
pal Church in the well-to-do farming community of New
Brunswick, New Jersey, about thirty-five miles from New
York.

By his side in a cheap blue dress with red polka dots
was Mrs Eleanor Mills, the best singer in his church
choir, a fact to which someone had drawn attention by

cutting out her tongue, her larynx and her upper windpipe.

What made that murder on the night of September 14, 1922, one of the most sensational in American criminal history was that it had more than the usual tabloid ingredients: a parson, a chorister; wealth on his side, poverty on hers; illicit love; sex; passion; and scattered round the lovebirds, torn-up love letters they had sent one another, to and from 'Babykins', her nickname for the parson, and 'My Gipsy Queen', his name for the chorister. Her letters referred to 'the man who made me smile today' and proclaimed 'my heart is his, my life is his.'

And, ironically, the parish and the local society, which lived and breathed gossip and scandal, divided over whether they had or had not the slightest suspicion that the couple were joined in unholy love or that the affair had been going on for years. Some maintained that the couple were even planning to elope. Among the last to discover the affair, others claimed, were Mrs Frances Stevens Hall, the homely rotund wife of the minister, seven years his senior and a member of one of the wealthiest families in the area, and Mrs Mills's husband James, sexton at St John's Church.

On top of that, the police bungled the case. Two county forces, one in Middlesex, one in Somerset, fought over which should investigate the case since the Lovers' Lane marked a boundary between their jurisdictions. While the official squabbling went on, thousands of sightseers arrived at De Russey's Lane to trample the scene of the crime, strip the crab-apple tree bare and remove any clues which might have been there. The law, in the confusion, did not bother to hold immediate post-mortem examinations on the bodies, nor to hold an inquest.

The murders remained unsolved for ten months and the case was all but forgotten when police surrounded the home of the cleric's fifty-two-year-old widow Frances Stevens Hall, dragged her from her bed and charged her with killing her husband. They also arrested Mrs Hall's two brothers, Henry Stevens, a stockbroker, and Willie Stevens, who was rather odd and thought to be half-witted.

The trial was sensational. The three defendants had, in customary American fashion, been tried in advance of the jury by the news media. The New York *Mirror* had claimed that Willie Stevens' fingerprints were on the visiting card left at the dead parson's feet. Willie, however, was reckoned so eccentric that he might well have allowed himself to be persuaded by newspapermen to handle the card long after the murder had been committed. Proceedings were delayed because notwithstanding the allegations, a grand jury, which under US law vets all criminal prosecutions and returns a 'true bill' if the trial is to proceed, did not think the police had sufficient evidence to indict the trio.

However, the Governor of New Jersey exercised his legal powers to overrule the grand jury. Another newspaper had revealed that the husband of Louise Geist, a parlourmaid at the Hall parsonage, was attempting to have the marriage annulled, one of the grounds given in his petition to the court being that his wife had been bribed by Mrs Hall and her brother Willie to give false evidence before the grand jury.

The trial finally got under way at Somerville, New Jersey, on November 3, 1926, four years after the murders, presided over by Charles W. Parker, New Jersey Supreme Court Justice, and Frank L. Cleary, Somerset County Judge, presumably settling the dispute over where the murders actually took place. From the start it became a fashion show as media attention focussed on the dignified, middle-aged widow, dressed on the first day of the trial in a black corded silk coat with a squirrel collar and a black ribboned hat.

Mr Alexander Simpson, a New Jersey senator and special prosecutor, blamed the tragedy squarely on Mrs Hall. He told the jury that she had wanted to catch her husband in a compromising position with the sexton's wife, Mrs Mills. Mrs Hall had overheard her husband making a date to meet Mrs Mills in De Russey's Lane on September 14 and asked her two brothers to accompany her to the confrontation. Their crime, unfortunately for them, said police, had been witnessed by Mrs Jane Gibson. Mrs Gibson, who described herself as a fifty-four-year-old widow and pig farmer, lived in De Russey's Lane, and on the night in question had seen shadowy figures in the act of killing the unholy lovers. There had been shouts of 'Don't, don't, don't!' and the name 'Henry' (one of Mrs Hall's brothers) had been mentioned.

When the young couple found the bodies on September 16, the older couple had been dead for thirty-six hours. The position of the bodies – he flat on his back, she in the crook of his arm, her left hand on his right knee – suggested a theatrical tableau deliberately arranged after death, for the impact of the bullets would almost certainly have upset any such posture if it had been natural.

The scarf removed from the singer's face revealed that

her throat had been cut from ear to ear right down to her chin and her wounds were covered in maggots, crawling witnesses to the length of time she had lain dead. The Reverend Hall's pockets were empty and his gold watch and a $50 bill were missing. His pocket book containing a driving licence, masonic and YMCA cards was scattered with the torn-up love letters on the grass, and the visiting card at his feet, appropriately printed in ecclesiastic Gothic lettering, identified him and his church.

Mr Simpson insisted that the idea of a suicide pact was ruled out by the nature of the wounds, by the emptying of the cleric's pockets, the disappearance of the $50 bill and the gold watch and the absence of any weapons near to the bodies. He felt he had a duty to tell the jury that a media-spread rumour that the priest had had his penis amputated and stuck in the chorister's mouth had been proved untrue by the autopsy report.

The love letters, written in pencil on cheap notepaper, included such passages as: 'There isn't a man who could make me smile as you did today. I know there are girls with more shapely bodies, but I do not care what they have. I have the greatest of all blessings, the deep, true and eternal love of a noble man . . .' 'My heart is his, my life is his, all I have is his, poor as my body is, scrawny as they say my skin may be, but I am his for ever . . .' 'I want to look up into your dear face for hours as you touch my body close.'

John S. Dickson, a Wall Street accountant, and his wife, who lived at North Plainfield, ten miles north of New Brunswick, told how a man called on them at 8.30 p.m. on the night of the murders. Mr Dickson said the caller said he was Willie Stevens and asked to be directed to Parker House old people's home where he had relatives. 'I thought he was drunk. He was agitated. He was anxious to get out of the neighbourhood.'

Mr and Mrs Dickson accompanied the caller to the trolley-bus stop and on the way the man said he was an epileptic. Unfortunately, both witnesses said the stranger did not wear glasses, but Willie Stevens could not walk anywhere without his spectacles because of his defective sight.

Charlotte Mills, twenty-year-old daughter of the murdered woman, identified a number of her mother's letters to the minister and said that she had a habit of leaving them for him in a big black book on the second shelf from the bottom of the bookcase in his study.

On the night of the murder, after dinner, Mrs Mills had cut out from the New York *World* an article by a well-known Episcopalian churchman advocating the liberalising of the church's canon law on divorce. She wanted to show it to the preacher, who was trying to make a date to see her. The Mills did not have a telephone and a neighbour brought the telephone message. Mrs Mills then left the house to phone the clergyman 'to see if there was anything he wanted'. That was the last time, said Charlotte, she saw her mother alive.

Miss Mills identified a second package of letters in the parson's handwriting which used to be kept in a crocheted bag which hung on the back of the living-room door. The bag also contained a diary in the minister's handwriting. The daughter (who had been working on the murder case for the New York *World*) said that her father had been given $500 for the letters by another newspaper but she did not know whether he had ever bothered to read them.

Mrs Ann Hoag, who lived near the scene of the crime,

took the stand wearing a fur coat and a fashionable turban, and told the jury that she had heard four shots at about ten o'clock on the night of the murder. A year later Henry Stevens, dressed in a dark suit and Panama hat, called to ask the way to Raritan which was up-river from the murder scene. 'I asked him to sit down and he sat on the porch. I thought the man was sick because he trembled so. Then he talked on Florida for a while. Then all at once he said, "Wasn't there a tragedy on this place?" and I said, "I know nothing about any tragedy." And with that I ran into the house because I was frightened.'

After that, the visitor walked to the local pump for water. 'Then I came out to watch him. I had my dog with me and I watched him [go] up the lane and the man nearly collapsed when he passed the place where the bodies were found, he nearly collapsed.'

Although, she said, Stevens had told her he was out for a walk, Mrs Hoag was convinced that there was a car waiting for him near De Russey's Lane. 'He must have had a car because he was so immaculate.'

Drama continued when the prosecution produced the visiting card from the murder scene and claimed it bore an unmistakable thumbprint of Willie Stevens. It was quickly proved by fingerprint experts to have been fraudulently superimposed over another. Then it was revealed that the state's star witness, pig farmer Mrs Gibson, was too ill to give evidence. The judges promptly adjourned and hurried to the hospital where she was being treated for cancer of the kidneys.

Sexton James Mills, husband of the murdered woman, said Mrs Hall had called on him soon after the bodies were found. It was he who suggested that her husband

and his wife were going to elope. To this she replied bluntly, 'They're dead.' Under cross-examination, he confessed that, despite his earlier denials, he had read a good part of the clergyman's love letters to his wife. Asked if he had not told a detective at the time of the murders that he had quarrelled with his wife because of her affair with the minister, he said he could not remember.

The former parlourmaid, whose marital troubles had prompted the Governor of New Jersey to order the trial, was another failure for the prosecution. Louise Geist told the court that her husband's affidavit of her being bribed to give false evidence had been nonsense. He had married her, she said, only to obtain from her the under-stairs secrets of the murderers. He discovered too late that she did not know anything about the affair and he had brought the annulment suit and charges out of revenge.

Mrs Gibson, the much-publicised pig farmer, was later brought to court on a stretcher, attended by a nurse and a doctor who kept taking her pulse. Because she groaned and grunted constantly and because she kept pigs she was immediately and unkindly dubbed 'the Pig Woman' by the media. In a weak voice she related how a few nights before the murders a thief had robbed her of four rows of Indian corn. To try to catch him if he returned for more, she tied her dog to a tree between her shanty home and the corn field. The dog began barking and she went out and could, at first, see nothing. But in her search, mounted on her mule, she had lost her slipper.

Looking for it, she saw two men and two women quarrelling in the lane. One of the couples, a white-haired woman and a bushy-haired man, were standing beneath the crab-apple tree. 'Explain these letters,' the white-haired woman had cried. There was a struggle. Something silvery glinted in the moonlight. The man shouted, 'Let's go.' The other woman screamed, four shots were fired and the Pig Woman fled.

Shown pictures of Mrs Hall and Willie Stevens, the witness showed no hesitation in identifying the white-haired woman and the bushy-haired man as Mrs Hall and her brother Willie Stevens. At this, the defence's secret weapon spoke up. They had tracked down the Pig Woman's mother, who, unseen by her daughter, occupied a prominent seat in the courtroom.

Suddenly, the mother shouted, 'She's a liar, a liar, a liar. That's what she is and that's what she has always been!' The Pig Woman, it was claimed, had made up the story for newspaper publicity and the money it might bring her. She had actually boasted, 'I'll be the Babe Ruth of the trial,' a reference to George Herman 'Babe' Ruth (1895–1948) regarded by some as the greatest baseball player of all time.

Mrs Gibson's evidence was further discredited when the defence counsel tested her memory in cross-examination and discovered that she could no longer remember the simplest things such as whom she had married, when and where, and whether she had been divorced. Nevertheless, after the scandal had ended in acquittals, the Pig Woman went to her death four years later still insisting that Mrs Hall and the two Stevens brothers had got away with murder.

Mrs Hall, in the witness box, was cool and self-possessed. She denied the Pig Woman's story, saying she had played no part in the tragedy. As far as she knew, she said, her husband was devoted to her and his conduct had never given her any cause to suspect his morals.

She had known Eleanor Mills as a chorister and an active churchgoer and had helped her with her hospital and doctors' bills made necessary by a kidney operation. She knew that her husband received letters from Eleanor but 'they were, as near as I remember, descriptions of evening services at church.'

On the night of the murders, as a result of a telephone call from Mrs Mills, her husband said that he must go and see the sexton (Mr Mills) about his wife's hospital bills. She was surprised how long he was away from home. She woke her brother Willie, who lived with them, and they both went to look for him. They went to the sexton's house but they could get no answer. They thought he might have fallen asleep in the church, but the church was empty and also in darkness.

She was asked why she did not alert the police sooner. Mrs Hall said that early next morning, although she did not give her name, she rang the police and asked if there had been any accidents in the neighbourhood. She was told there had been none. As a result, she contacted a number of members of her husband's family and instructed a lawyer to carry on the investigation from there.

Asked why she had sent a brown coat, believed to be stained with blood, to a dyer soon after the murders, she retorted that she wanted a black coat for the funeral.

Walrus-moustached Willie Stevens was no more shaken by the cross-examination than his sister. The eccentric brother who used to ride around town on fire trucks in a specially tailored fireman's uniform, corroborated Mrs Hall's account of how she had wakened him and they had gone to the church together, and how they had returned home without finding her husband. 'If a person sees me go upstairs and doesn't see me come downstairs isn't that a conclusion that I was in my room?'

Prosecutor Senator Simpson said, 'Certainly.'

'Well, that's all there is to it.'

By the fifth week of the trial the strain was beginning to show. Simpson appealed to the judges to declare a mistrial because the jurors were not paying proper attention to his arguments. The judges refused. Robert J. McCarter, for the defence, suggested that Mrs Gibson, the Pig Woman, might have shot the clergyman and the chorister because she thought they were stealing her corn.

Senator Simpson interpreted Mrs Hall's coolness as a lack of emotion at her husband's death. She was a Messalina, the immoral third wife executed by her husband, the Roman Emperor Claudius; a Lucretia Borgia, who committed incest with her father, the Pope; and a 'Bloody Mary', the Tudor queen who had persecuted Protestants. He pointed at Mrs Hall and asked the jury, 'Has she even batted an eyelid?'

On December 6, 1926, the all-male jury returned a verdict of not guilty in the case of all four defendants. Mrs Hall and her two brothers, and the fourth, Henry Carpender, a cousin of Mrs Hall, awaiting separate trial on a charge of complicity in the murders, were all released. New Jersey taxpayers had to foot a hefty bill to pay for the police investigation and the trial. The Hall family had spent a fortune arguing their freedom but they sued the New York *Mirror* for $3 million, eventually accepting a generous out-of-court settlement. James Mills, the church sexton, said, 'Money can buy anything.'

The Hall-Mills case remains one of the great unsolved mysteries of all time. More than forty years later William

M. Kunstler, a New York civil rights lawyer, produced new evidence that the killings were the work of the Ku Klux Klan, which was well represented in New Jersey at the time. The KKK was not only racist but sometimes a fierce defender of the church's strict moral code. And that included the seventh commandment, 'Thou shalt not commit adultery.'

Sixty years after the tableau of death, a holy killer who showed no respect whatever for the sanctity of marriage left no doubt as to his guilt.

Imagine the grief among the congregation when it is announced that the minister's wife has died. The euphemisms for death are used aplenty. She passed away, was taken from us, paid her debt to nature, answered the last summons, crossed the river Jordan to the other side. There is something in the character of a clergyman's wife which demands such carefully worded sympathy. A woman, mother, counsellor, friend – indeed she represents the very heart of so many faiths.

In the ministry of the Reverend Donald Lewis Clark, it was particularly sad when his first wife died, but what about the second and the third? Lutheran worshippers at the Macedonia United Brethren Church at Greencastle, Pennsylvania, were asked to pray for Norma, the first (about whom they knew nothing, neither how she died or even where her birth, marriage or death were registered); for Phyllis, the second, who appeared to have had an accident on the stairs; and Ronaele, the third, who took a bath into which fell an electric heater.

The Reverend Clark, a chubby, bespectacled father-figure, appeared thrice grief-stricken. Then the services, hymns and dirges were interrupted by a police investigation which was conducted more by perusing accounts books than prayer books.

Clark, a native of Marion, Alabama, had served in the United States Navy in his early twenties, and it was at this time that his first wife, Norma, suddenly vanished without trace. He then wed Phyllis Miller at Hagerstown, Maryland. She bore him two daughters and for twenty years he supported the family working as an advertising salesman and later as a typesetter in a commercial printers. At the same time he served as a lay minister and the strong call of the Lutheran faith made him quit business for the church full-time.

The pastor was forty-five years old when he was ordained and installed as the minister of Lurgan United Brethren Church near Shipensberg, Pennsylvania. Four years later, when he was approaching fifty, he took on the work at Greencastle in the same state. On October 17, 1981, his wife, Phyllis, a usually healthy and robust woman, complained of excruciatingly painful stomach cramps. She fell down the stairs in the parsonage and was admitted to hospital where she died seven days later. The Reverend Clark was so distressed that no one thought it odd that he asked the doctors not to perform a post-mortem because she was so beautiful and it would be a desecration of one of God's creatures. One close friend said the minister took her death so badly 'he went off the highway.'

He added, 'We were driving with him on a small mission when he suddenly made an expression that I never dreamed I would ever hear from a minister of God. It was so blue that he got it into his head to let go of the wheel and let the car go where it would.'

The church elders feared for the state of his mind and for the welfare of his congregation and on February 28, 1983, passed a motion of no confidence in him. He resigned and was due to move out of the clergy-house on a month's notice. What the elders and most of the congregation did not know was that in the January he had secretly married forty-year-old Ronaele 'Candy' Rotz, wife number three. She was a religious woman; a chorister at the First Evangelical Lutheran Church, a member of the Lutheran Church Women and the Altar Guild, and she taught at Sunday School. The minister had put his age on the marriage certificate as forty-six instead of fifty-three. He had told his bride he was an undercover drug squad detective so he registered his occupation not as a 'minister of religion' but 'policeman'.

For some reason, the couple did not occupy the same address. He may have anticipated being sacked from the ministry for he remained in the parsonage a month after the expiry date while she lived at Chambersburg ten miles away. On April 7, 1983, she was found dead in the bath. With her in the water was an electric fan heater.

The fact that the preacher had described himself on his marriage certificate as a 'policeman', which he was not, alerted the investigating officers to other suspicions. Clark had received $50,000 in benefits from a life insurance policy on his second wife, Phyllis, which he had taken out in April, 1981, only six months before she died.

On January 28, 1983, eight days after his marriage to Candy, he had insured his bride for $50,000. Under the policy, if she died accidentally he would receive $200,000. At the same time he had agreed to buy a house from a local estate agent for $89,000, although he had lost his ministry, his only source of income, and did not own any property on which to raise that sort of money.

Detectives never solved the mystery of the first wife, Norma. After her body was exhumed and a post-mortem performed they concluded that his second wife, Phyllis, had been weakened by small, repeated doses of arsenic before she fell downstairs in extreme pain and died. The third wife, Candy, according to medical evidence, had been struck on the back of the head by a pointed instrument, had been placed in the water unconscious and a 'live' electric fan heater thrown in after her, killing her. In addition, they had traced a teenager Clark had been courting with promises of marriage at the same time as he was asking Candy to marry him.

Armed with search and arrest warrants, police called at the parsonage and found the Reverend Donald Lewis Clark naked on the bathroom floor, dead from poisoning. Five suicide notes lay around him.

The debate about the background of the Reverend Clark continued long after his death. Everything was queried, even his qualifications to become a minister in the first place, although these were defended by the church elders. But such arguments are typical of the controversies which holy killings arouse.

*Chapter Seventeen*

# MISSION OF MURDER

'He felt that the Latter Day Saints' religion
was a fairy-tale, and he wanted all Mormons
to know that they had been misled.'

Former girlfriend of Mark Hofmann.

Most young housewives have at some time in their lives answered the doorbell or knocker to a handsome, well-groomed young American male with a smile and an engaging conversation about the benefits of becoming a Mormon. Mark William Hofmann, a good-looking nineteen-year-old with a mop of black hair and a cherubic grin, spent almost two years in the 1970s as such a missionary in the Bristol area of England. It was the dutiful religious task for those brought up as Mark had been, in a family who strictly adhered to the teaching of the Church of Jesus Christ of Latter Day Saints, to spread the word, just as their forefathers had done for a century and a half.

The difference was that Mark and others passed on the message of the restoration of the one and only true gospel of Christ, while their forebears had encouraged members to enter into polygamous marriages and obey the injunction, 'Go forth and multiply.'

Mark Hofmann returned from Bristol to Salt Lake City, Utah and enrolled at the state university where he fell in love with a music student, Kate Reid. Meanwhile he developed an interest in rare and antique books and manuscripts, some of which he thought threw doubt on the beliefs passed on by the founder of the Mormon faith, Joseph Smith. Kate talked to Mark about his beliefs and eventually rejected him after 'Mark professed to me that he was an atheist and wished me to share this belief. He felt that the Latter Day Saints' religion was a fairy-tale, and he wanted all Mormons to know that they had been misled.'

In 1979 Mark married Doralee Olds, a homely local girl, by whom he had three children. His interest in old papers had multiplied when he found a 'blessing' from the hand of Joseph Smith himself, pinned in an old Bible. Other historic Mormon letters which came into his possession included a document signed by Martin Harris, the first person converted to Mormonism by Smith. In November, 1983, Hofmann sold this missive, known as the Salamander Letter, to a benefactor of the Mormon Church for $40,000. Other valuable manuscripts followed.

Another Hofmann triumph came when he told the Mormon Church that he had found the papers of William McLellin, a one-time disciple of Smith, who had become disillusioned in 1838 and left the Church. He asked the Church for $185,000 to buy the collection.

Rumours suggested that the epistles were forgeries. They contained passages which threw doubts on fundamental parts of Mormon history and the documents had not yet been made public after the purchase. That was the position, when on Tuesday, October 15, 1985, three bombs exploded in Salt Lake City, killing two people and seriously injuring a third.

Bruce Passey, a jeweller, remembered travelling that morning in the lift of the Judge Building in the business section of the city with a dark-haired young man, who was wearing a green jacket with leather sleeves and carrying a parcel addressed to Steve Christensen. Just before 8 a.m. Janet McDonald, a saleswoman with the Minnesota Mutual Life Company in the same building, noticed a dark-haired man walking quickly away from her. That was odd, she thought, because he was going along a corridor which led nowhere. She then noticed a box leaning against the door of suite 609, the office of Steve Christensen and his partner, Randy Rigby.

It was addressed to Christensen, looked like a present, and Janet wondered whether she should take it into her office for safe-keeping. She decided not to do so because she suddenly remembered a telephone call she had to make. The young, stocky, dark-haired stranger walked back from the cul-de-sac corridor and vanished. And Steve Christensen, her neighbour, entered his own sanctum.

Within seconds, a terrific explosion rocked the building. Janet thought the wall opposite her was flying through the air. What was left of the corridor and the offices opposite almost buried Christensen, his face blackened, one of his eyes missing, his mouth making the whimpering sounds of a child. Within minutes he was dead.

Ninety minutes later, out in the suburb of Holladay, Kathy Sheets returned from her brisk morning walk. She was fifty years of age, the wife of Gary Sheets, millionaire head of the CFS (Coordinated Financial Services) Corporation. Propped against their garage door she saw a parcel addressed to her husband. She picked it up, tucked it under her arm, and bent down to pick up the morning paper, when the second bomb exploded.

Police were still interviewing bystanders and passers-by at 2.30 p.m., six and a half hours after the first explosion, when a dark-haired young man walked out of the gymnasium on Main Street, unlocked the door of his blue Toyota sports car, and leaned inside to pick up a package from the seat. A loud explosion followed. The car was wrecked; the motorist blown backwards with a hole in his head, his fingers blown off; and he looked as if he had lost a knee-cap. He was Mark Hofmann.

What was the connection between the three bombs and the three victims? Christensen had been a vice-president of Sheets' financial services company which was in grave financial trouble, and fears had been expressed that many investors would be ruined. Connecting Hofmann to the other two was more difficult.

Hofmann, in a hospital bed, connected to a saline drip and a heart monitor with nurses in attendance, said he could remember driving to the gym and noticed that he was being followed by a light tan pick-up truck. He had made a note of its licence number and written it down in his notebook. When he returned to his car he had noticed a parcel on the seat, and wondered what it was. When he opened the door, it exploded and that was all he remembered.

The police bag-man, who collects pieces of removable forensic evidence, searched Hofmann's home. He could not find the licence number of the pick-up truck in the notebook to which he had been directed. He did find a green jacket with leather sleeves similar to that worn by the man in the lift. In the boot of Hofmann's Toyota was a pair of rubber gloves and a length of piping. All the exploded bombs had been made with lengths of piping but not one fragment bore fingerprints. Amongst the debris left by the bomb which killed Kathy Sheets was discovered a fragment of black plastic bearing the name of 'Radio Shack', a well-known nationwide retailer of electronic parts.

Detectives went through the receipt books of every

Utah branch of the business. At one outlet they discovered that a plastic battery holder and mercury switch, the kind employed in the making of bombs, had been sold to 'M. Hansen'. The date of the purchase was October 9, six days before the explosions. The address on the receipt proved to be fictitious, but in the Hofmann house the officers found a piece of paper bearing the name 'M. Hansen' and a telephone number. Again, no fingerprints could be found on any of the documents.

The fact that the initials of M. Hansen and M. Hofmann were the same bothered the police. They were certain that Hofmann was the bomber, and that the Mormon Church was a significant factor in the murders, but they did not have sufficient evidence to prosecute the chubby, smiling, former missionary. He left hospital on crutches a free man.

The Salt Lake City police included many faithful Mormons who found the investigation distasteful, but they were meticulous in their pursuit of the killer.

One seemingly good clue was the telephone number against the name of M. Hansen which they had found in Hofmann's house. It bore no dialling code but was eventually traced to an address over the state border in Colorado. It belonged to Cock's Clark, an engraving shop, but there was no M. Hansen there.

A tour of engravers in Salt Lake City took them to DeBouzek Engraving. A detective handed the engraver a postcard-sized piece of paper titled *Oath of a Freeman*. Hofmann had claimed to have discovered one of fifty copies of that original document which was printed in the American colonies in 1658. The oath written on it was sworn by twenty or so self-styled freemen of the Massachusetts Bay Company. It was a unique historic document because it bore no words of allegiance to the English monarch, Charles I, who then ruled the American colonies. And all fifty copies of the original were thought by historians to have disappeared for good or even been destroyed many years ago.

Hofmann claimed to have found that one original in a collection of old English colonial pamphlets which he bought as a job lot for little more than $50 from an antiquarian bookseller in New York. Kenneth Rendell, an expert on historical documents, who had been called in to prove that the so-called Hitler Diaries were a hoax, certified that Hofmann's copy of the oath was genuine. Valuers said it was worth $1.5 million, the price it could fetch if offered to the US Library of Congress.

The engraver at DeBouzek's put on his spectacles, placed the document under a powerful lamp, and said, 'Yes, I made that to order. I should know my own craftsmanship.' The artist pulled down a receipt book from the shelf and added that it had been ordered by a 'Mike Hansen' and had been paid by personal cheque by a 'Mike Hofmann'.

Another investigator was looking at a number of documents, including the Mormon Salamander Letter, all sold by Hofmann, and had them analysed by Bill Flynn, a document examiner from Arizona. Flynn knew that while ancient inks did not crack when dry but turned to a rusty brown, forgers used gum Arabic which when it dries forms many tiny cracks, like a mosaic, which can only be seen when placed under a powerful microscope. Flynn saw cracks.

Another expert who had declared the Salamander Letter genuine was now no longer convinced. In those far-off days people wrote on one side of a piece of paper, then folded the four corners into the centre, forming it into a natural envelope, and sealed it with wax. The Letter was only folded three ways. The seal was wrongly positioned. And there were discrepancies in the hand-writing.

Yet another document analyst, Roderick McNeil, con-cluded that none of Hofmann's ancient documents was earlier than 1970!

Even so, if Hofmann had sold all these historic finds as he had planned they would have made him a millionaire. Why then would he murder Steve Christensen and Mrs Sheets, albeit with a bomb intended for her once-wealthy husband, Gary?

The elders of the Mormon Church had the explanation. The Church had arranged a bank loan for Hofmann to buy the McLellin collection, but he had not delivered the manuscripts and he was late with his repayments. They had asked Christensen to collect the money due from him. They did not know that the McLellin collection was still in the possession of Otis Traughber of Houston, Texas, who had never even heard of Mr Hofmann let alone sold anything to him. At the same time, Hofmann owed investors in his rare books and manuscripts com-pany $400,000.

The only solution to pressing debts and to being found out, in Hofmann's mind, was to kill Christensen, the debt collector. Then, knowing that Christensen had connec-tions with Sheets, who was in financial difficulties, he should kill Sheets as a diversion. Police would think the bombing was entirely a matter between the two victims. When Christensen was dead, no one would be able to prove that Hofmann had not repaid the money he owed. No one could connect him directly with Sheets.

Hofmann's own lawyer, Ronald Yengich, had described the prosecution's tale of forgery and murder as 'bull'. But when prosecutors arrived at the defence lawyer's house, the murderer, free on bail, was there and described in detail how he had made the bombs. He claimed that he was ashamed and had tried to commit suicide by blowing himself up. Prosecutors did not believe him. They thought the third bomb had gone off by accident. And eventually the forger and murderer was sentenced to life imprisonment without hope of parole.

It was by no means the first time the Mormon faith had had to suffer the indignities of its members falling foul of the law. The religion was founded in 1830 by Joseph Smith. Adherents were guided by the book of Mormon, which purported to be a record of certain ancient peoples, written originally by the prophet Mormon on golden plates and discovered and translated by Smith between 1827 and 1830.

Acceptability of the new faith was made difficult by a number of its beliefs, particularly that of polygamy. The prospect of marriage to an unlimited number of wives guaranteed crowded churches and packed prayer meetings. But to its critics it was criminal, and to other powerful religious authorities it was anathema.

Abraham, according to Smith, had been a polygamist by divine command, and continuing the works of Abraham was the only way which led to eternal salvation. When Smith told this divine revelation to his wife, Emma, she threw him out of the marital home. She was not the only disbeliever. Although Smith acquired a number of wives his religious activities were halted in a dramatic manner.

310

As mayor of Nauvoo, Illinois, he had attacked newspapers hostile to Mormonism (although there had been no official public reference to polygamy) and had the city marshal and troops destroy the printing press. As a result, Smith and his brother, Hyrum, were held in jail on charges of treason for their assault on such a fundamental liberty as the freedom of the Press. On June 27, 1844, a lynch mob with blackened faces broke into the jail and murdered the two brothers.

Brigham Young, the painter and decorator who became the Mormon leader, Lion of the Lord, was powerful in build, ideas and action. He and his followers, persecuted and hounded, trekked across the arid deserts of America to reach their final home in Salt Lake City, capital of the future state of Utah.

Although Young had said it was 'better to feed the Indians than kill them', travelling Mormons became involved in a number of battles from which they did not emerge with credit, notably the Utah Indian War (1849–50), the Walker War (1853–54) and the Black Hawk War (1865–68). Biggest embarrassment to them was the work of fanatical Mormon Bishop John Doyle Lee, who became an Indian agent in the early 1850s. He intended the post to make him rich; arming his white followers and renegades, in 1857 he dressed them as Indians and began attacking wagon trains heading for California, falsely claiming that the migrants were rival settlers who would take their land in Utah. With a large body of men, Lee stopped a wagon train of 140 immigrants at Mountain Meadows but after three days of fighting there was no victory. Lee, fearing a lengthy stalemate or having to let them proceed, sent word that they should lay down their arms to prevent antagonising the 'Indians' any further. If they surrendered, giving up their gold and some of their livestock, they could continue their journey in peace.

The immigrants threw down their arms and came out of their defensive circle of wagons. Lee ordered them to be slaughtered. Only seventeen children, who could be used to expand the faith, were spared. It was not until 1875 that the truth about the Mountain Massacre was discovered.

Lee was tried, but the jury could not agree. Tried again a year later and convicted of first degree murder, he was taken to the scene of the massacre and shot dead.

By then Brigham Young, the black-bearded pulpiteer, had expounded the doctrine of polygamy to a conference of missionaries in Salt Lake City. Many Mormons already had more than one wife, but the idea of publicising and boasting about it put them in a turmoil. They feared the civil law would punish them.

Young himself acquired so many wives he lost count. Various writers put it at between nineteen and fifty, but the true figure was probably twenty-seven, and he fathered fifty-six children. A memorial stone to the Mormon leader says, 'Brigham Young born on this spot, 1801, a man of courage and superb equipment.'

Young reassured his followers, 'The Revelation [of polygamy] will ride triumphantly above all the prejudice and priestcraft of the day. It will be fostered and believed in by the more intelligent portions of the world as one of the best doctrines ever proclaimed to any people.'

The first major scandal to rock the Church over the practice of polygamy was the defection of Ann Eliza Webb Young, Young's twenty-seventh wife. She was the most influential and favourite of his wives, until she fled the marital home, told the world what happened in the

Young *ménage*, gave lectures on 'My Life Of Bondage' and rallied disaffected Mormons and opponents to her side.

She won $9,500 alimony. When Young refused to pay it he was jailed, but the judge who made the order was dismissed from office. When the amount of money was reduced to $3,600, Young hesitated but, warned that all his assets could be seized in the event of non-payment, paid up.

This century was only two years old when the body of Mrs Joseph P. Pullitzer was found in a ditch near Newark, New Jersey. A very heavy iron brake-shoe usually tied to wagons and put under wheels on steep hills was tied round her neck. Police checked with livery stables in New York and New Jersey and found one carriage had been let out to William Hooper Young and returned without the tie-weight.

Police thought they had a double-celebrity killer and victim, Young and Pullitzer, on their hands. Mrs Pullitzer, though, did not belong to the family of the famous Joseph Pulitzer (1847–1911) newspaper owner and founder of the literary and journalistic prizes which still bear his name. But the missing killer who had hired the buggy was notable.

William Hooper Young was the idle, thriftless grandson of the Mormon leader, Brigham Young. Since he had been expelled from the Mormon Church he had been making a living on the name of his illustrious forebears, sometimes speaking in their favour, sometimes against. He escaped the police posse seeking him and travelled to upstate New York, posing as a tramp and avoiding law officers for many months.

Without using his famous name he could earn or beg little, so he was identified, confessed that his act of murder was downright sadism, was found guilty and sent to the electric chair.

The Mormon Church is no more prone to murderous scandals than any other denomination. Nevertheless, the faith attracts its share of killers. Roger W. Downs was a Mormon missionary to the motor-cycle gangs who rode the flats around Salt Lake City. Like so many teenagers they needed counselling and the prospect of salvation from a wasteful future. The missionary's neighbours thought that while Downs himself was bespectacled, moustached, quiet, reserved, neatly dressed and soft-spoken, the visitors to his modest home – dubbed by bikers 'the nesting place' – were coarse, noisy and behaved like vandals. Quarrelling and fighting were frequent and there had been complaints against them, even of arson.

For nearly four years Salt Lake City police had been troubled by the disappearance of five young boys. Two were only four years old, one was six, one eleven and the eldest thirteen. All came from middle-class homes. In none of the cases was there any clear evidence of abduction, but the more police looked at the mounting file of missing boys the more they suspected the work of a sexual deviant.

On October 6, 1979, Alonzo Daniels, aged four, with a mass of dark curly hair, asked his mother's permission to go out to play. She wrapped him up against the cold and told him not to wander too far from the front door; but in spite of her warnings he vanished. Little more than a year later, on November 8, 1980, tousle-haired Claude Kimley

Peterson, an eleven-year-old with an impish grin, picked up his roller-skates and announced that he was going to sell them to a man. He was never seen again.

Eleven months went by and on October 25, 1981, Danny Davis, four years old, his blond hair cut in a fringe, went to the supermarket with his grandfather. One moment Danny was gazing at the bubble-gum machine, next he was gone. A child answering Danny's description had been seen near a blue car but the car was never found. July 22, 1983, was Troy Ward's sixth birthday and he lisped through his two missing front teeth that he was going to be given a motor-cycle ride by a friend as a present. Troy never returned.

While there were gaps of approximately a year between the dates each of the first four boys vanished, only twenty-two days elapsed before the next lad went out and did not return. Graeme Cunningham, always brushing his hair out of his eyes, was older; more mature; wanted to become an air pilot; would love to give his mother a ride in a Lear jet. His mother, impressed by his grown-up approach to life, bought him a small number of shares in a company for his future. On Thursday, July 14, he said he was meeting 'a friend at the grocery store and I'll be right back'. He too was never seen again.

Mr and Mrs Cunningham did not know the name of Graeme's friend. Police interviewed his class-mates one by one and discovered that one of them, Leon, had gone on a trip to California with his stepfather two days after Graeme had melted into thin air. The stepfather's address, a rented brick bungalow, was vacant. When the police fed his name into their computer the print-out read, 'Roger W. Downs, also known as Arthur W. Davis, aged 32, book-keeper, last known employed by lumber yard at Murray, Utah. Missionary to motorcycle gangs. Arrest warrants issued in name of Downs alleging forgery . . . Also sought re violation of probation . . .'

Salt Lake City broadcast an alert but to their surprise, on Sunday, July 24, ten days after Graeme's disappearance, Mrs Cunningham opened her front door to find Downs on the doorstep. 'I'm Leon's stepfather. I've been out of town,' he said, 'and I've just heard about Graeme. I thought I'd better come straight round and say how sorry I am . . .'

Mrs Cunningham, who had been waiting constantly by the phone for any news of her son, knew police were looking for Downs. She invited him inside, kept him talking, and when her husband returned he called the police, who asked him to keep Downs in conversation to give them time to reach the Cunningham home.

'The police want to talk to you,' said Cunningham evenly. 'Can you wait twenty minutes?'

'Twenty minutes! I can wait a week if I can help find Graeme.'

While officers were searching for the wanted man, investigators had profiled a wide range of abductors. They described child molesters who touch, pet, cuddle and fondle children; paedophiles who have sex with the under-aged; and deviants who sodomise, torture and kill their victims.

Officers were certain the abductor was one of the latter but they could not imagine why he would wait a year between victims to satisfy his wilful lust. Then it occurred to them that the missionary might be entertaining his bikers to pornographic movies for which innocent children had to be recruited as live participants, 'film stars' who were then expendable.

From Downs's stepson Leon they learned that the older man was not really his stepfather at all, but had merely taken him in after the boy's own father had been stabbed in a street brawl.

Leon's account was fed, incident by incident, back to the book-keeper and eventually he confessed. He led them to a number of shallow graves within a sixty-five-mile radius where they found the bodies of the five missing boys. One had been shot, one had been strangled, three had been beaten to death. While lawyers prepared to charge him with five first degree murders, police completed their own file on the killer.

Neither Downs nor Davis was his real name. He was really Arthur G. Bishop, also known as Lyn E. Jones, aged thirty, one of nine children from Hinckley, Utah, 180 miles southwest of Salt Lake City. He had been an honours student, an Eagle Scout, a Mormon missionary in the Philippines for two years and for most of his life a devout and active member of the Mormon Church. Only shortly before the boys began to disappear did the Church throw him out, but they refused to give the reason – as a matter of church policy – for the excommunication even after he was arrested.

Downs could have been expelled for sexual offences against children or embezzling employers of between $18,000 and $20,000. He changed his name several times and his jobs often; and police just prayed that if any church ever expelled someone for such offences again, they might just glean in advance an idea of what a holy killer looked like.

They closed the file thankfully with a line straight from Noel Coward. 'Uncle Harry's not a missionary now.'

317

*Chapter Eighteen*

# HARE KRISHNA, HARE KRISHNA

'I have done my work . . . I have done my work.'

John Tierney (Navaniticara),
killer of James Immel (Jayatirtha).

The world has never been short of religious cults, which offer more attractive rites and ceremonies than those of conventional worship, or fanatics, who claim to perform better miracles than those previously recorded. They promise to out-perform the Biblical prophets and in the attempt may even offer suicide or murder in the name of the Almighty as part of their great plans.

Margaret Peter, a Swiss, decided that she had to be crucified if Satan was to be defeated. She ordered her followers to murder her, nail her to the cross and wait three days for her to rise again. They did so but when she did not rise, a local clergyman called the police who had the disciples jailed.

James Naylor claimed he was the new Messiah, and rode into Bristol on an ass, just as Christ rode into Jerusalem. Women cried, 'Holy, holy, holy is the Lord God of Israel' and threw down their cloaks beneath the animal's hoofs. Naylor was sentenced to have his tongue burned and his forehead branded with the letter B for Blasphemer. He was whipped and imprisoned in a damp cell where he died.

While most latterday messiahs have tried to imitate the works of Christ, some invented their own religions. Charles Manson of California believed in free love, drug experiments and oddball religious ceremonies. In 1969 he ordered members of his 'Family' to break into the home of film director Roman Polanski where they shot, stabbed and clubbed his pregnant wife, Sharon Tate, and four others. The following night they repeated the act by slaughtering Leonard and Rosemary Le Bianca. Manson, described by the prosecution as 'one of the most evil, satanic men who ever walked the face of the earth' and three of his female followers were sentenced to death, a sentence commuted to life imprisonment.

Today's continuing nightmare surrounds the activities of the Hare Krishna movement in Britain and elsewhere. The shaven heads of the disciples, the saffron robes, the sandalled feet, the sacred hand cymbals are all a familiar sight as they jingle to the continuous chant of 'Hare Krishna, Hare Krishna . . .' They wend their way from their Soho Street, London, headquarters to Oxford Street and beyond, wherever there are people with money to give. How many who give money suspect that it is to finance the taking of sons and daughters from their homes or riches from their parents or to finance communes featuring child abuse, torture, prostitution, illicit drug dealing, arson, and murder?

The London centre of the movement is just one of a world-wide chain in sixty different countries, with many thousands of followers funded by many millions in sterling, dollars and other currencies. They all belong to the International Society for Krishna Consciousness (ISKCON), started by A. C. Bhaktivedanta Swami Prabhupada with less than £5 in 1965. When he died in 1977 he had built an international empire.

The movement was founded with the best of intentions to preach a development of a well-known religious philosophy. Krishna Consciousness teaches us that man is not merely a body but an eternal spirit. The body goes through incarnations too numerous to count. The eternal spirit buried deep within each one of us is unchanging and always with us. What we must do is to merge the eternal spirit – the Christian soul, the Krishna *atman* – and the body so that they become one. This may take many incarnations, many lifetimes. To achieve it we must abandon ego, self, the desire for pleasure, food, sex, money, luxury and power. The ego can only be defeated by giving everything to God.

Unfortunately, as so often happens in such apparently attractive religions, human nature interferes. The evil devotees seek to divert the aims, break the rules, destroy triumphs and gain control of the organisation. The death of Swami Prabhupada in Vrindaban, India, left the way open for others to fight for a share of the power in the vacuum he left.

More fundamental to the criticism of such cults is that they encourage recruits to abandon their identities. Who knew that Jayatirtha was really James Immel, a London recruit and spiritual guide, who mixed the mind-bending drug, LSD, with his devotions, was expelled from the movement and started a new sect called Tirthapada? Who knew that Immel's disciple Navaniticara was actually John Tierney, from London, a member of that splinter group, who was accused of decapitating his spiritual master in London? The list is endless, for once a novice shaves his head, dons the saffron robes and sandals, takes up the hand cymbals and begins reciting 'Hare Krishna, Hare Krishna . . .' he or she has another name.

When distraught parents inquire of their out-of-touch or missing offspring, they cannot find or contact them because they have taken another name for a new religion and a new existence and probably gone to one of the

323

many other shrines of Krishna Consciousness round the world. That is why FAIR (Family Action Information and Rescue) tries, often in vain, to put anguished parents, relatives or friends in touch with those caught up with cults who have vanished without trace.

Even they could not find James Immel, because he had become Jayatirtha; or John Tierney, now Navaniticara. Immel joined the movement soon after its foundation in 1967; moved to the United States, Canada, India; worshipped in several temples in various cities and returned to London. He was revered as a fine guru, or spiritual teacher, a worthy successor (said some) to the founder-swami. One woman disciple wanted to put his picture on a shrine immediately underneath that of the founder, Swami Prabhupada.

To obtain the picture she followed the spiritual teacher at 5 a.m. from his bedroom at Bahktivedenta Manor, the estate just outside London which Beatle George Harrison had purchased and given to the Krishna Consciousness movement. She knew Immel made his rounds chanting the 'Hare Krishna' at this time every morning. And she probably knew that he seduced any woman who was available and was a regular user of the drug LSD (lysergic acid diethylamide).

LSD is a crystalline solid that produces temporary hallucinations and a schizophrenia-like psychotic state. Used in medical research into mental disorders, it was taken up in the 1960s by the Hippie movement, with their philosophy of Peace and Love, and the rejection of material things. This was sustained by marijuana and LSD, communal life-styles and libertarian sexual behaviour and marked by the devotees' fashion of wearing beads, bells and long hair. The use of LSD was responsible for a part of the movement degenerating into a form of violence known as 'acid fascism' such as that demonstrated by Charles Manson's 'Family', mentioned above.

The woman who wanted Immel's photograph for her shrine was in luck. On this particular morning, his sexual peccadillos were about to be revealed; he was chanting his way to an ancient oak behind which waited the young woman.

He helped her to her feet, they danced, and as they whirled each other round, she slipped out of her sari, he let his dhoti fall to the ground. They stood naked for a moment, then she fell to her knees and took his penis in her mouth until he groaned with ecstasy, threw back his head and cried (said the observer later) like a vixen, a mixture of a baby crying and a dog howling. The couple fell to the grass where they made love.

What the holy man, Jayatirtha, alias Immel, did not know was that he was being observed and that he was being photographed. The husband of the photographer showed him the blown-up pictures of his dawn sexual escapade and gently pressurised Immel to arrange for him and his camera-enthusiast wife to go to India at the movement's expense; for spiritual renewal, of course. Immel readily agreed and one wonders whether he was aware, through his psychadelic haze, that he was becoming very vulnerable to blackmail.

Because of his drug abuse, Immel was reported to the Governing Body Commission of the movement in Bombay. He was so highly regarded as a personal disciple of the founder that no one wanted to take summary action. Members produced all sorts of excuses for him: it was all the fault of his wife, a sexually demanding woman. But that did not explain the drugs. Immel had been a follower of Dr Timothy Leary, a leading exponent of LSD use, while Swami Prabhupada had taught that such substances were evil and not the way to Krishna Consciousness. Immel on the other hand found that LSD helped the constant rhythmic chant of 'Hare Krishna, Hare Krishna'.

Eventually, at the Commission's annual meeting at Mayapur in April, 1982, Jayatirtha-Immel was suspended for one year, ordered to become celibate and give up drugs. He was in Nepal when a former disciple, Nataipada – another Englishman whose real identity had been lost in the transfer to the cult – complained that he had come all the way to Kathmandu, paying his own fare, only to discover that his guru was a drug addict. He wanted his return fare to London. Immel replied angrily that he had not invited Nataipada to Nepal and it was not his responsibility to pay his way.

When the complainant suggested that the police would be interested in his drug habit, Immel changed his tune. He suggested that Nataipada return in the morning to see for himself how the ceremonies were conducted. Meanwhile Immel handed him $500 which would cover his air fare home.

Next morning Nataipada arrived early and was told that there was to be a ceremony on the far shore of a lake and they would row across. When they were half-way across, Nataipada was seized, forced overboard, and when he hung on to the boat his hands were beaten until he let go, then his head held under the water until he vanished from sight. Nepalese police recovered the body when it was washed up some days later. They found the $500 in the pocket of his dhoti. Despite his broken fingers the verdict entered in their report was accidental drowning – and that was that.

Drugs eventually took their toll of the disciple Tierney (Navaniticara) and indirectly his guru, Immel (Jayatirtha). They were staying at an antique shop in London called Knobs and Knockers – no connection with the public limited liability company of that name – run by a Peace Krishna movement. Tierney had been tormented by drugs and could not understand exactly what was going on. As he told police afterwards he saw his guru, Immel: tall, untidily bearded, with piercing eyes and dirty fingernails. At last he realised that Immel was, in fact, not James Immel, not Jayatirtha, but the mad, evil monk, Rasputin.

Tierney waited in the recess behind the door and when the key turned in the lock and Immel entered, the disciple plunged a knife into his stomach. Immel's blood poured on to his attacker's body and the guru fell to the floor dead. But the realisation that he had killed Immel did not satisfy the disciple Tierney. He began to cry with the thought that Rasputin was not dead so he plunged his knife into the corpse again and again. 'I put the stake through his heart,' he said.

Even that was not enough. He grabbed Immel's hair and hacked at his throat until he had decapitated him. And he was still nursing the head when police found the two 'missing' Hare Krishna followers.

All Tierney could say was 'I have done my work', over and over again.

Francis Pencovic was another who appropriated the name of the Hindu avatar Krishna for his own irreligious and criminal ends. This boilermaker, shipyard worker and dishwasher was born in 1911. He spent many of his formative years in jail for burglary, theft, passing cheques with no funds to meet them, failing to support his wife, and – at the instigation of the FBI – for sending a threatening letter to President Roosevelt of the United States.

During World War Two, when Francis was eminently eligible for the services, he registered as a conscientious objector, but was turned down and recruited into the army. On demobilisation, he changed his name to Krishna Venta, donned flowing oriental robes, sported shoulder-length hair and a beard, walked bare-footed and told people that he had been born in Nepal with the gift of transcendentalism. He could, he claimed, go beyond normal human experience in time, backwards as well as forwards, a continuing existence outside the created world.

Krishna Venta, head of the WKFL (wisdom, knowledge, faith and love) Foundation had, he claimed, visited Rome in AD 600. On a more recent visit the Papal guards had refused him admission to the Vatican. Asked how long he had been in America he said he had been 'teleported' to the USA in 1932. He settled his cult near Box Canyon in Ventura County, California, and began issuing predictions about the end of the world.

According to his calculations there would be a communist revolution in 1965 and ten years later, in 1975, he and his 144,000 followers would take over global government. Unfortunately he did not live to see the realisation of his dream. On December 6, 1958, two disillusioned disciples, Ralph Miller and Peter Kamenoff, called on him in his San Fernando Valley monastery just outside Hollywood and demanded that he confess he was a fraud. His cult was a cover for sexual promiscuity, the recruitment of 'brides' to the Foundation. These soul-mates included his accusers' own wives.

Krishna denied their accusations. He refused to confess. One of the avengers opened a canvas bag. A loud explosion tore the monastery apart, killing accusers and accused. In a pick-up truck nearby police found a recorded tape listing the sins of the prophet and declaring, 'He isn't Christ. He is only a man.'

## Chapter Nineteen

# DRINK THIS, ALL YE . . .

'They are not crying out of pain, it's just a little bitter tasting.'

From the Last Supper of Cyanide.

Every suicide is a solution to a problem, but what about the mass suicide of more than 900 people within minutes? These pitiful souls were ordered by the charismatic Reverend James Warren Jones to end their lives by taking soft drinks laced with Valium and cyanide. On November 18, 1978, they did so.

Contrary to popular novelists' belief cyanide is not always fatal. (The reverend murderer John Selby Watson, page 123, took it and survived.) But a dosage sufficient to produce a rapid pulse, headache, convulsions and coma, in that order, is usually a very certain means to an end.

Jones's method of mass destruction was unique. He gathered around him sycophants, appointing from them lieutenants and recruiting officers to lead a whole army of men, women and children who would believe his every word, even to the final order to kill themselves.

Jim Jones was born in 1931 in Lynn, Indiana, USA. His father had been gassed in battle in World War One and became an alcoholic barfly, touring taverns and bumming free drinks from other customers. He had been a life-long Ku Klux Klansman and believed in white Anglo-Saxon Protestant (WASP) supremacy. Even his son called him 'a mean old redneck racist'.

His mother paraded the streets in slacks and smoked in public, which was frowned upon, as was her pose as a self-styled mystic who could see visions and truths to which others were blind. She was a great story-teller who spun adventure yarns of her meetings with aborigines, pygmies, Amazonian head-hunters and their strange creeds. Jim looked in the mirror, noted his own dark complexion and pronounced that he was a Red Indian from the Cherokee tribe. He did not realise that his mother's tales had been gained from the most recent copies of the *National Geographic* magazine; but he was also impressed by her prediction that he was born to help the poor and oppressed.

Most local children of his age sang about their Indiana homes and the smell of new-mown hay and the sight of candles on the sycamores gleaming on the banks of the Wabash, while their parents were hewing trees and planing wood for coffins – the town's principal industry. In this funereal atmosphere the Jones boy, from the age of twelve, held church services in a disused attic, full of live and dead animals and pictures of the crucifixion, where he preached to an even younger congregation his visions of hell and damnation. He had developed a curious fondness for neighbours' animals, claiming to heal them and sometimes even conducting animal funerals. That was before neighbours began counting how many of their pets had mysteriously disappeared.

The more the teenaged preacher saw how the Methodist and other institutional churches were run, the more he believed he could do better, gather more faithful worshippers and collect more money in the name of the Lord. He gained admission to Indiana University with the ambition of becoming a doctor or a priest, but he dropped out after meeting his future wife, Marceline ('Marcie') Baldwin, a nurse five years his senior. With Marcie he went door to door collecting money and converts for the Methodist Mission.

The largely white conservative congregation objected to the number of new black believers Jones was bringing into the Church. His style of making converts was offensive to them. Some of his claims and visions were wildly exaggerated, and when he claimed he had met God, had sat next to Him, a fellow-passenger on a train to Philadelphia, the Methodists showed him the church door. At the tender age of twenty-three he branched out to found his own church.

Premises for the Community National Church were difficult to find and expensive and eventually Jones had to settle on an abandoned Jewish synagogue in the predominantly black neighbourhood around North Delaware Street, in the state capital of Indianapolis. Sermonising was all very well but he knew that the poor, jobless, run-down, multi-racial community needed more tangible rewards. So he started a business importing and selling monkeys at $29 each, the profits enabling him to open soup kitchens, cheap clothing stores and two nursing homes.

If Christianity entails the common ownership by the people of the means of production, distribution and exchange, as adopted by communists, then Jones was its new Messiah. He joined the Communist Party but he owed his pavement and pulpit appeal and activities more to Robin Hood. He would seek out the poor, the aged, the lonely, the most obviously ethnically isolated, and hand them gifts, hug them and kiss them, telling them that he loved them and would save them. They believed him.

He then made a very significant financial move by merging his People's Temple with the Disciples of Christ,

335

which in terms of members in full employment, of pay packets and property ownership, was one of the six most powerful churches in America. The Disciples gave him new respectability by ordaining him a minister of God. The people turned to him in droves and the mayor of Indianpolis, recognising his popularity among electoral opponents, appointed him to the City Human Rights Commission. Jones showed a practical example of his multi-racial Christian philosophy by adopting eight Korean and black children and by leading a two-year mission of his followers to the *favelas*, the desperately poor shanty-town homes of Rio de Janeiro, Brazil.

Pastor Jim Jones had become, in political terms, a person who could not be ignored, even if he might not always be trusted or liked. He took up every popular cause: the civil rights campaign of Martin Luther King; the armed struggle of Black Muslim Malcolm X; opposition to America's involvement in Vietnam. He made several pilgrimages to the Peace Mission of the black clergyman Father Divine, from whom Jones picked up the idea that to succeed he must project himself as divine to his followers.

As a result, the People's Temple Full Gospel Church fast became an evangelical circus with hired people vomiting chicken livers, claiming they were cancers their bodies had rejected at the call of Pastor Jones. Make-up artists turned handsome young folk into deformed invalids in wheelchairs nursing beautiful hired babies they said they had sired or to whom they had given birth under the guidance of their preacher.

With such show-business successes, Jones found Indianapolis was quickly becoming too small. The tinseltown state beckoned. God, he told his flock, had called on them to go to California, just as He had called on the Israelites to quit Egypt. He would lead the oppressed and the depressed to a new-found promised land. It was a valley called Ukiah, in the redwood forest of America's fastest-growing state, and to add support to his claim he could cite the American magazine *Esquire* which had declared Ukiah a nuclear-safe zone.

His followers piled into buses for this twentieth-century exodus to their camp in the valley, while Jones headed for San Francisco where he bought another run-down church in the depressed Fillmore district. The poor ethnic minorities flocked to his altar where he offered them food and care as well as religious nourishment. They gave him, in return, a political power the City Hall could not ignore. Mayor George Moscone appointed the Reverend Jones to the city housing authority where he used the position to get preferential treatment for his followers, passing it off as further proof of his divine intervention.

The new housing representative dined with Rosalyn Carter during the 1976 Presidential campaign for the election of her husband, Jimmy Carter. 'I enjoyed being with you,' she wrote to him. In the 1984 campaign he flew with would-be Presidential candidate, Walter Mondale.

The sexual morals of the Reverend Jones were at that time being kept secret from the faithful. He had met a fellow church member, Tim Stoen, an ambitious Californian lawyer, who like many had been disillusioned by the assassination of President John F. Kennedy and was seeking a revolutionary future for the people. Stoen had recently married and asked Jones to go to bed with his wife, Grace, and sire him a child. In an affidavit Stoen signed, he admitted the appointment of the surrogate father 'with the steadfast hope that the said child will

337

become the devoted follower of Jesus Christ and be instrumental in bringing God's kingdom here on earth, as has been his wonderful natural father'. Stoen's signature was witnessed by Jones's wife, Marcie.

Eventually, in 1974, the threat of an impending courtroom battle for the custody of that child, John-John Stoen, prompted Jones to take not only the child out of the country but the whole congregation. He had seen the future escapist Eden when he had stopped off in Guyana years before after his two-year missionary stint in Brazil.

The reason he gave for the move was that the People's Temple was looking for a practical paradise, a Utopia, which he visualised as being just like Sir Thomas More's imaginary island of that name, enjoying the utmost perfection of Christian beliefs, justice and politics. He did not specify whether his paradise would be a dictatorship or a democracy, and the blindly faithful who followed him did not ask. He found his Utopia not on an island but on mainland Guyana, near the Venezuelan border, in 27,000 acres of rainforest which he chopped down and cleared for the new Jonestown, as he immodestly named it.

Supplies were shipped up-river and the people built their own planned and orderly-spaced bungalows on land free from what they were told and believed was a corrupt American society. The Co-operative Republic of Guyana, which had achieved independence from Britain, gave Jones $1 million to cut down the rainforest for 'development'. The Temple elders welcomed 380 pioneers, a number which grew to 1,000, including 150 or more children, the latecomers having to surrender their worldly possessions to settle permanently in Jonestown.

Sex was an important weapon in the preacher's religious armoury. He took to his bed members of both sexes, knowing that he was driving a wedge between married couples, weakening their marriage bonds, binding them closer to him, filling the 'pews' and enhancing his power. At the same time he forbade sex with 'outcasts' who were not members of their faith. 'Your head is between your legs,' he would bawl at them from the open-air makeshift wooden throne 'pulpit'. 'Sex is not for pleasure,' he preached. 'It is a revolutionary act.'

Jones fathered three children in the commune. One expectant mother had an abortion rather than bear his child. And his bizarre sexual excesses included demonstrating that his revolutionary faith was without racial prejudice by persuading a white man to have oral sex with a black woman in the presence of a large congregation. Sex in public without shame was like urinating, he declaimed, another proof that his church had nothing to hide.

A secretary kept a diary of times and dates and sleeping partners which Jones boastfully displayed to those he thought did not believe his sexual prowess and potency.

Jones's hold over his worshippers was demonstrated by the experiences of Elmer and Deanna Mertle, starry-eyed newlyweds, who visited the People's Temple in Redwood Valley in 1968. They were mesmerised by the happiness, the friendship and communal spirit they found there. They did not need asking twice to sell up their home, hand over their possessions, move into a farm and take jobs Jones found for them.

They were elected to the church's Planning Commission, whose task was to work out the details of Jones's earlier political philosophy; that the poor and oppressed, when they could not persuade the rich and powerful to assist them, should be willing to take part in the ultimate act of mass disobedience and commit revolutionary suicide. The Mertles became increasingly worried about their leader's bizarre behaviour and when their daughter was spanked for a minor behavioural offence – at a daily disciplinary ritual in which the cries of the punished could be heard over the loudspeaker system – they decided they had had enough and announced they were quitting.

To do so was not easy. The church had their money and possessions. Two of their three children were living in the homes of other members of the congregation and, as part of the Jones plan, were refused contact with the outside world. They were being brought up as Temple children and must not leave, said Jones and his followers. When the parents insisted, a delegation called on them to try to make them change their minds.

In the ensuing battle of words, Jones threatened to broadcast that Elmer Mertle was a child molester. The couple retorted that they would take their story to the Press. Jones offered them their freedom on receiving the gift of a profitable nursing home in Berkeley, California, 'donated' by Mrs Mertle's mother. But by then they had ensured their freedom by claiming they had sworn affidavits about Jones's indecent behaviour and put them in safety deposit boxes. Jones countered by accusing the Mertles of 'selling their brothers and sisters for [the freedom of] a pocketful of credit cards and a fancy car'.

As a result of the Mertles' defection, members and even ex-members of the Temple suspected of talking about church secrets to the Press were kept under surveillance. Pastor Jones boasted that his political friends would pour scorn on any revelations. On other occasions, however, as part of his mania for security, he warned the faithful that FBI agents were tapping their telephones and following them.

The faithful did not question whether they were living in a free, democratic society or under a totalitarian dictatorship. Among Jones's rules was one forbidding sex for pleasure. Anyone suspected of having lustful thoughts or unlawful sex – that is, not approved by the leader – was punished with beatings and torture, as were those who fell asleep or whose attention seemed to wander during Jones's increasingly incoherent sermons.

One child was put down a well where a waiting assistant dunked the juvenile in icy water before pulling the terrified and tearful youngster out. Another was buried in a metal box for twenty-four hours. Even when chastisements were not witnessed it was important to make sure that the flock believed that such corrective discipline was being carried out by broadcasting screams and letting weals and bruises be seen. Children who did not smile and mention the leader's name sufficiently often or loudly were taken away and reputed to have had electrodes attached to them to give them shocks.

Suspected defectors were warned that trying to escape from Jonestown would be like trying to flee from Devil's Island penal colony, one of the Safety Islands, off the coast of the former French Guyana. The *Ile du Diable* was sufficiently well known to the literate and the story-tellers among the worshippers to dissuade those thinking of slipping away.

Jones monitored the news from the USA, censored it and re-broadcast his own version of events in the outside world. He became paranoiac about the safety of the congregation or more correctly the secrecy of his depravity. He preached that American big business which had kept the people oppressed in America was jealous of their faith and opposed to their work of building a better land, and was sending in the CIA (Central Intelligence Agency) to attack Jonestown. That was why he had posted armed guards round the perimeter fences – not to keep the faithful in but to keep the ungodly out.

On the first day of 1976, Jones was ready to put his master plan, the revolutionary suicide of protest, to the test. He commanded the congregation to drink a liquid which he said was poisonous. Some, mesmerised by his leadership qualities, were quite prepared to do so; some hesitated and one who was planted in the congregation refused and began to run away. A sniper appeared and 'shot him dead', the people were told. The 'dead' man was spirited away. Only after everybody else present had taken a drink of the 'harmful' cup did the Reverend Jim reveal it was not really poisonous, and thanked them for their selfless gesture, loyalty and belief in him. So successful was the trick that mock suicide services, known as rehearsals or 'white nights', were held with increasing frequency.

At first, Jones intended that all his followers except himself should die voluntarily but he would survive in order to tell the world the reason why. Curiously, when that story was told back in the United States, few if any believed it.

Parents anxious about their missing children reported to be living in his commune and relatives of others with similar worries had complained to newspapers, congressmen and senators and set up the Committee of Concerned Relatives.

Stories of extortion, embezzlement, blackmail, torture and beatings went either unbelieved or unheeded. Revelations about Grace Stoen's sexual relationship with Jones were dismissed as entertaining domestic gossip. The San Francisco *Examiner* revealed some of what was going on in Jonestown. Journalist Sam Houston lobbied Leo Ryan, a Californian Congressman, alleging that his son had had a violent quarrel with Jones, defected and next day died in a particularly suspicious road 'accident'.

Ryan alerted the State Department to the possibility that Jones was holding cult members who wanted to leave as prisoners so that their relatives would send contributions to the cause. The House of Representatives Foreign Affairs Committee authorised a fact-finding mission of officials, parents of cult members and journalists to fly to Jonestown on November 14, 1978.

They landed at Port Kaituma, a few miles from Jonestown, where the leader of the cult tried to impose conditions. He would not, he said, admit 'enemies', by which he meant defectors or newsmen. Jones was warned of the harm a film of Congressman Ryan being turned away would do him. Such an international incident would spark a Congressional inquiry and Guyanan government intervention.

As a result, Ryan and the media went in. At first the visitors found the reception friendly. Cult members were ordered to keep smiling. Guests were dined, and entertained by the Jonestown Band. Young and old went on the floor to dance.

But all was not as it seemed. Monica Bagby, a young black woman, actually slipped a note to a radio reporter asking him to take her with him out of Jonestown. Ryan, on the other hand, seemed to have been converted. He

343

made a speech in which he said, 'From what I have seen, there are a lot of people who believe this is the best thing that ever happened to them.' Even the sect members, always suspicious of outsiders, clapped him and continued clapping.

Jones was being interviewed on camera, telling a reporter that sex stories about him were 'bullshit'. He proudly listed the undeniable achievements of his work on behalf of minorities. But the questioner was well-briefed and the answers became more and more heated. 'The only thing that I regret is that somebody hasn't shot me. We're a small community. We are no threat to anyone. But they won't rest until they destroy us. I wish they would shoot me and get it over with. But I guess the media smear is what they use now. In the long run it's as good as assassination.'

The Guyanan courts had announced that they were ready to pronounce on the custody of John-John, the son of Mrs Grace Stoen, alleged to have been fathered by Jones. 'If it is not true, why have you refused to allow him to rejoin his mother?' asked the reporter. The Reverend Jones began to sweat. By now the questions were coming faster and harder. 'Why do the guards carry guns?' 'Why are threats made to people who want to leave?'

'It's all lies,' he cried.

Unfortunately for him, at that moment an aide told him that Edith Parks, the grandmother of a family who had wanted to leave for some time, had asked Ryan whether she could return with him.

'I've been betrayed. It never stops,' Jones shouted.

Twenty more people asked Ryan for the same help. Ryan suggested that to avoid any accusations of coercion those who wanted to leave the Temple should be allowed

344

to go. As the visitors and defectors left, Don Sly, a Jones acolyte in his twenties, stabbed Ryan in the arm. Two other Jones loyalists pulled Sly away.

On November 18, 1978, visitors and defectors reached the small airport, to find the runway blocked by a truck and trailer carrying twenty armed Jonestown guards.

Larry Layton, so close a confidant of Jones that he was known as the 'Jones robot' or 'Jobot', had somehow duped the visitors into believing that he too wanted to defect. Once inside the plane, Layton pulled out a gun and started shooting. Outside, guards from the truck opened fire. Congressman Ryan, three journalists and three defectors were shot dead. By the time news of the killings reached the United States the Jonestown apocalypse was under way.

What was supposed to have happened was that Layton would shoot the pilot in the head during the flight, the plane would crash and Jones would be able to report the mishap to the faithful as an accident. According to his planned script, the twenty 'soldiers' in the truck and trailer were only there to protect the travellers.

When the news reached Jonestown the final drama began, as the 'white nights' became a black day. The mass 'revolutionary suicide' of which Jones had dreamed was about to become a reality. He mounted his wooden throne and told them that the CIA would force the left-wing Guyanan government to send the army to attack them. 'They are our black socialist brothers and we cannot resist them. We cannot fight back.'

He had (he said) dispatched a suitcase containing half a

million dollars to the Russian embassy in Georgetown, the capital, with the request that the Soviet Union grant them all asylum, but it was too late. 'We will meet in another place,' he promised.

Two 50-gallon drums of Kool-Aid already laced with Valium, the trade-name for diazepam, a sedative and tranquilliser, and cyanide were rolled to the gathering. Jones bid them drink. Even before that some mothers had just poured the liquid down their babies' throats and swallowed the rest themselves. Others fed their babies the refreshment through feeding bottles with rubber teats. Brimful paper picnic cups were handed to adults. Those who hesitated were prodded with rifles and other hand-guns.

The congregation had been promised that death would be quick and painless. When children went into convulsions there were screams and cries. 'They are not crying out of pain,' Jones shouted into the microphone, 'it's just a little bitter tasting.'

When the flock lay dead, the guards and Jones's own children – including John-John, the tug-of-sinful-love child – took their poison without a murmur. 'They just laid down and died,' said an official statement later. Jones took a gun and shot himself in the head. Annie Moore, a Jonestown nurse, picked up the gun and killed herself. The counting began: 900 plus – 911, 912, 913, 914, 915 is hardly worth dispute – men, women and children, mostly but not all illiterate blacks, lay where they had drunk from the deathly cups. The Reverend Jim Jones, satisfied that his earthly work had been accomplished, before putting the revolver to his head ensured that he would be remembered by posterity. The hidden tape-recorders, so useful for spying on the faithful, were still recording.

The last words, however, came from accidental survivors. Grover Davis was partially deaf, hadn't heard the summons to suicide and slept on. Hyacinth Thrush, frail and bedridden, got up to demand to know where her breakfast was and saw the killing fields. 'I'm sorry. I would have liked to have died with my brothers and sisters,' she said.

## Chapter Twenty

# APOCALYPSE NOW

'My hand made heaven and earth. My hand shall also bring it to an end.'

David Koresh.

In 1993, at least fourteen Britons were among those who perished when law enforcement officers twice attacked the fortress Ranch Apocalypse of David Koresh, leader of the Branch Davidians. Koresh, who claimed to be Jesus Christ, was wanted on unspecified firearms and other charges. Within minutes, the first assault operation, in February, exploded into the bloodiest defeat the US Bureau of Alcohol, Tobacco and Firearms (ATF) had ever experienced. Four of their agents were killed, sixteen injured. Six cultists also died. Six weeks later, in April, there was a repeat performance by Federal Bureau of Investigation (FBI) agents and this time eighty-five Davidians, including at least seventeen children, met their deaths. Only eighteen survived.

Perversely, the public debate centred not on the evil influence of Koresh: his weapon-storing, his sinister recruitment of followers, his sexual immorality, his own death wish or the demise of so many; but on whether the forces of the law should have attacked the fortress in the first place.

Anyone who thinks such a cult could never exist in Britain or that Britons could not have belonged to it should consult FAIR, the acronym for Family Action Information and Rescue. FAIR operates from a terraced house in the East End of London, unidentifiable from any other, except by appointment to visit. Officials man telephones, waiting for the next call which will tell them,

'My daughter is missing,' or 'my son has joined some cult,' or '. . . may be dead,' or '. . . is believed to have been murdered by a cult.'

They keep track of ideologies and lifestyles advocated in Britain and established all around the world by the growing number of cults and quasi-religious groups whose methods of recruitment are weird and whose activities may well lead to suicides and even murders. They advise and counsel.

'We were in France on holiday,' said one caller, 'and we were introduced to these people in flowing white robes who told us about their extra-terrestrial excursions in a flying saucer. The children wanted to go for a trip with them.' A woman at FAIR told the caller that about 140 children between two months and seventeen years old had been taken into custody as a result of raids in French cities on houses run by Children of God (The Family). More than twenty-one men and women had been arrested and charged with 'enticing minors into debauchery'.

In one house in Aix-en-Provence in the South of France police found forty children. Eight women and four men were later charged. The Aix prosecutor said he had found texts of speeches by leading members calling for the initiation of very young children, as well as pornographic drawings made by the children themselves. A British couple with eight children were arrested at a house in Condrieu near Lyons who were part of a group of seven English-speaking families with thirty-four children. And that, said the monitor, was the biggest operation against Children of God (COG) since 120 children were taken into care the previous year. COG also circulates curse prayers asking Jesus to destroy specific persons, like the officers of FAIR; to give them painful deaths after having 'their vitals eaten by cancer'.

FAIR warns all callers: 'If you are at a crossroads in life, feeling alone, facing difficult decisions or coping with great changes you are the most vulnerable to such invitations [to join a cult]. They offer emotional support. Once you are a member of such a group it is often difficult to extricate yourself. It could take years for you to adjust to a real world. If you live that long.'

The organisation identifies the oddball sects as characterised by leaders who claim divinity or a special mission delegated personally by a supreme power. Such leaders demand absolute and unquestioning obedience and are the sole judges of the members' faith and commitment. Members become mainly preoccupied with fund-raising, recruiting and attending seminars and are subjected to iron discipline and sometimes outrageous sexual abuse.

Members usually find that the denomination requires them to live away from home. Communication with family and friends is sharply curtailed or completely broken, for the cult becomes the new family. A convert to such ideas can usually be identified by the way he or she puts the organisation ahead of individual concerns like education or career; even health. Sophisticated techniques are designed to destroy the ego, reform the whole pattern of thought and make the members wholly and totally dependent on the group they have joined.

Established members are guarded, vague, deceptive or even secretive about their beliefs, goals, demands and activities until the recruit is caught in a bizarre intellectual atmosphere. A typical method of recruitment is to maintain members in a state of heightened suggestibility through lack of sleep, a carefully engineered diet, intense spiritual exercises, repetitive indoctrination and controlled group therapy.

Converts display symptoms of extreme tension and stress; fear, guilt, lack of humour, regression in communicating and in critical judgment. They are encouraged to believe they are exclusive, cut off from the outside world, because, they are told, that world is evil or satanic. Suddenly they find their bank balances are depleted. They probably did not read too closely the membership contract they signed handing over their wealth and even their worldly possessions, so mesmerised were they by the offer of a 'new way of living'.

That is why FAIR warned people against joining the Ranch Apocalypse at Waco, Texas. Founder David Koresh believed in the literal interpretation of the Bible and particularly the last Book of the New Testament, the Revelations of St John the Divine, in which the final battle is fought at Armageddon between the forces of good and evil. To illustrate his behaviour and what occurred as a result, passages from Revelations in this chapter are in italics.

Waco was the ideal place for a commune: a town of 100,000 souls, once an important crossing for the old cattle trails south-west of Dallas, and still a hub for national and state highways. FAIR had answered many calls from people worried about friends or relatives who had been traced to the stronghold. They had been recruited in places as far apart as Australia, Hawaii and the United Kingdom.

Even from the outside, the ranch was forbidding. It was a cheap building internally, made of yellow pine, plasterboard and tar-paper, furnished with park benches and wooden bunks, but looked for all the world like a military barracks, complete with watchtower and an underground bunker, guarded by trusties with powerful weapons and night-vision telescopes, manning their posts round the clock.

David Koresh, who changed his name from Vernon Howell in 1990, was thirty-three years of age, a good-looking high school drop-out, another Messiah. Koresh was a curious choice of name. He took it from Cyrus Koresh, formerly Dr Cyrus Tweed, who, a century previously, had founded the 'cellularists', a community which believed the earth was flat.

This Koresh moved his community from Chicago to the Gulf of Mexico resort of Estero in Florida where the flat coastline would provide proof of his theory.

When he died three days before Christmas, 1908, his followers believed that he would rise from the dead within three days. When he did not, the state health authorities ordered them to bury their founder for hygienic reasons. Burial within the earth was offensive to their principles. It would mean that their immortal founder would be interred in a place where nothing could exist. When they could not get permission to erect a tomb for the master on the mainland, they built one on the surface on Estero Island and the body of Koresh was taken there. Some years later, Koresh and tomb were washed away to sea leaving no trace of the founder, but his successors still maintain a college in the area to promote his ideas.

The ideas of the more recent Koresh, formerly the Reverend Vernon Howell, stemmed partly from his having been a Seventh Day Adventist, to whose congregations he had preached in Britain, notably at their Watford, Hertfordshire, headquarters. The Adventists grew out of a movement begun by William Miller in the United States in 1831. He prophesied that the present world would end in 1843; suffered the First Disappointment, put the date back a couple of years and suffered the Great Disappointment. When the imminent second coming of Christ did not occur, the sect vanished, but later emerged as the Seventh Day Adventists, adopted their name in 1860 and were formally organised three years later. They observe Saturday as the seventh day and, therefore, the Sabbath.

That faith did not satisfy Koresh so he founded the Branch Davidians. Some maintain that this was based on an earlier church, the Davidists, founded by David Joris (1501–1556), an eccentric Belgian famous for his extraordinary posthumous execution. Joris claimed to be the third David, the first being David, King of Israel; the second, Christ the son of David. His scurrilous attacks on the Roman Catholic Church brought him a fine, whipping, tongue-boring and three years' banishment. He died in 1556 and three years later a trial was held over his corpse in which an *auto da fé*, the ceremonial procedure of reading sentences against heretics during the Spanish Inquisition, was carried out. His body was reduced to ashes and the sect died out.

Others reckoned that David Koresh thought he was the reincarnation of John of Leiden, a mad Anabaptist who in 1534 at the age of twenty-five proclaimed himself King of Zion and turned Münster, Germany, into a communal theocracy in which God was proclaimed the civil ruler. He took multiple 'wives', in his case to establish a new race of 'Israelites'. His captors eventually dismembered him with red-hot pincers.

As in most cults, Koresh required members to surrender their worldly possessions. The car park at Ranch

Apocalypse looked like a second-hand car lot after the Davidians found they couldn't sell or afford to replace the cars that had been generously 'donated' with better or newer models.

Koresh also enforced strict physical discipline. Offenders were beaten with an oar on which was inscribed, 'It is written: *He shall rule them with a rod of iron.*' A discipline room was kept for dealing with serious offenders and the really damned were made to wade in a pit of raw sewage and then forbidden to bathe.

He banned sex between the lawfully married and took women and girls at random – one a child of eleven – to his own bed, even though his lawful wife, Rachel, whom he married when she was fourteen, and their children, Cyrus, aged eight, and six-year-old Star, lived on the compound. In this way, he fathered seven more children, and retained nineteen 'wives'.

More irrational than Jones, Koresh rationed the food of the faithful because, he said, fasting was good for the soul. Chicken was good for the members one day, but so was a diet of popcorn the next. Sugar and ice-cream were good today, bad tomorrow. When the hungry went to town they had to surreptitiously buy and hoard ready-packaged victuals from fast-food stores.

Temperance and abstinence from tobacco, alcohol and similar substances was mandatory. After the first massacre at Waco, a spokesman for the Bureau of Alcohol, Tobacco and Firearms muttered, 'Two out of three ain't bad. Pity they didn't abstain from firearms.'

There were two raids on the Waco fortress, both bloody and, according to critics, both bungled. Both in a sense were miscalculations, but the duty of the ATF and the FBI was to enforce the law, and they had plenty of evidence to justify entering the compound on both occasions.

Long before the first assault on February 28, 1993, a neighbour complained to police that he had heard the sound of machine-gun fire coming from within the fortress. A United Parcel Service deliveryman told them, 'I just dropped off at the ranch two cases of pineapple-type hand grenades and some boxes marked "black gunpowder". I ain't supposed to carry that sort of stuff.' Another whisper said that the people inside were developing a radio-controlled aircraft to carry explosives.

In addition there were the usual complaints by anxious relatives that their kin were being held hostage in the camp. Investigations revealed evidence that David Koresh had spent $119,715 on ammunition and weapons in the seventeen months before the raid. His arsenal included 123 M-16 rifles and the parts necessary to turn semi-automatic rifles into machine guns. Surely that was sufficient reason to insist on a search of the ranch. Local officials, refused entry for two years even to check that local laws and ordinances were kept, now believed that whether or not the fortress was impregnable they would have to try to storm it.

*Rest a little longer, until the number would be complete both of their fellow servants and of their brothers and sisters, who were soon to be killed as they themselves had been killed.*

There is compelling evidence that Koresh deliberately invited the raid by publicising the size of his armoury and, therefore, stage-managed the confrontation. In any case, he had advance warning of the first raid. ATF officials knew that.

Postman David Jones, who was a Davidian, the

brother of Rachel Jones Koresh, legal wife of David Koresh, was finishing his morning round and returning to the compound when he saw an unfamiliar white car. He asked the driver, a journalist, if he was lost, and from the ensuing conversation gathered that something big was about to happen. He reported what he had learned back to his brother-in-law, David Koresh.

The ATF had an undercover agent, Robert Rodriguez, inside the compound, who confirmed that information. Rodriguez was actually talking to David Koresh at about the same time on the morning of February 28, when the leader was called away by one of his disciples. Later, the agent heard Koresh say, 'Neither the ATF or the National Guard will ever get me. They got me once [a reference to a previous brush with the law] and they will never get me again. They are coming. The time has come.'

Rodriguez quit the compound soon after, alerted officials, and forty minutes later the ATF, in a convoy of trucks, stormed the fortress. Word went round the citadel that 'the Assyrians are coming,' an allusion to Lord Byron's *Destruction of Sennacherib*:

The Assyrian came down like the wolf on the fold,
And his cohorts were gleaming in purple and gold;
And the sheen of their spears was like stars on the sea,
When the blue wave rolls nightly on deep Galilee.

By 9.30 a.m. on this bloody Sunday, nearly one hundred ATF agents were in the forecourt. Most of the cultists inside were armed. An agent, brandishing a search warrant, approached the front door. The door was slammed, the guns pointed and the firing began. *And if anyone wants to harm them, fire pours from their mouth and consumes their foes*. Koresh's lawyer has always maintained that the ATF fired first. The ATF denies it. No mention of Koresh himself, the self-styled Lamb of God, garbed entirely in black, seen with an AR-15 rifle in his hands before he was wounded. *They will make war on the Lamb, and the Lamb will conquer them*.

Agents said they were so overwhelmed by the Davidians' fire power that many did not have time to squeeze off a single shot. Four agents were killed and sixteen wounded, some thought to have been shot by their comrades in the panic of friendly fire, although this too was denied by the ATF. Six cultists died, but the fortress withstood the attack, the surviving agents recovered their dead and injured and the inquest began. The engagement had resulted in a deathly stalemate.

The FBI were called in to mount a seige on the fortress. The inhabitants, behind their barbed wire, stout walls, locked and barred doors, were self-sufficient. They had a storage plant for water, a gymnasium used as a food store and enough to keep them for two years. There had to be negotiations. Fourteen adults were released along with twenty-one of the thirty-eight children.

Those who left the compound voluntarily were held as possible witnesses to Koresh's lawbreaking but were unco-operative. Women admitted, however, that they were 'wives' of David Koresh. Their attitude was summed up by thirty-five-year-old Rita Fay Riddle. 'If we're a cult, then all churches are cults. If I've been brainwashed then anyone who practises Bible teachings is brainwashed. The difference is that we live the Bible. Other people go to church on Saturday or Sunday and the rest of the week do their own thing. We lived it.'

For fifty-one days the electricity was cut off, and there was uneasy talk by the one working telephone – all others had been cut off, by order – as the law and the cult faced each other across the wind-swept plains of Texas, the one with their law books, answerable to the government and the people, the others with their Holy Bibles, answerable only to a higher authority. The stand-off diplomacy by agents was followed by broken promises, glimmers of hope, crushing disappointments, failed negotiations and the official use of blaring music, day and night, to upset, unnerve and persuade the fortress dwellers to surrender. They played Nancy Sinatra and the chanting of Tibetan monks full blast and put searchlights on the windows of the barricaded stronghold.

Inside, the cult members relied on Koresh, the chosen one. Asked to give himself up, he demanded that he be allowed to preach on a Christian radio network to his flock while in jail. *You must prophesy again about many peoples and nations and languages and kings.* The FBI agreed to his request in writing, but he screwed the letter into a ball and threw it away. He said he would surrender when he had finished a book he was writing about the Seven Seals. *And I saw in the right hand of him that sat on the throne a book written within and on the backside, sealed with seven seals. And I saw a strong angel proclaiming with a loud voice, Who is worthy to open the book, and to loose the seals thereof? And no man in heaven, nor in earth, neither under the earth, was able to open the book, neither to look thereon . . . When he had opened the seventh seal, there was silence in heaven about the space of half an hour.*

Then Koresh said he would submit after his people had celebrated Passover. Then only after he had talked to God.

Ranch Apocalypse had never had proper toilet facilities. Now there were fresh water problems. Members allegedly refused to take their human waste outside the buildings in case FBI snipers shot at them. US Attorney-General Janet Reno, who had only been in office a month, feared that children might die in the insanitary conditions if she did not authorise another raid, and feared other deaths if she did so. Outside, agents talked to psychologists who saw Koresh as a grand-standing fanatic who prophesied awful disasters and probably believed and hoped they would come true.

Some FBI negotiators suggested they could walk in through the front door without trouble; some agents believed the stockade was booby-trapped. Whenever they approached the compound, the inmates held up babies to the windows. They even sent out videotapes showing how happy were the children playing inside.

Koresh wrote a letter on April 10 in which he said:

The Law is mine, the Truth is Mine. I AM your God and You will bow under my feet. I AM your life & your death. I AM the Spirit of the prophets and the Author of their testimonies. Look and see, you fools, you will not proceed much further. Do you think you have power to stop My will. My seven thunders are to be revealed. Do you want me to laugh at your pending torments. Do you want me to pull the heavens back and show you MY anger. Fear Me, for I have you in my snare. I forewarn you, the

Lake Waco area of Old Mount Carmel will be terribly shaken. The waters of the lake will be emptied through the broken dam.

Next day he penned another epistle:

My hand made heaven and earth. My hand shall also bring it to an end. Your sins are more than you can bear. Show mercy and kindness and you shall receive mercy and kindness. You have a chance to learn My Salvation. Do not find yourselves to be fighting against Me. Please listen and show mercy and learn of the marriage of the Lamb. Why will you be lost. [signed] Yahweh Koresh. [Yahweh is a Hebrew form for God.]

Even taking into account the copied Biblical references and allowing for legitimate religious belief, cult deprogrammers, psychologists and psychiatrists were all convinced that this was the work of a psychopath. The time was coming for the authorities to act. After more than a hundred hours in telephone negotiations, the fear was that David Koresh was bent on his followers committing suicide; and because he would do nothing to stop them, he would be, in effect, their killer. Their duty was to prevent such a crime.

They all knew the risks. Battering-ram poles would punch holes in the side walls and into the holes compressed air would pump a fine mist of non-lethal CS gas. This would temporarily incapacitate those inside the fortress, causing eye irritation, crying, runny noses, coughing, sneezing, and difficulty in breathing. It was unanimously held to be the best way to prevent the ranchers from shooting and killing the law officers or taking their own lives.

The Attorney-General called President Clinton on the spot, told him there was no reasonable alternative, and obtained his approval for the raid.

Before dawn on April 19, many of the Branch Davidians were still sleeping. Some were awake reading their Bibles. The FBI agent with the portable public address system said, 'This is not an assault! Do not fire! Come out now and you will not be harmed!' Other agents toured houses in the neighbourhood telling the householders to 'stay indoors, there may be some noise'. Those words had a different meaning for some of the brainwashed Davidians. According to one of the group's lawyers, 'Some of the very religious people thought it was the last day of the world.' It was Judgment Day.

Dick Rogers, head of the FBI's Hostage Rescue Team, led the operation mounted on his A-1 Abrams tank. *And I looked, and behold a pale horse: and his name that sat on him was Death*. He had 170 agents on duty, manning M-60 tanks converted into combat engineering vehicles, and four Bradley armoured personnel carriers outside the perimeter fence of the ranch. They would poke booms through the side walls of the ranch and fire CS gas into the upper floors of the building. This, they reasoned, would force the inhabitants into the centre and out through the ground-floor doors. Snipers were posted a hundred yards away in case anything went wrong. Ambulances were on stand-by a mile away in case they were needed.

What could go wrong? They had not forgotten but could not control the Texan prairie wind. In a few days' time Waco folk would be holding a memorial service to those who died in the tornado of May 11, 1953, which killed 114 people, injuring 597 and causing more than $40 million worth of property damage. On April 19, 1993, the wind was blowing, billowing clouds of dust through the grass. At 4 a.m., it was still blowing. At 5.55, Byron Sage, the FBI's chief negotiator, phoned the ranch and asked for Koresh or Steve Schneider, his forty-three-year-old deputy.

Schneider, like Koresh, had been a Seventh Day Adventist. He graduated from Hawaii University, tried to start his own church, was refused permission, and married. His wife, Judy, introduced him to one of Koresh's recruiting agents. Both were converted. Judy became one of Koresh's 'wives' and there was doubt about the paternity of Judy's child, although Schneider claimed it was his.

As Koresh was tired and worn out after many hours of negotiating, Schneider, who advised the leader on theology and finance, came to the phone. Sage put a lot of pressure on him and said, 'Do not shoot. We are not entering your compound. There's going to be tear gas injected into the compound. This is not an assault. Do not fire. The idea is to get you out of the compound. You are responsible for your own actions. Come out now and you will not be harmed.'

*Do not fear what you are about to suffer. Be faithful unto death, and I will give you the crown of life.* Schneider panicked. 'Everybody, grab your masks,' he screamed and he threw the phone out of the window and left it dangling. Sporadic small arms fire erupted. Schneider recovered the handset. Sage pleaded, 'Don't do it to these people.' But the firing began again.

*Then the angel took the censer and filled it with fire from the altar and cast it into the earth*. Armoured car booms crashed into the buildings making holes through which more gas was pumped. All told, eighteen bottles of tear gas were injected into the compound. No one came out. Maybe they couldn't escape. Some doors were barricaded from within with potatoes, tinned foods, even a piano and a dangerous large metal drum of propane gas. By then the wind was gusting at thirty-five knots and it was impossible for those outside the compound to know what effect it was having on those inside.

At 11.50 the gassing was over and the assault team stood back to see what would happen. Suddenly, at 12.05 p.m. smoke curled from the front of the building. Almost simultaneously four other fires started. Someone had toured the building puncturing kerosene cans and maybe the propane cannister, too.

A fireball rose from the ranch house. Buzzards doing aerobatics overhead told how the wind was turning small fires into a mighty inferno. *And the sun became black as sackcloth of hair, and the moon became as blood*. Smoke covered the prairie, interrupted in its wind-blown path by more fireballs as stored ammunition exploded, making death in the afternoon a spectacular if tragic apocalypse.

The FBI insisted it was part of a suicide plan. *Be thou faithful unto death, and I will give thee a crown of life*. Lanterns had been knocked over, igniting hay stacked around kerosene cans, and the wind drove the resultant flames down long corridors. 'It was a mass murder,' said Special Agent In Charge Geoff Jamar. 'It wasn't a mass suicide. Those people would have done whatever he said. If he had told them to "leave, I will stay here and burn," they would have left.' A cult member, Jaime Castillo, agreed, for another reason. Blaming the FBI, he said, 'It was mass murder. It wasn't a mass suicide.' But he couldn't explain the behaviour of people like Ruth Riddle who emerged from the flames clutching her Bible and tried to go back into the compound before she was prevented by an agent. She tried to fight him off as he yelled, 'Where are the kids? What did you do with them?' She just shook her head and said nothing as she was dragged to safety.

A man appeared on the roof, his clothes ablaze, but when agents moved towards him, he waved them away. He fell off the roof, but for all that was rescued and taken to safety. *And in those days people will seek death but not find it; they will long to die, but death will fly from them.*

Away in Manchester, England, Nellie Morrison screamed at her television set as she saw on the screen the compound go up in flames with her daughter and granddaughter, Melissa, aged six, inside. Renos Aavram, a twenty-eight-year-old Londoner, survived, but his girlfriend, Alison Bernadette Monbelly, from Manchester, who had been his partner in a computer business before leaving Britain, died in the inferno. In Birmingham, Samuel Henry, another Briton, stared into the TV cameras and when asked whom he had lost, replied, 'My wife and our five children. There's no point in anger. My family's dead already.' Derwent Lovelock, a thirty-seven-year-old chef from Bristol, a meticulous Biblical scholar, survived.

Everyone inside knew what to expect. Armageddon, the final battle between the forces of good and evil, was to take place at Waco, Texas. Was it not written in Revelations, the central authority for their beliefs, what would happen? *And the devil who deceived them was thrown into the lake of fire and sulphur, where the beast*

*and the false prophet were, and they will be tormented day
and night forever and ever.*

David Koresh, his wife and children, his father-in-law,
Perry Jones, Schneider, his wife Judy, and more all
suffered the same fate, most likely as a result of their own
determination to remain inside Ranch Apocalypse.
David Koresh's grandmother said, 'There were law-
abiding, God-fearing people in there. He [David] used to
say he'd be killed for his beliefs, but I didn't believe him.
He said, "Grandma, dying's not so bad, I'll be resur-
rected." '

*POSTSCRIPT:* In February, 1994, a San Antonio,
Texas, court acquitted eleven cultists, including three
Britons, of conspiring and murdering four Federal
agents. Jurors believed their claim that they opened fire
believing the sect was under a 'Domesday' government
attack. It was impossible to tell who shot first in the
forty-five minute battle at Ranch Apocalypse. Norman
Allison, aged thirty, a one-time Seventh Day Adventist
and rap singer from Manchester, who went to Waco to
play with Koresh's religious rock band, was cleared of all
charges but faced deportation as an illegal immigrant.
Livingstone Fagan, aged thirty-two, from Nottingham,
and Renos Aavram, from Tottenham, London, were
convicted of aiding and abetting manslaughter. They
faced ten years in jail.

# INDEX